Strategies for Struggling Writers

Strategies for Struggling Writers

JAMES L. COLLINS

THE GUILFORD PRESS
New York London

To my family

© 1998 The Guilford Press
A Division of Guilford Publications, Inc.
72 Spring Street, New York, NY 10012
www.guilford.com

Printed in the United States of America

This book is printed on acid-free paper.

Last digit is print number: 9 8 7 6 5 4 3 2 1

Library of Congress Cataloging-in-Publication Data
Collins, James L.
    Strategies for struggling writers / James L. Collins.
        p. cm.
    Includes bibliographical references (p.   ) and index.
    ISBN 1-57230-299-2.–ISBN 1-57230-300-X (pbk.)
    1. English language–Composition and exercises–Study and teaching (Secondary) 2. Report writing–Study and teaching (Secondary) I. Title
    LB1631.C64 1998
    808′.042′0712–dc21   97-3145
                                                              CIP

Acknowledgments

I am, first, deeply grateful to the students and teachers who participated in the research reported in these pages. To them I owe an infinite debt.

Seven very special colleagues, members of our "Strategies Group" at the State University of New York at Buffalo, are Janice Almasi, Elfreda Blue, Jack Cawley, Laura Klenk, Suzanne Miller, Rene Parmar, and Diane Zigo. Through meetings and informal discussions they contributed to my ideas on writing strategies and kept me focused on sociocognitive concerns.

Many other friends and colleagues were generous in sharing their ideas and research and in talking with me about their work and mine. They include Arnetha Ball, Carol Sue Englert, Steve Graham, Karen Harris, and Ann Marie Palincsar. I am also grateful to Chris Jennison for encouraging me to go ahead with this project and for the advice he offered throughout the writing.

Finally, I am grateful to my family for their willingness to talk about ideas in this book. My wife, Roma McSweeney Collins, made many contributions to my thinking through her insights as a teacher and her support as a companion. My daughter, Kathleen M. Collins, was a constant collaborator and contributor to my thinking. And I am grateful to my son, James M. Collins, for his support and for helping me balance work and play.

Preface

This is a book about helping students who have difficulties with writing. The book focuses on secondary students and English classes, but its message is relevant for teachers in every classroom where students struggle with literacy learning. The message is an encouraging one: Struggling writers benefit greatly from collaborative assistance that focuses on helping them to think strategically about writing.

Thinking strategically about writing means taking deliberate control over writing skills and processes. Until quite recently, teachers were encouraged to think of skills and processes as separate aspects of written composition, so separate, in fact, that most of us probably participated in or witnessed debates over whether we should teach writing skills *or* writing processes to help low-achieving writers. The assumption in such debates was always that we couldn't do both at once. Historically, for example, we had only two basic options in the past 50 years for working with struggling writers: the traditional skills approach, which advocates teaching component skills, structures, and rules for writing; and the process-writing approach, which advocates facilitating writing through processes of prewriting, drafting, revising, and editing. We embraced these options one at a time, as if writing skills and writing processes could not possibly have anything to do with each other.

This book presents a more balanced approach, which I call

strategic writing instruction after its main characteristic, collaboratively teaching writers to recognize and use strategies for controlling writing skills and writing processes with the goal of mastering academic and lifelong literacy.

During the past 20 years, and in a variety of fields—especially English and language arts education, literacy studies, cognitive science, and special education—a great deal of research was conducted on learning strategies and writing strategies. This book synthesizes the research and gleans from it key findings and implications for teaching struggling writers in middle schools and high schools. Much of the research was originally conducted with elementary students and, when appropriate, I extended the findings to secondary students through observational studies, probes, and inquiries in the classrooms of teacher-researchers working with me. The schools we worked in were in urban, suburban, and rural districts, the classrooms included every grade from 5th through 12th, and the students included both general education and special education students with mild disabilities. Strategic writing instruction is the result of this research program.

In the book I present general recommendations for strategy-based writing instruction and offer many writing strategies we have used with struggling writers. My overall purpose, though, is not to provide the reader with an exhaustive list of writing strategies but rather to encourage teachers to think strategically about writing and the teaching of writing so that they can help writers identify and use strategies to control their own writing skills and writing processes.

A strategy is a sequence of cognitive steps designed to accomplish a particular outcome. Writing strategies are deliberate thinking procedures writers use to solve problems they encounter while writing—problems ranging from spelling a word to planning a whole project. Strategies, furthermore, are acquired or learned in social and cultural contexts. Some strategies are acquired intuitively from experience with reading and writing, others are learned more directly from instruction and practice. Using reports from case studies in our research, I show how strategies are learned interactively and how teachers can co-construct learning strategies with students to help them overcome difficulties with writing.

This interactive nature of strategic writing instruction is its main pedagogical feature. Strategies are not learned best by reading textbooks or by listening to teachers. Hence, we focused our inquiries into strategic writing instruction especially on studying how teaching and learning work together to build an understanding of learning difficulties and strategies for overcoming them. Early on we decided not to separate teaching and learning, but instead to study how they blend together and work in tandem. We looked at how teachers and students negotiate understandings of texts and control of writing processes and how collaboration, especially in the form of co-construction of writing strategies, supports learning. We paid particular attention to our emerging observation that certain key strategies, which I describe as "default writing strategies," show up repeatedly when writers are faced with challenging tasks. The book discusses three main default strategies—*copying, visualizing, and narrating*—and shows how they influence the work of struggling writers and how teachers can use them as starting points to help writers build other strategies to guide their writing.

Without exception, we found that students who cooperated with us in co-constructing writing strategies took greater control of their writing skills and writing processes. This co-construction of writing strategies is the main component of strategic writing instruction. Our research taught us that it is best not to think of writing strategies as controls provided by teachers or transmitted from teachers to students. Strategies, to be most effective in overcoming writing difficulties, must be understood and used by students in the midst of their struggles to express themselves in writing. The role of the teacher is to aid in the understanding and use of appropriate strategies by studying the difficulties writers are having and by co-constructing with them ways out of the difficulty. Writing strategies for struggling writers must be tailored to fit their struggles, and the teacher's role includes the most crucial step of working with the student to co-construct a custom fit of strategy to struggle.

Throughout the book, I show how strategic writing instruction can be used with writing workshops and process-oriented teaching methods. This demonstration is important because the process revolution brought many positive changes to writing instruction, but its strength is not in helping struggling writers.

Workshops replaced workbooks; purposeful writing and multiple drafts took the place of contrived exercises and grammar study; and teachers adopted the role of facilitators, circulating among writers and providing response, guidance, and support. Such activities are generally beneficial to all student writers, and undoubtedly they provide some support for struggling writers. By itself, however, process-based writing instruction is not sufficient to overcome many of the difficulties struggling writers face. Process approaches tend to downplay the teaching of skills and text regularities, as if they trust that skills and text regularities will be acquired intuitively as a by-product of writing and revising.

What distinguishes strategic writing instruction from process writing by itself is an emphasis on goals for writing and strategies for achieving these goals. Strategic writing instruction is compatible with most of the tenets of process teaching. Where process teaching would have teachers confer in a supportive manner with writers, however, strategic instruction also allows for the systematic, explicit teaching of options for goal and strategy selection and a gradual, scaffolded transfer of responsibility for their selection from teachers to writers. Where process teaching advocates a separate and greatly diminished role for skills instruction, strategic writing instruction sees skills, united with processes through writing strategies, as integrally related to the achievement of writing goals. Where process teaching believes writing abilities are naturally acquired by everyone, strategic writing instruction ensures that they will be learned, even when acquisition is difficult.

This book, then, is about helping struggling writers, but it is also about collaborative teaching and learning and balancing skills and processes in writing instruction. Above all, its meaning is that writing struggles survive in isolation and that success comes from strategic co-construction of writing abilities.

Contents

Acquisition and Learning and Writing Instruction

Jason[1] sits in ninth-grade English, head in hand, staring at a spot on his desk somewhere between his textbook and a blank piece of paper. The class has read the first half of Langston Hughes's short story "Thank You, Ma'am," and the teacher asked them to write about what happened so far in the story and what they think will happen next. It's obvious that Jason is having trouble, so I move to his desk and ask him to tell me about the story. His response is tentative but suggests that he understands both the story and the assignment:

> "Sounds like the boy really, kinda like sounds like he's lying just a little bit. Sounds like he's got no family, and trying to take her purse for money so he can live. And, sounds like the woman wasn't too mad about it and wanted to take him home, clean him up, and maybe have him for her son."

When I ask Jason to write down those ideas, however, he tells a different story. He leaves out the crucial idea that the boy was

---

[1]All names of students have been changed.

trying to steal the woman's purse and instead provides a summary of more minor events in the story. He also comments on some of the events, and his comments are separated by quotation marks from the plot summary:

```
I have just read a story about a boy who ran
into a women knocking her down and braking her
purse. The boy fell down from hitting her purse.
The women turned around and picked him up buy
his shirt. The boy said he didn't mean to hit
the women and knock her purse to the ground.
"But I think the boy was lieing to the women."
The boy had a dirty face and the women said to
the boy if I let you go will you run away, and
the boy said yes. So the women said I should
bring you home and wash your face and give
dinner. "I think the women thinks that the boy
lives on the street and I agree with the women."
The women says that the boy should come live
with her.
    "I think the rest of the story the boy will
live with this women and stay with her for the
rest of his life."
```

Jason is fairly typical of students who have difficulty with writing. He's clearly more comfortable with talk than writing, and talking about his ideas in response to the reading allows him to identify main points in a way that writing does not. Writing about the story instead seems to tie his thinking closely to the text he read, as if repeating parts of the story might help solve the problem of writing about it. His own comments are brief and tentative and separated from the rest by quotation marks. Like many struggling writers, Jason substitutes plot summary for gist, copies and lists ideas without developing them, and at times juxtaposes ideas instead of connecting them. He also frequently spells words according to the way they sound and uses some punctuation marks unconventionally.

In this book I intend to help students, both regular and special education, who have difficulties such as Jason's. Until quite recently, teachers had only two basic options for working with struggling writers, each merely an extension of prevailing instructional approaches recommended for all student writers.

The traditional skills approach, which advocates teaching component skills, structures, and rules for writing, and the process-writing approach, which advocates teaching writing as a process of prewriting, drafting, revising, and editing are still very much in vogue. I'll have more to say about them momentarily, but first I want to introduce a third approach—strategic writing instruction—which this book is about. Its name comes from its main characteristic, teaching writers to recognize and use strategies for controlling writing skills and writing processes.

The Sociocognitive Basis of Learning and Strategy Instruction

Throughout the book, my main theoretical assumption is that learning difficulties reflect differences, not deficiencies. Some students don't do their best learning through the conventional analytical, text-based methods of writing instruction that schools have favored for about a century. Analytical, text-based instruction is best exemplified by grammar books, textbooks, and workbooks, but it also includes verbal admonitions that sound like they are straight out of a textbook, advice such as the following: "If you use an 'either,' you have to come up with an 'or,' and if you don't come up with an 'or,' your sentence is incomplete." I call these methods "text based" because they are built on the assumption that by the time they are in middle school, students are sufficiently familiar with the workings of standard written text to understand how to analyze and construct text by reading or hearing about its underlying rules and structures. Struggling writers, however, tend to see text-based rules and structures for writing as unattached to the problems they encounter during the act of writing. For them, alternatives to text-based literacy learning can be useful. Jason again provides an example; his preferred mode of learning seems to be through visualization, and strategies that help him visualize written text can help him write, as I demonstrate when I discuss his case in more detail in the next chapter. Conventional advice, like that found in composition textbooks, is likely to contribute to Jason's difficulty with writing because such advice is oriented toward a mode of understanding based on familiarity with text structures. His misuse of quotation marks is an example. Jason uses quotation marks to visually separate one category of ideas from another; at the same time, as I discuss later, he is wondering whether he used the marks correctly. He is not using familiar text structures to build an understanding of his topic because the text structure he is attempting to use is not all that familiar and because it doesn't match the writing objective he's trying to achieve, which is to make a distinction between what the book says and what he thinks about the story. Skilled writers rather automatically use text structures to help plan and express their thoughts in writing, but Jason does not. For him, writing involves thinking about text structures as much as it involves thinking with them.

It appears that Jason is doing something wrong when he writes about the story, but what he is really doing is thinking visually instead of textually. Unfortunately, visual intelligence can be one source of the notion of academic deficiency because schools favor linguistic intelligence (Gardner, 1983) and a narrow definition of literacy as skill with reading and writing (Gee, 1990, 1993). Whenever literacy is used as a primary measure of achievement and intelligence—which, of course, is often done in schools—achievement measures assume familiarity with the workings of print media. Print is only one of the culturally based ways social groups encourage the development of specific skills in children (Gee, 1990, p. 29), and others (oral storytelling and other forms of talk, sign language, imagination, imitation, modeling, etc.) are easily recognized. Schools, however, place an enormous value on print literacy, and this emphasis may contribute to the idea that struggling writers are somehow deficient. Literacy is at the heart of the academic enterprise, and students who have trouble with literacy learning are usually consigned to the lower half of the academic achievement range, to slower groups and lower tracks.

There is a tendency, furthermore, to provide remedial instruction for students in the lower half of the achievement range because of a long-standing and widely accepted medical model for treating academic difficulties: Diagnose what's wrong, label the condition, and prescribe certain remedies. More recently, we have seen a reaction to both ability grouping and remedial instruction. Current books on teaching reading and writing to struggling elementary students (e.g., Strickland, 1995; Roller,

1996) suggest that such labels as *learning disabled, dyslexic,* and *mildly mentally disabled,* and even more common ones such as *at risk, resistant,* or *unmotivated,* should be used carefully and sparingly because they can be too negative and limiting, too readily suggestive of deficiency, weakness, or failed learning. Applying such labels to students who have persistent difficulties with writing runs the risk of circular reasoning: Labels suggestive of deficit can create a need for remedial programs, and remedial programs can teach students to think of themselves as deficient writers. Classrooms are similar to other cultural settings in that they contribute to the social formation of participant identities. Remedial instruction may create remedial learners.

Instead of text-based or remedial instruction, this book presents an approach to teaching writing based on sociocognitive strategies for controlling writing skills and writing processes. Early descriptions of strategy-based writing instruction (e.g., Flower & Hayes, 1977; Flower, 1979) took a predominantly cognitive perspective on writing strategies and advocated teaching cognitive strategies used by expert writers to novices. The intention was to add problem-solving techniques to the popular belief that writing results from following the urgings of either prescription or inspiration. Current research on strategic writing instruction takes a broader, sociocognitive perspective on literacy learning, one that holds that the development of cognitive strategies takes place in social and cultural contexts and can follow different pathways, including the adoption of strategies used by experts, but also including the use of strategies prompted by students' own cognitive preferences and social interactions. Deaf students, for example, do not need to learn the sound-based literacy strategies that work for hearing students, and deaf learners report that forcing them to do so can be harmful to both their literacy learning and their identities as readers and writers (Kimmel, 1996).

From the sociocognitive perspective, contexts for literate activities are extremely important because it is through the individual's interaction with texts within social and cultural contexts that he or she acquires or learns writing abilities. Krashen (1982) initially made the distinction between acquisition and learning in the case of second-language learning and Gee (1993) later applied it to literacy. According to Gee (1993), *acquisition* is a process of attaining abilities through largely intuitive or subconscious means, by exposure to models and through trial and error, without formal teaching, whereas *learning* is a process that involves conscious knowledge gained from instruction, explanation, and analysis (p. 259). Gee adds that acquisition is the principal means by which we get our first language, our ways of speaking in home and local communities, which he calls our "primary discourse." Primary discourses consist of the forms of language we use with intimates, our ways of communicating with family and friends. Literacy involves the learning of secondary discourses, specialized forms and functions of language which may or may not be close to the primary discourse with which one is already familiar. Gee (1993), in fact, defines literacy as control of secondary discourses, and he includes all discourses, not just scholarly ones: A person can be literate by controlling the specialized language of space exploration, automobile repair, dramatic performance, and so on. When literacy activities involve language forms and functions close to one's primary discourse, they can be achieved through a balance between acquisition and learning which favors acquisition. The typical writing workshop shows this balance in favor of acquisition, owing to its pronounced student-centered methods, including student-generated topics and genres for writing, multiple drafts to gradually improve writing, and supportive feedback from teachers and peers. When literacy activities involve ways of using language substantially different from one's primary discourse, the balance shifts in favor of learning. In this case, workshop methods should be supplemented with explicit instruction in appropriate strategies for writing because an emphasis on acquisition, by itself, would not be enough to learn to use structures and strategies with which one is not familiar. Part of Jason's problem as he sat staring at his desk, for example, was the fact that he was facing the writing task alone, and working alone limited him to knowledge he could acquire by himself through interaction with two texts, the one he was reading and the one he was writing. Thinking about the text he was writing seems to have displaced some of his comprehension of the text he was reading. Perhaps this is why his writing, unlike the spoken version of his response to the story, repeated or copied events from the story instead of stating a main idea. His copying the plot of the story can be understood as a "default" writing strategy, as I discuss in Chapter 5. My recommendation for this situation is that teachers consider copying such as Jason's as a starting point in the process of writing about texts being studied. Instead of telling students not to copy or accepting copied material for partial credit, we should teach students how to make reference to and transform copied material so that it supports and expresses their own ideas. Jason, in other words, is faced with a difficult task and is not in complete control of his writing process. In turn, he copies material from another writer, the one he is studying and trying to write about. This is a signal that he is ready for explicit help from others to learn how to regulate his own skills and processes in writing about text.

It might seem obvious that in the case of struggling writers, explicit instruction should be added to the largely intuitive development of writing abilities at the heart of workshop methods. Given the popularity of workshop methods, teachers seem to have only two fundamental choices: We can immerse struggling writers in a reading/writing workshop and wait for the secondary discourse we recognize as schooled literacy to take hold; or we can speed things up by adding direct instruction to the process of literacy acquisition, teaching the forms and functions of literate discourse explicitly. But it's not that simple. Recognizing literacy as a secondary discourse doesn't tell us how to teach its forms and functions to students who are having difficulty mastering them. Struggling writers at the secondary level, that is, are not just inexperienced with literacy or un-schooled in its workings; it is not the case that they continue to struggle, as two popular explanations would have it, because they missed the reading and writing practice usually responsible for the acquisition of literacy or because they missed what their teachers were teaching all along. Indeed, if that were the case, the approach labeled "text-based writing instruction" would show much more success than it does, as that approach offers considerable practice and instruction in written language. What complicates the picture is the fact that struggling writers come to middle school and high school with cognitive preferences and culturally influenced primary discourses already in place and with varying degrees of success and failure with school-spon-sored literacy tasks. Certainly the cognitive processes and primary discourses they use daily for making sense of their lives, their cognitively and culturally inspired ways of knowing the world and communicating their knowledge, and their prior experience with the secondary discourse of schooling must influence the way they approach writing tasks and the strategies they use while writing.

This is where the culture of the home and community meets the culture of the classroom. Following Vygotsky (1978) and in company with contemporary theorists and researchers (e.g., Resnick, 1989; Englert, 1992), strategic writing instruction takes the view that literacy abilities are acquired and learned through meaningful participation in communities. People become as literate as they need to be to participate in the cultures in which they hold membership. Struggling writers are no exception to this general rule. They can learn to control the language of school as successfully as they control the primary discourses they use outside school, but the learning has to go hand in hand with achieving full membership in the classroom community and it cannot deny or invalidate the primary discourse used outside school. Most people, quite understandably I think, would rather give up a secondary discourse than a primary one. Many struggling writers in our studies, for example, limit their writing vocabularies to simple words they can spell with confidence because they would rather look less intelligent than make mistakes that they expect will bring criticism from teachers or laughter from peers. Similarly, adding a secondary discourse to a primary one is more acceptable than choosing between them, especially if adding a secondary discourse happens in a manner respectful of the primary discourse. Most writers in our studies, for example are more willing to accept advice aimed at adding new strategies to their writing repertoires than toward eliminating strategies they are already using.

Students for whom school literacy is acquired easily come to school with primary discourses that correspond closely to the secondary discourse used for most school reading and writing tasks. For struggling writers, the correspondence between the language structures and control strategies in primary and secondary discourses is not as close, and the secondary discourse involved in school writing must be learned more deliberately. In the latter case—as happens readily in the former—instruction must strike an appropriate balance between acquisition and learning by connecting primary and secondary discourses through culturally responsive instruction and supportive classroom mentoring and networking.

Writing-workshop approaches such as Atwell's (1987) most likely view writing abilities as developing primarily through the *acquisition* of a secondary discourse: school literacy. Workshop approaches, furthermore, are built on the theoretical assumption that literacy is an extension of primary discourses; this assumption is especially evident in the workshop's emphasis on self-discovery of topics and content and self-selection of genres for writing. Feedback about writing is also an important part of the writing workshop, especially feedback provided during teacher and peer conferences, but feedback again favors acquisition because it generally takes the form of questions and prompts to elicit more information. Feedback during the writing workshop is definitely serving a useful purpose when it guides revision of written products in the direction of increased elaboration of meaning. By itself, though, such feedback constitutes a relatively slow and indirect attempt to shape and control writing processes. In one recent report, for example, sixth-grade teacher Virginia Smith (1994) describes the 7-week process used by Mike, a student classified as learning disabled and attention-deficit/hyperactivity disorder, to write and revise a short personal narrative. The workshop approach in this case hardly seems a promising way to help Mike develop his writing abilities and certainly wouldn't help Mike catch up to his peers if the production of one piece takes so many weeks. Interestingly, Smith attributes one of the more significant changes in Mike's piece to several minilessons on openings and leads (from Atwell, 1987). And in another section of her report, in which she describes Mike's struggles with expository writing, she mentions how the special programs (inclusion) teacher provided a successful, valuable scaffold for note taking and relieved Mike's frustration by giving him help in the form of topic sentence guidelines and examples (Smith, 1994, p. 14). The learning achieved through elements such as these—minilessons, scaffolds, guidelines, and more—are examples of what this book calls "writing strategies," and adding them systematically to workshop-style writing practice is what I mean by *strategic writing instruction*. The main idea is that students who struggle with academic literacy are more likely to benefit from *both* process-based writing practice *and* instruction in strategies for regulating writing processes. Together, these two modes of instruction activate literacy development through both acquisition and learning.

Problems with Process Writing

Process approaches—in spite of their frequent claims to teaching ownership and voice and independence—do not teach writers to control specific strategies for writing because process writing was a reaction to an earlier skills-based model of writing instruction. The process movement was literally born in reaction to a long tradition of teaching writing by assuming a direct transmission of skills and rules from teachers and textbooks to student writers. The result is a general tendency when using process-based instructional methods to downplay the teaching of skills and text regularities, to trust that skills and text regularities will be acquired intuitively as a by-product of writing and revising. This tendency, furthermore, creates an unfortunate dilemma for teachers who work with struggling writers. Teachers are supposed to emphasize process more than product, but it is extremely hard at times, for both writers and teachers, to avoid focusing on errors and other surface qualities of written products. For example, it's difficult to imagine helping the 11th-grade writer who wrote the following essay without noticing errors and wanting to talk with him about specific writing skills he apparently needs to learn:

> There are many school events, one of wich are Pep Rallys. Pep rallys are supposed to Build up School Spirit to get the energy flowing through the blood and your Body. You get siked for the sport events for the foot Ball teem Basket Ball, Swiming, etc. You must Be mentally and phisicly prepaired for a sport event
>   The thing you see done are one teem come out and every Body cheers for them one at a time: foot Ball, soccer, track, etc. They come out and we cheer for them then they have a cheering contest the gym is divided up into four parts

freshmen, Sophmores, juniors, Seniors. one class
at a time cheers and whoevers the loudest gets
a class prize. Then the cheerleaders come out
and do hole mess of cheers and nobody can
understand what they are saying. Then every Body
runs of the bleacher and runs around and yells
a lot. "Were the Best"! etc. then every Body
goes home and then the sport events start and
Nobody else cares but the jocks.

In its brevity, narrative form, and focus on observed events, and in many of the problems it manifests, this writing sample is typical of the writing of struggling writers in middle and high schools. The writing is interesting, even amusing, but it shows a confusion of purpose, and its meaning is underdeveloped; we can't tell, for example, whether the writer wants to describe pep rallies or make fun of them. Granted, these problems may be approached through conferences that prod the writer to say more and to focus the writing. However, the act of revising may be more efficient, and the resultant learning more generalizable to future writing tasks, if we ask the writer to formulate an objective for the piece by deciding whether he really wants to describe or satirize pep rallies, or both, and then offer a strategy for moving the writing in that direction. The many surface and mechanical problems, such as the variations in punctuation and capitalization and the apparent attempt to spell some words (e.g., *siked, prepaired, teem*) by sound or by analogy with similar-sounding words, make it safe to predict, furthermore, that content-oriented feedback about the writing will not be enough to transform the piece into successful, well-formed prose. In this case, we need to give attention and considerable help to improving *both* the acquisition of an understanding of the important qualities of pep rallies *and* the learning of specific strategies and conventions for writing about those qualities.

This book makes a case for just that, for putting acquisition and learning together in our work with struggling writers. My emphasis, however, is not on learning discrete skills or rules or decontextualized writing techniques, or even a long list of seemingly universal writing strategies, but, rather, on teaching students to think strategically about writing. For example, let's say that we determine that the writer of the "pep rallies" essay could benefit from being asked to do some planning to come up with a better organization for the piece. But how should he accomplish the planning? For about 50 years prior to the process revolution, formal outlining was the only method of planning to write recognized by most textbooks and handbooks on the teaching of writing. In the book that started the process revolution, Emig (1971) pointed out that studies of the writing processes of professionals and skilled high school students show that they seldom use formal outlining but do use a variety of planning activities, including informal outlines and prewriting activities which may last as long as 2 years, as in the self-sponsored writing of one of the students in her study. The implication in Emig's argument is that we should stop teaching formal outlining and allow students to discover their own best methods of planning their writing. This argument suggests, again, a reliance on acquisition, this time as the means of achieving planning abilities, and although it is probably good advice when working with skilled writers such as those in Emig's study, it is less appropriate for struggling writers like the author of the pep rallies piece. Left to their own designs, in a development-by-acquisition mode, many struggling writers would most likely continue to struggle in inappropriate ways because they are unaware of their planning abilities and how to put them in the service of writing. It's better to shift the balance toward development by learning by providing instruction in writing strategies that tap into the planning preferences of struggling writers. As teachers who are familiar with using webs, charts, diagrams, and discussions know, there are many ways we can help writers plan by focusing and organizing the thinking that goes into writing. Later chapters present many of these planning strategies in detail and show how they are frequently based on imitative, visual, and narrative learning—three strengths of many struggling writers. For now, my point is simply that such methods of making thinking about writing more visible, efficient, and deliberate illustrate the use of instruction in writing strategies to enhance the development of writing abilities through strategic learning rather than solely through acquisition.

Current research has much to say about using strategy instruction with struggling writers. Researchers recognized strategies useful for literacy learning both in the primary discourses students bring to school and in the secondary discourses of schools. Researchers also emphasized both social and cognitive aspects of language and language learning. In the following chapters I take a close look at research that focuses on using these sociocognitive resources to help struggling writers strategically develop their writing abilities, and I show how explicit instruction within a social–cognitive framework can help writers identify and use strategies to gain greater control over their work at each stage of the writing process.

Writing as Process and Skill

Historically, as I mentioned earlier, the process movement represented a turning away from skills-based writing instruction in which writing skills were often thought of as "things," as reified objects passed from teacher to student. One of the earliest references to this turn was made at the Dartmouth Conference on the teaching of English in 1966, where participants decided to move "from an attempt to define *What* English is—a question that throws the emphasis on nouns like *skills*, and *proficiencies*, set *books*, and the *heritage*—to a definition by process, a description of the activities we engage in through language" (Dixon, 1967, p. 7, emphasis in original). As even that brief quote suggests, this view of language as process and activity assumed that writing is acquired rather than learned; like speech, writing is a naturally occurring phenomenon, latent within each student, an emergent ability the alert teacher will notice and draw on. Once writing came to be considered an activity, as in Emig's (1971) pioneering study of the writing processes of 12th graders, pedagogical emphasis began to be placed on emergent abilities and on the means of drawing them out, as in the content-oriented conferences between teachers and students that were so much a part of Graves's (1975) research on the writing processes of second-graders.

Process teaching thus assumes that students will develop their own reading and writing abilities through acquisition, that is, through practice and supportive feedback rather than through learning in the traditional sense of a transmission of skills from teachers and textbooks. Hillocks (1986), in fact, refers to the process model as the "natural process" mode of writing instruction because the dominant metaphor in the model is one of natural development. As Cook-Gumperz (1993) pointed out, the model has its basis in the self-discovery function of expressive writing, a kind of personal writing resembling written-down speech (Britton, Burgess, Martin, McLeod, & Rosen, 1975). Through reading and writing practice, writers internalize the forms of written language at the same time they learn to transform expressive writing into conventional, communicative writing (Britton et al., 1975). Methods texts for teachers of writing using the natural process model, such as Romano (1987), Kirby and Liner with Vinz (1988), and Noden and Vacca (1994), repeatedly stress the naturalness of learning to write from an expressive base by internalizing the forms of written language through reading and writing experience. Underpinning this expectation are two related central metaphors. The first is the metaphor of natural development, as if literacy development were governed by a graphic version of Chomsky's language acquisition device; this is the source of the belief that writing develops as naturally as speech. The second is the metaphor of instruction as the facilitation of writing development, as if the teacher's work were primarily to support writing development rather than to initiate, shape, or lead it.

Recent critiques of process approaches question their assumption of natural acquisition, the belief that nearly all writers will learn to write through experience with reading and writing and facilitative instruction. Researchers and theorists, for example, recognized a possible bias against nonmainstream students in the assumption that written forms will be more or less automatically internalized through reading and writing experience (Delpit, 1986, 1988; Gee, 1990; Hillocks, 1986; Kutz & Roskelly, 1991; Siddle-Walker, 1992). Siddle-Walker (1992), for example, finds "a lack of cultural synchronization" (p. 325) between what she sees as the process theorists' nondirective methods and African American students' general valuing of teachers who are directive (Delpit, 1988; Foster, 1987; Siddle, 1988). Dunn (1995) similarly finds a bias against learning-disabled students in the process movement's beliefs that inexperience with literacy is the primary cause of writing problems (see, e.g., Shaughnessy, 1977) and that natural language learning mechanisms will eliminate the problems through practice. The message in these new studies that learning differences are based on cultural or cognitive preferences supports the need for adding strategic writing instruction to process approaches. Researchers in special education (see, e.g., Englert, 1995; Harris & Graham, 1992, 1996) have taken the lead in combining process and strategies in writing instruction.

Many teachers, of course, also realize that the process assumption of natural acquisition of writing abilities is usually not justified in the case of writers who are having serious difficulties. Most secondary teachers who work with struggling writers know that some explicit teaching of knowledge and skill and some advice on adapting knowledge and skill to the achievement of particular goals must be added to a general process orientation. But what knowledge and what skill? How explicit do we need to be in our teaching? And where do we start? Do we begin with familiar forms of spoken language and tasks students can already do? Should we start with personal narrative writing, because that most closely resembles the familiar linguistic patterns used in everyday speech? Or, is an apparent dependence on the forms of spoken language one of the problems inexperienced writers bring to the classroom? Should we focus writing tasks on this week's course content, on the competency test at the end of the year, on writing typically required in content area courses, on local or national standards, or on expectations for writing in college and work contexts? This book answers these questions and more through a strategic learning model of writing processes. The main idea is that instead of attempting to teach struggling writers the content knowledge and the particular writing skills they need for every form of writing and every important writing task they may encounter in and out of school, we should teach them sociocognitive learning strategies for achieving self-regulation of the processes and codes necessary for the writing they encounter in a variety of settings. To put the matter another way, in place of a generic process approach, and without going back to traditional teaching of specific skills and rules, this book shows teachers how to teach students to control their own writing processes and writing skills.

Writing as Control and Identity

Control is the heart of writing development. Control over writing processes and written forms is where acquisition and learning come together. Control also ties process to product, cognition to motivation, community to school contexts. Teaching control over writing, to put the matter concisely, contributes to the social formation of identities as writers. To illustrate the crucial matter of the social formation of writing identity, I introduce Greg, a 17-year-old African American 10th-grader. Like many struggling writers, Greg was usually willing to work during writing workshop, and he seemed to work hard, even though he had a difficult time and generally produced writing that showed a lack of focus and contained many errors in spelling and mechanics, much like Jason and the author of the pep rallies piece.

What makes Greg's voice representative of struggling writers, however, is what he said on the day he *stopped* writing. Right in the middle of a writing workshop class, Greg suddenly put his pencil down, looked up at his teacher and asked, "Why do I have to do this writing? You know, and I know, I'm going to get a job working with my hands."

Greg had concluded that literacy did not matter much in his life. Somehow, he had acquired an identity of nonliteracy. Writing was for other students, more academically successful ones, those destined for jobs requiring mental work. It is not possible to identify specific reasons why Greg decided writing was not for him, but we can notice that he saw both the writing he was doing and the choice of careers open to him as out of his control, as governed by someone else. He saw writing as something one is told to do, not as a self-selected and self-directed means of exploring thought and constructing understanding. The teacher, or the school, was responsible for Greg's attempts at writing, just as forces beyond his control were responsible for the job limitations he perceived. It is reasonable to infer from Greg's question that he had a low level of belief in his identity as a writer because he did not believe in his own agency, his ability to affect his environment and control his writing and his life. Greg saw the work he did, both in school and out, as in the control of others.

The issue of control over learning and achievement is at the heart of strategic literacy, and I come back to it later in this chapter. For now, I want to point out a possible connection between Greg's perceived lack of agency and what I earlier called the "writing process by itself" approach to writing instruction. I am not claiming the two are causally related, but process teaching, perhaps ironically because of its nondirective qualities, does seem to have contributed to Greg's belief that his life is being directed by others. Greg's school had placed him in a lower-track program and given him a process-based writing program that allowed him nearly always to choose his own topics, to write at his own pace, and to postpone attention to spelling and other conventions. In a workshop setting Greg usually wrote about what he knew well, such as sports, in forms with which he was already familiar, such as personal narrative. He received plenty of feedback from his teacher and his peers but little specific advice on improving his writing. He seldom received explicit instruction in skills or strategies for writing, and when he did it was in the form of brief, generic minilessons offered to the whole class that usually had little to do with the writing Greg was working on at the moment. Certainly these experiences in the writing workshop were meant to give Greg a sense of accomplishment and confidence in his writing, but his question, "Why do I have to do this writing?", suggests that he knew better, perhaps because he knew his writing wasn't getting much better. Writing about familiar topics in familiar forms, receiving little help with mastering conventions of written language, and writing to revise in directions that may not have seemed clear were quite possibly holding back Greg's development of a sense of control over his writing. Greg's question, "Why do I have to do this writing?", suggests another one: Why is he questioning, right in the middle of a writing workshop, the connection between literacy and his achievement of success in school and career?

Tension in the Teaching of Writing

From interviews and observations of dozens of students like Greg, I concluded that frequently for them, literacy is not tied to a sense of control and identity, to self-determination and self-regulation of learning (Harris & Graham, 1992, 1996). Especially in matters of academic achievement and preparation for employment, writing is perceived by them as having no instrumentality, no meaningful effect on their lives. Greg's writing, furthermore, was unfocused and showed occasional serious problems in structure, logic, and mechanics, and it often stayed that way in spite of multiple drafts. Here again Greg is certainly not alone. The writing workshop and process approaches underplay the importance of being shown how to produce writing that conforms to conventions governing form and mechanics. For struggling writers, writing is something one attempts when told to, without sufficiently understanding why or how.

This analysis suggests that process approaches are giving writers control in inappropriate ways. Control over choice of topics, for example, is a hallmark of workshop teaching (Atwell, 1987), but choosing topics for writing is of questionable value if writers choose topics with which they are already familiar and then wonder why they have to write about those topics. And if control over form and mechanics remains elusive, how successful can writing be in academic and career settings?

In the teaching of writing, process is often contrasted with product, but that's just alliteration. The real contrast, as I suggest throughout this chapter, is between process and skills, primarily because the process movement has meant a nearly total turning away from an earlier model of writing instruction in which skills were the main focus of attention. Thanks to the writing-process movement, we have come a long way since Braddock, Lloyd-Jones, and Schoer (1963) launched an attack on the teaching of grammar that lasted several decades by stating that "the teaching of formal grammar has a negligible or, because it usually displaces some instruction and practice in actual composition, even a harmful effect on the improvement of writing" (pp. 37–38). Process-based writing instruction brought a turning away from studying the rules of prescriptive grammar, but this turn also brought avoidance of the study of model pieces of writing, the presentation of criteria for finished pieces, the structuring of instruction around sets of skills or rhetorical concepts, and the use of teachers as sources of explicit instruction. This turning away from traditional approaches found its fullest expression in *Writing without Teachers* (Elbow, 1973), where the emphasis is almost entirely on acquisition, on "natural" literacy development and implicit instruction to help students discover and elaborate meaning while allowing them to choose their own writing topics, free-write to identify and develop ideas, and postpone attention to matters of conventional form, style, diction, and editing. Generally speaking, the writing-process literature shows a neglect of skills-based teaching, the most notable exception being when Graves (1983), Atwell (1987), and Calkins (1994) recommend minilessons to teach matters of procedure and skill.

Of course, even though the writing-process literature neglected writing skills, the need for the teaching of skills and conventions never went away entirely. Throughout the 30-year history of the process movement, skills-based instruction was preserved in handbooks, workbooks, and professional texts such as *Errors and Expectations* (Shaughnessy, 1977). What's more, the general neglect of skills during the process movement had the ironic effect of preserving mid-1960s methods of instruction in writing skills. Compare any contemporary handbook on grammar and usage to one from 20 or 30 years ago and you'll see what I mean: The same rules are taught, they are often printed in the same bright shade of red ink, and they are illustrated with the same types of decontextualized, generic, and frequently vapid sentences. In spite of the process paradigm's constant effort to downplay the importance of skills, instruction in specific writing skills has not disappeared; indeed, such instruction in some schools appears to have been enhanced by the process movement's amplification of the debate over teaching skills and usage. Judging by reports and observations in secondary classrooms, it appears that skills instruction has often gone underground. For the most part, high school and middle school teachers still recognize the need for teaching skills, but they are often apologetic during discussion of skills instruction, perhaps because a discussion of writing skills, and especially grammar and usage, so frequently leads to disagreement in the teachers' room and at department meetings. The need to teach conventional forms and skills ranging from content generation and organization through error finding and correction is still with us, but the process movement both downplays and enhances the importance of such teaching, depending on where particular teachers stand in the debate over skills instruction.

With reference to the challenge of teaching struggling writers, Shaughnessy (1976) described a tension between what she called format and freedom:

Still, the special conditions of the remedial situation, that is, the need to develop within a short time a style of writing and thinking and a background of cultural information that prepare the student to cope with academic work, create a distinctive tension that almost defines the profession—a constant, uneasy hovering between the imperatives of format and freedom, convention and individuality, the practical and the ideal. Just where the boundaries between these claims are to be drawn in basic writing is by no means clear. (p. 152)

What Shaughnessy referred to as "the imperatives of format and freedom, convention and individuality, the practical and the ideal" describes the same distinction I discuss in terms of skills and process. Both formulations reflect the central challenge in teaching struggling writers by describing a double necessity—a need to reconcile conformity and creativity, convention and invention, skills and discovery, product and process. Where Shaughnessy saw tension and boundaries between opposites, however, strategic writing instruction advocates a combination of both ends, a balance between skills and processes.

Perhaps it is the tendency, as in Shaughnessy (1976), to see the debate over educational issues as reconcilable only by choosing between options arranged as a set of binary oppositions that gives us a seemingly constant tension in the teaching of writing. Or, perhaps we expect too much from educational innovation, as if abandoning one set of ideas completely and adopting another, opposite one, were the only path to reform. Certainly the writing-process movement fits this description. Zemelman and Daniels (1988), for example, use a table to "identify the key points of contrast between the old and new paradigms" (p. 340), that is, between traditional teaching and process-based instruction. Here are excerpts from their table, which they call a "comparison of polarities":

Old/traditional view	New/process view
Writing is a product to be evaluated.	Writing is a process to be experienced.
Writing is taught rather than learned.	Writing is predominantly learned rather than taught.
The process of writing is largely conscious.	Writing often engages unconscious processes.

What strikes me as peculiar about this way of thinking is not so much the alternative choices the table offers—though I do take strong exception to the view that writing is largely an unconscious process; control over writing, even at a level where it is automatic, is still conscious. What bothers me most is that we separate the two sides of the table. According to this way of thinking, innovation is only a reaction to tradition, and process and product, teaching and learning are forever isolated from each other. Historically, process writing was a reaction to directive, skills-oriented teaching, but that does not mean that once process writing itself becomes the dominant tradition, we must abandon explicit teaching of writing skills completely. Such a view runs the risk of oversimplifying education by suggesting that teaching always involves choosing between alternatives and establishing one alternative as the authoritative one. The problem with this stance is that it leaves educators who are in tune with the realities of classrooms and the needs of students with an ongoing tension between opposite choices, such as skills and process, or the "constant, uneasy hovering between the imperatives of format and freedom" which Shaughnessy (1976, p. 152) described.

The teaching of writing to struggling writers would benefit from rejecting notions of incompatible extremes in the teaching of writing in favor of a view that integrates seemingly discrete alternatives—skills and process, tradition and innovation, development and socialization, cognition and culture, nature and nurture. Reconciling these differences gives us the necessity of *both* process and skill, creativity and conformity, invention and convention, discovery and communication, and acquisition and learning. Such a reconciliation is at the heart of the strategic writing approach as it is presented in these pages.

The common ground between process and skill in the teaching of writing which I emphasize in this book is self-regulated, culturally responsive strategic writing—exactly what was missing in Greg's experience in the writing workshop. Writing strategies stand midway between process and skill. A strategy is a sequence of cognitive steps designed to accomplish a particular outcome, and therefore we can think of strategies as controls over inward processes which result in outward manifestations of skills. Writing strategies, accordingly, are cognitive controls or procedures that transform the intention to write into marks on paper. Strategies, furthermore, are acquired or learned in social contexts. Some strategies are acquired intuitively from experience in situational contexts, and others are learned deliberately, usually in educational contexts, but the acquisition or learning is always accomplished through social interaction with people or texts or both. This book argues that one way of integrating the writing-process movement with recent calls for explicit, goals-oriented, culturally responsive instruction (e.g., Ball, 1992, 1994; Collins, 1995a; Delpit, 1986, 1988; Gee, 1990; Hillocks, 1986; Kutz & Roskelly, 1991; Lee, 1995; Siddle-Walker, 1992) is to build instruction around strategic learning opportunities writers can use to produce purposeful, contextually meaningful writing and to achieve self-regulation of processes and skills involved in writing.

That last sentence provides a good framework for introducing strategic writing instruction. I use the term "strategic writing instruction" throughout this book to refer to a pedagogical stance focused on helping writers learn to identify and use strategies for writing through sociocognitive mediation: sociocognitive in the sense of combining social and cognitive aspects of writing and also in the sense of combining teaching and learning so that learning and acquisition supplement the traditional transmission of knowledge and skills from teachers to students. Process and skill become integrated as writers learn to look for and work with strategies for managing writing and for achieving communicative goals through writing. People formulating and achieving goals is what constitutes strategic behavior: "*[L]earners,* not actions are strategic because it is their decisions, purposes and efforts that determine their behavior in large measure" (Paris, Lipson, & Wixson, 1983, p. 298, emphasis in original). Greg's question earlier in this chapter now takes on greater significance because we see that it is the focus of his question, the recognition of goals, that drives strategic literacy. "Why do I have to do this writing?" is a very real question for all writers and an especially difficult one for students, because teachers usually provide their motives for writing, but the role of instruction in identifying goals for writing does not have to stop at the traditional assignment. Rather, we can give writers the sense that writing is a means of solving problems in school and in life. The answer to "Why do I have to do this writing?" should not be focused on the value of producing certain texts as much as on the value of literacy for acting intelligently in a challenging world. The role of instruction in helping students to answer questions about why they have to write can be to provide a gradual transfer of responsibility for writing, and for control over writing purposes, processes, and skills, from teachers to students through the attainment of personally and socially meaningful, goal-directed strategic writing abilities.

Chapter Two

Strategies and Performances

Seven years ago I decided to take saxophone lessons. I wanted to see whether I could learn to play rock tunes from the 1950s and '60s, including some of the saxophone solos in much of that music. So I signed up at night school and rented a saxophone. Only when I held the instrument in my hands for the first time, then let it hang from my neck, loose and awkward and heavy, did it dawn on me that I had absolutely no idea what to do with it.

I remember thinking that I would prefer reading about playing the sax to actually playing it. I'm very much a text-oriented person, and reading is the primary way I learn new skills. I have books on gardening, home remodeling, deck building, automobile repairing, and much more. Reading helped me learn to use my microcomputer and to coach my son's baseball team. When I started running again after a 20-year layoff, the first thing I did was read about training techniques, even though I was on the varsity track and cross country teams in college and coached the same sports when I taught high school. Reading, in short, is my preferred approach to difficult new tasks.

And reading is how I initially wanted to learn the saxophone. At the music store I asked for a book on playing the sax, but the salesperson sold me a book without words, certainly not what I in mind when I had asked for a book. I wanted a book that said things like, "If you wear a shirt with a collar, the neck strap will be more comfortable," and, "The following stretching exercises will help prevent the lower back pain that comes from standing tense and motionless for a couple of hours with a saxophone dangling from your neck." All I wanted was the usual self-help advice, clearly and simply presented in the familiar medium of written text, but the only book available had nothing but music in it. Of course, I couldn't read it.

Instead of self-help, I asked several people to show me how to get started. My wife used to play the clarinet, and she led me through putting the sax together and wetting the reed and blowing hard enough for sound—noise, not music—to come out. A colleague showed me the six basic finger positions, the "home keys" of the saxophone, and a graduate student showed me how to use these keys to produce my first notes: B, A, G, by holding down one, two, and three keys with my left hand, then F, E, D by also holding down one, two, and three keys with my right hand.

Then classes started. We had five students in class, and Larry, our instructor, divided us into three groups on the second night we met. Dick could already play the saxophone and therefore comprised the advanced group all by himself. Pam and Steve could already read music and became the middle group. Dave and I, the nonreaders, were sent next door to the band room, where Larry said he would join us later. I remember that there was no heat in the band room and that Dave liked to walk around and quickly play notes up and down the scale, probably to keep warm. When Larry joined us, I told him about trouble I was having establishing the length of notes; for me, whole notes, half notes, and quarter notes all sounded the same so that what I produced was not music but rather a string of seemingly unrelated sounds. I told him I had practiced for hours, but the tunes from our book didn't sound like they were supposed to sound. He told me not to worry, that my ability would improve with practice.

Dave and I had no idea how to help each other learn to play the saxophone. While we waited for Larry each week, we practiced alone, even though we were in the same room. What little we said to each other seemed designed to compensate for our shared ineptitude at playing the sax. One night, for example, Dave told me that he always succeeds at tasks he sets his mind to complete, and he illustrated the truth of that statement with several examples from his work as a salesperson. Another night we went out to my car where I played "Yackety Yak" for Dave so he could hear my favorite 1950s rock saxophone solo. He was more impressed with the car, especially the radio and leather seats, and I remember being glad Dave knew I had a sports car with leather seats. I felt my musical ability was stuck on hold and I didn't want him to think I was a failure in other ways as well. In fact, occasionally I had to fight that perception myself. One night Dave was absent, and the highlight of my lesson was locking myself out of the band room. I went to the other room, where Pam, Steve, and Larry were practicing, to get a new reed from my case. I stayed and listened to them for a while, thinking I might learn more from them than I was learning by myself in the other room, blaming myself for not being good enough to belong to their group. Then I discovered the band room door had locked behind me when I left. I spent 20 minutes roaming the halls looking for a janitor to let me back in.

On another night, after I practiced four melodies until I could really play them well at home, I discovered that I still couldn't play them along with Larry. We were looking at his book, not mine, and I couldn't read the notes. In my book I had penciled in the note names above each note so that I wouldn't have to think about each note and decide what it was. I just read the penciled-in names. It sure beat looking at each note, identifying it, thinking about finger positions, and then blowing the horn. Penciling in the note names, however, prevented me from learning them. I couldn't read the notes in Larry's book and I played miserably.

Lest you think I failed entirely, I quickly add that I finally hit upon a learning strategy that worked for me. I taped Larry playing several practice melodies from our book to see if that would help me practice by playing tunes the way they were supposed to sound. At most, Larry was spending 10 minutes each night with Dave and me, and his primary instructional method consisted of the three of us playing together. Larry, Moe, and Curly. Perhaps this was why Dave stopped coming after 3 weeks. My new method—recording Larry playing clear and deliberate renditions of the tunes and striving to imitate his playing while I practiced at home—rather suddenly had me playing tunes directly by reproducing whole patterns of sound. Learning to read music went more quickly once I could read the notes as sounds because I had heard Larry play them. If I played a tune several times, in fact, fingering began to become automatic, through a kind of direct note-to-sound transfer. The next week in class Dick stuck around after his lesson and we played together. I managed to keep up with him most of the time. The following week Dick and I played songs together from a book I had picked up—*20 All-Time Hit Paraders.* The songs were straight out of 1958: "Witch Doctor," "Johnny B. Goode," "Twilight Time," "For Your Love." Larry heard us playing some rock music, and he joined right in. Later he told us that he had logged many hours in local bars playing jazz and rock and taught us a basic rock melody which repeats the same five notes in three different combinations. I was on my way to musical success.

Struggling Musician, Struggling Writer

The story of my saxophone lessons is true, and I tell it here because in many ways my experience was parallel to what struggling writers often go through. To begin with, my lessons were difficult because they didn't match my usual learning methods. I am good at processing knowledge through text, and I wanted to read and figure things out for myself, but the kind of reading I was good at was not the kind of reading the task required. Struggling writers, similarly, have ways of reading the world and processing knowledge, but their ways of reading don't include advanced skill with the complex literacy tasks schools value, the kind of reading skill, for example, which is assumed in this lesson from a popular handbook:

> Most paragraphs contain a topic sentence that states the paragraph's main idea. Usually the topic sentence is paced at or near the beginning of the paragraph. Placing the topic sentence at the beginning helps readers by giving them a clear idea of what is going to be discussed in the paragraph. Stating the main idea at the beginning of the paragraph also helps

writers keep clearly in mind the main idea they are going to develop. (Warriner, 1986, p. 408)

This is an example of the text-based writing instruction I described in Chapter 1. It is time-honored advice on using a topic sentence to focus the writing in a paragraph, and there is nothing wrong with such advice for writers who know what paragraphs and topic sentences are, who can read well enough to process rather abstract writing instructions, and who can put the advice to work while they are writing. Struggling writers, however, have difficulty meeting these criteria.

Other parallels between struggling musician and struggling writer are available. The teaching and modeling I finally benefited from was not the kind of teaching my instructor preferred. Larry seemed to think that our playing together would assist my development, but I couldn't keep up, even though he had grouped us by ability. I am sure Larry meant well, but dividing five students into three groups amounted to cutting his "remedial" students off from possible interactions with other learners, interactions that could provide much of the help we needed. At the same time, isolation from more talented musicians helped ensure that my identity as a musician would go nowhere. Dave and I didn't want to be perceived as failed musicians, so we resisted revealing our lack of skills, even to each other, by discussing subjects other than saxophone playing. This resistance helped to protect our identities from any threat of a perception of weakness. My resorting to penciling in the names of notes is another parallel in that it resembles the coping strategies often seen in the work of struggling writers. I am sure my penciling in the notes has the appearance of cheating, just as the beginning writer's tendency toward copying from the book or from other writers does, but in both cases we are attempting to solve a problem by resorting to a strategy that seems to make sense because it helps to get the job done. Finally, my success came when I discovered a useful strategy and when I moved out of the remedial class and became a member of a community of musicians. This last similarity between my saxophone lessons and the experience of struggling writers gets to two general principles regarding the development of new skills:

1. The acquisition of increased ability can be assisted by the learning of strategies for managing performance.
2. Strategies for managing performance are best learned in social contexts which support both acquisition and learning.

Taken together, these two principles stand midway between learning and acquisition and combine both modes of development. When ability is not picked up "naturally," when it is not easily or automatically acquired in the course of attempting a performance, the ability must be learned through deliberate effort. Strategic thinking and strategies are ways of focusing that effort, ways of controlling and managing the attempted performance so that deliberate learning assists the acquisition of ability. The social context, furthermore, is important for combining learning and acquisition in situations where "going it alone" is not possible. I was stuck at the beginning of the process of learning to play the saxophone, and I needed help. My reading ability with text wasn't useful in overcoming my lack of reading ability with music. Rote learning of the notes as I practiced at home didn't help because the notes weren't forming musical patterns. Penciling in the note names above the notes on the page provided a shortcut to performance that failed to transfer to other situations. In short, I needed help from skilled performers to get past my inability to read music. Larry seemed to believe there was no *direct* way to teach me to decode musical notation. To me, it seemed reasonable to expect that a lesson about musical notes and how to control their variations in length would contribute to my interpretive understanding of the notes on the page, that is, how to recognize and replicate patterns in the notes, not just decode them into individual sounds. Larry, however, favored *indirect* methods of teaching, which means of course that he favored acquisition as a way of developing musical abilities. He was a talented musician, and learning by acquisition probably worked well for him, but his tendency to let me simply discover playing techniques and relations among notes by myself didn't work for me. What did finally work was a combination of both direct learning from instruction and indirect acquisition through practice without instruction. The combination took the form of a learning strategy that included modeling (my recordings of Larry playing the tunes to show how they were supposed to sound), performance (my playing the same tunes in imitation of his renditions), and practice (repetition to achieve closer approximations of Larry's performance). It is also important that the strategy became effective when I left the solitude of the band room and joined an apprenticeship (Larry allowing me to tape-record his playing) and a community of helpful and supportive musicians (what our group of saxophone players quickly became once Dick and I, and then Larry, started playing together). The combination of *strategic thinking and supportive social context* served both acquisition and learning—acquisition, for example, when Larry's tape-recorded playing guided my efforts, and learning from direct instruction when we practiced the versatile rock melody Larry showed us.

Learning Strategies for Managing Performance

Strategies and supportive social contexts are also important in writing instruction. More about our work with Jason, the ninth-grader I introduced at the beginning of Chapter 1, clarifies and illustrates that point. Recall that in his spoken response to the Hughes story, Jason briefly but successfully responded to the request for a summary of what had happened so far in the story and a prediction about what would happen next:

> "Sounds like the boy really, kinda like sounds like he's lying just a little bit. Sounds like he's got no family, and trying to take her purse for money so he can live. And, sounds like the woman wasn't too mad about it and wanted to take him home, clean him up, and maybe have him for her son."

His writing on the same task, however, provided an unfocused summary of a few details from the plot of the story and several interpretive statements set off by quotation marks, including a prediction about the rest of the story:

> I have just read a story about a boy who ran into a women knocking her down and braking

her purse. The boy fell down from hitting her
purse. The women turned around and picked him
up buy his shirt. The boy said he didn't mean
to hit the women and knock her purse to the
ground. "But I think the boy was lieing to the
women." The boy had a dirty face and the women
said to the boy if I let you go will you run
away, and the boy said yes. So the women said
I should bring you home and wash your face and
give dinner. "I think the women thinks that the
boy lives on the street and I agree with the
women." The women says that the boy should come
live with her.
    "I think the rest of the story the boy will
live with this women and stay with her for the
rest of his life."

The cognitive demands of writing seem to call out a tendency in struggling writers toward "knowledge telling," Bereiter
and Scardamalia's (1987) label for a model of cognitive processing involved in writing which uses a familiar genre and repeats
what one knows about a given subject. Jason relied on the
original story to frame his written response. Rather than stating
the gist of the story and his own response to it as he did in the
brief spoken version of his response to the assignment, his
writing listed events in the story. Jason tells what he knows about
the story by reviewing the text and summarizing selected details
and by providing a running commentary on what he thinks of
events in the story. The result was that Jason's writing leaned
heavily on the content and form of the original text. In fact, he
copied some details almost verbatim from the story, and he
organized his summary by following the story's narrative line,
interspersing his own comments along the way. As I noted earlier
and explain fully in later chapters, these tendencies toward
copying and plot summary are often typical of struggling writers
and seem to resemble coping or default strategies, similar in
their effects to my penciling in the names of musical notes.
    When the teacher and I first read Jason's writing aloud with
him, he interrupted the reading just after the first sentence with
quotation marks—"But I think the boy was lieing to the
women."—and asked, "Should that be a quote right there?" In
our work with struggling writers, as I explain more fully in

Chapter 3, we ask them to share their struggles with us by voicing the questions and concerns that seem to indicate important trouble spots or difficulties they encounter while writing. Jason's question about quotation marks, it turned out, was one such indicator of trouble. Before answering the question, we asked why he had used quotation marks, and he said, "because I was writing for myself." We prompted him for a further explanation, and it became clear that Jason was writing with a distinction in mind between recording what the book said and interpreting what he thinks and writes "for himself," marking the latter in accordance with a misinterpretation of what a teacher once told him about quotation marks to set off "direct" statements. His reliance on "copying" the content and plot from the story was his attempt to capture what the book said, and the three sentences in quotation marks were his attempt to formulate his own opinions about events in the story. Jason was following a "summarize and give your opinion" plan in his writing, certainly a plan appropriate for completing many school assignments. He also sensed that summary and opinion should be separated somehow in his writing, and he achieved the separation by setting off his own remarks with quotation marks instead of placing them in a separate paragraph or using some other means that would be more conventional than quotation marks.

Taken together, Jason's spoken response and his written one suggested that he could do what was called for in the task we gave him, except (ironically) when directly focusing his attention on writing about the story. Writing about the story seemed to pull Jason in the direction of carefully copying and listing the events in the story instead of reshaping and condensing them as the spoken version of his response to the reading had done. Our observations of Jason's writing process seemed to indicate that he accomplished the "summarize and give your opinion" plan in two ways: by referring repeatedly to the text of the story, borrowing events for his summary and writing them down and by interspersing his own thoughts throughout the plot summary by juxtaposing them with items from the summary but setting them off with quotation marks. When we interviewed him about his writing process, he indicated that he learned to pay close attention to his reading from previous teachers who, in his words, "kept telling me to be specific." We decided, accordingly, that Jason's "summarize and give your opinion" strategy was appropriate for this task—as it is for so much school writing requiring close analytical attention to text—as long as Jason met the terms of the assignment by also including a prediction about what will happen in the rest of the story, which he did in the last sentence of his essay. Notice that this decision precludes asking Jason to avoid using strategies he was having some success with in his school writing, such as repeating some events from the text he was writing about. This acceptance of strategies that struggling writers are already using is a crucial aspect of strategic writing instruction, and I say more about recognizing and supporting strategies students bring to the classroom when I discuss default strategies and ways of combining old and new writing strategies in later chapters.

What we decided to help Jason with was constructing and using a strategy for paragraphing. As I noted earlier, Jason's question about quotation marks ("Should that be a quote right there?") was really a question about arranging his ideas on the page. His explanation of the trouble he was having with writing at the point at which he asked the question showed that he was really wondering about marking his own ideas as distinct from those in the book. In asking his question, he was beginning to think strategically about his writing because he was pausing and wondering about his options for creating his meaning. Jason was having difficulty, we decided, not because he wasn't thinking strategically but because he didn't control an appropriate strategy for sorting and grouping his ideas, for establishing at least two categories, what the book says and what he thinks. Accordingly, learning a strategy for organizing ideas into paragraphs is what we decided to help him with. Paragraph structure is more than an arbitrary convention of written language; our research suggests that paragraph structure reflects underlying cognitive processes involved in shaping, focusing, and organizing one's thinking. At the same time, paragraph structure entails the socialization of thought because it includes regularized patterns of writing, well-established ways of organizing ideas that provide firm but flexible guidelines for recognizing the shape and direction of an argument or a narrative for both writers and readers. It's probably not making too much of my comparison between text and music to say that paragraphs are like stanzas, complete with structural markers and regularities that construct form: indenting, topic sentences, and clarifying information in the case of paragraphs and meter, rhyme, and rhythm in the case of stanzas.

Once we decided to help Jason focus his writing by using paragraphs instead of quotation marks to signal the organization of his ideas, we started working with him by showing him a short essay containing two well-structured paragraphs written by an English teacher on the same topic Jason's teacher originally assigned. Using a drawing program on a microcomputer, we had him draw boxes to identify the two paragraphs in the model essay. We first asked him to draw a box around each of the paragraphs, and Figure 2.1 shows the results.

Next, we asked Jason how he knew where to draw the boxes. He said he relied on the author's use of indenting, and we congratulated him on taking advantage of one of the ways writers mark paragraph structure. Then we asked Jason to identify other clues to the shape of the two paragraphs. Jason noticed that they were about the same size and shape, features we did not consciously strive for in selecting the model paragraphs, but nevertheless features that might help Jason think about formulating a paragraph-structured response to the task that was given him. Next, we asked him to compare the first sentence in each paragraph with the other sentences. He became excited when he noticed that, in his words, the first sentence "leads" the paragraph and the other sentences "follow the leader." At this moment, with our help in establishing a procedure for identifying topic sentences, Jason discovered the gist-

> A boy tries to snatch a woman's purse, but fails miserably. He is overcome by the weight of the purse, he falls, and the woman captures him. The boy apologizes, wanting to get away. But the woman wouldn't let him leave her side.

> In the rest of the story Mrs. Jones will take him home, wash his face, and feed him. She will try to find out if he has a home. If he doesn't, she'll probably try to care for him or will make sure he's cared for by someone else.

FIGURE 2.1. Boxed paragraphs.

stating function of "leading" sentences and began to formulate his own knowledge about them. This is an example of modeling and instruction leading the acquisition of strategic writing knowledge; our model paragraphs and calling Jason's attention to differences between sentences according to their placement in the paragraphs helped him come up with the metaphor of leading and following sentences. We next asked him to underline the lead sentences, and he did, as in Figure 2.2.

The method we used helped Jason acquire an understanding of two key elements of paragraph structure, topic sentences, and clarifying information. Notice, however, that the method did not mention topic sentences or clarifying information at all. Instead, we started with two well-formed model paragraphs and used them to help Jason create a *graphic representation of paragraph structure* to set the stage for him to discover, or invent, a distinction between leading and following sentences. Presumably the graphic representation and the idea of leading and following sentences were registered cognitively as a corresponding mental image and verbal knowledge that can help Jason write focused paragraphs and build a conscious understanding of paragraph structure. My reasoning here is that struggling writers like Jason can build knowledge of writing processes and structures through visual or spatial means, such as "the capacity to produce a graphic likeness of spatial information," or "the capacity to conjure up mental imagery and then to transform that imagery" which form part of Gardner's (1983, p. 176) description of spatial intelligence. Following this logic, it is possible that by asking Jason to talk about the function of the first sentence in

```
   A boy tries to snatch a woman's purse, but fails
miserably. He is overcome by the weight of the purse,
he  falls,  and  the  woman  captures  him.  The  boy
apologizes,  wanting  to  get  away.  But  the  woman
wouldn't let him leave her side.
```

```
   In the rest of the story Mrs. Jones will take him
home, wash his face, and feed him. She will try to
find  out  if  he  has  a  home.  If  he  doesn't,  she'll
probably try to care for him or will make sure he's
cared for by someone else.
```

FIGURE 2.2. Boxed paragraphs with underlined topic sentences.

each paragraph, we were encouraging the learning of knowledge of paragraph structure through conversion from spatial and visual forms of cognitive representation.

Jason's expressed understanding of paragraph structure in terms of sentences that lead and others that follow exemplifies what I mean by learning through strategies. One of the most often cited challenges facing teachers in their work with students who struggle with literacy is to find ways to make up for reading and writing practice that simply hasn't happened with sufficient regularity. Many writers—and probably most writing teachers—have indeed acquired their understanding of text and paragraph structure and other written conventions intuitively from extensive reading and writing practice. Struggling readers and writers are likely to be working with more limited practice in reading and writing, and thus they have acquired fewer written forms by intuition or inference from reading and writing. Alternative means of achieving awareness of written forms, therefore, are likely to be extremely helpful for them. The key is to realize that struggling writers are not lazy or ignorant just because they struggle with conventional literacy. When Jason asked about quotation marks, we realized that what he was really asking about was a way of marking his own ideas as distinct from the ideas he borrowed from his reading. We now realize, in addition, that he was looking for a visible means, rather than a textual one, to categorize types of ideas, his own and the story's. The "visual representation of text" strategy we used with Jason played to one of his apparent strengths, visual learning. We resisted the temptation to teach Jason about the correct use of quotation marks, or to teach information about "topic sentences," or even about "leading and following sentences" or visual imagery. Instead, we started with two well-formed model paragraphs and asked him to think about their regularities. Jason then proved himself to be good at using visual imagery to help himself acquire a strategy for marking paragraph structure to signal the types of ideas he wanted to categorize.

Once we noticed his abilities with visual modes of learning, our instructional objectives focused on helping Jason to form a picture in his mind of what paragraphs generally look like, a mental model of paragraph structure which would be accessible while writing. Mentally representing "finished" writing is something experienced writers do rather automatically (Bereiter &

Scardamalia, 1987). For experienced writers, for example, it is difficult to read the words "business letter" without forming a mental image of one. The strategy we used to teach the use of a mental representation of paragraph structure to Jason consisted of having him create a "flexible template" comprised of paragraphs to draw on, first literally as he drew boxes and underlinings and then figuratively as he drew on his spatial knowledge of the general shape of paragraphs to express a verbal understanding of relations between leading and following sentences. Figure 2.3 demonstrates this use of boxes and lines to represent paragraph structure. The boxes represent the general shape of short paragraphs, and the lines represent topic sentences within the paragraphs.

The use of a visual template as a writing strategy, I want to quickly add, is *not* the same as using a formula or a workbook page with blank spaces to be filled in. Teaching writing by offering formulas for guiding the production of writing is not what strategic writing instruction is about, as I make abundantly clear in Chapter 4. The template is instead a flexible guide, a think sheet (Englert, Raphael, & Anderson, 1992), for helping to manage part of a writing performance by organizing ideas into paragraphs, for assisting in the construction of an understanding of paragraph structure and the function of topic sentences, and for focusing the instructional conferences taking place between writer and teacher. Having access to a computer, furthermore, helps with the drawing of paragraph-shaped boxes over written text and with copying the boxes for use as flexible templates with subsequent pieces of writing, but the computer

FIGURE 2.3. Graphic representation of paragraph structure for a two-paragraph essay.

is not absolutely necessary; teacher-researchers working with me have tried drawing boxes around paragraphs and highlighting topic sentences by hand on paper, and these techniques work just as well as drawing on the computer.

The strategy of mentally representing the structure of a paragraph so that it can be understood as a group of ideas placed in a certain relation to each other met the goal of focusing Jason's writing within paragraphs. Next we applied Jason's new visual representation of text strategy to revising his own essay. Using his writing and the computer drawing program, we asked Jason to draw boxes around his paragraphs. This time indenting and paragraph length were not such reliable clues, and Jason had difficulty deciding where the boxes representing paragraphs should go. Figure 2.4 shows his first attempt.

At this point Jason admitted he was stuck and asked for help. He said he didn't know what to do with the sentences in quotation marks. They no longer seemed to belong in that they didn't fit the organizational pattern we worked on earlier with the model paragraphs. Recall, too, that they didn't really fit the assignment which asked for only two categories of information,

```
   I have just read a story about a boy who ran into
a women knocking her down and braking her purse. The
boy fell down from hitting her purse. The women
turned around and picked him up buy his shirt. The
boy said he didn't mean to hit the women and knock
her purse to the ground.
```

"But I think the boy was lieing to the women."

```
The boy had a dirty face and the women said to the
boy if I let you go will you run away, and the boy
said yes.
```

```
So the women said I should bring you home and wash
your face and give dinner.
```

"I think the women thinks that the boy lives on the street and I agree with the women." The women says that the boy should come live with her.

"I think the rest of the story the boy will live with this women and stay with her for the rest of his life."

FIGURE 2.4. Jason's first attempt at locating paragraphs in his text.

what has happened and what will happen. Also, we suspected that Jason had trouble "finding" paragraphs in his own text because he had used a different organizing marker, the quotation marks, to distinguish his opinions from his plot summary. At this point, therefore, we gave him explicit help. We told Jason he was making the assignment harder than it had to be by including three "leading ideas" instead of only two as the other writer had done. We asked Jason to compare his essay to the other one we worked on and to underline the same two possible "leading ideas" in his essay. He underlined "I have just read a story about a boy who ran into a woman knocking her down and braking her purse," and "I think the rest of the story the boy will live with this women and stay with her for the rest of his life." We then asked him to look for his third set of ideas, and together with him we decided it included the ideas marked by quotation marks and the phrase "I think," but did not include the "rest of the idea" lead we had already underlined. In response to our request, Jason selected "I think the boy was lieing to the woman" as the lead idea in the third paragraph, or quotation marks group, and underlined it. We asked Jason to create boxes, as he did for the earlier essay, for his three leading ideas, which he did, as in Figure 2.5.

At this point, we asked Jason how he might describe the similarities among the three underlined ideas in the latest

---

I have just read a story about a boy who ran into a women knocking her down and braking her purse. The boy fell down from hitting her purse.

I think the boy was lieing to the woman

I think the rest of the story the boy will live with this women and stay with her for the rest of his life.

FIGURE 2.5. Graphic representation of paragraph structure for Jason's planned revision.

version of the drawing. He thought for a moment and then said that each is a leading idea that introduces other ideas. He further explained that the lead item earns its leadership position because it works to introduce the information that follows. We asked Jason how we could represent that in our drawing, and he came up with the notion of thinking of the lead item as contained within a box which, in turn, contained the other ideas in another box. We modified the computer drawing to represent his idea of using nested boxes for "leading" and "following" items, as in Figure 2.6.

We next told Jason that this new drawing could be used as a plan to revise his essay. We asked him to fill in the empty boxes with ideas that follow the leads of each of the leading statements. Before letting him get started, though, we asked Jason to compare his opening—"I have just read a story about a boy who ran into a woman knocking her down and braking her purse."—to the earlier one from the model essay—"A boy tries to snatch a woman's purse, but fails miserably." He picked up on the difference right away. He said the story was not about the boy

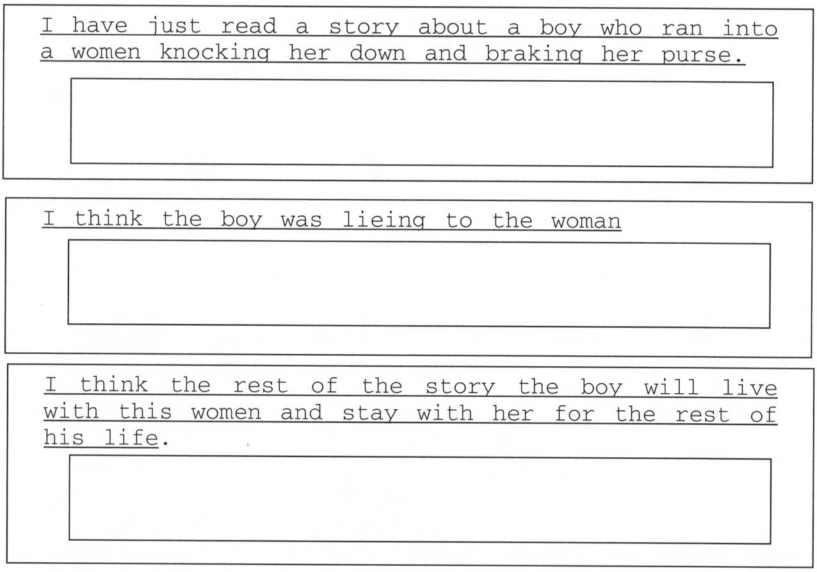

I have just read a story about a boy who ran into a women knocking her down and braking her purse.

I think the boy was lieing to the woman

I think the rest of the story the boy will live with this women and stay with her for the rest of his life.

FIGURE 2.6. Graphic representation of paragraph structure for Jason's planned revision.

breaking the woman's purse, as he had written, but instead was about the boy trying to steal the woman's purse. We asked Jason to change his drawing to reflect the purse stealing and to be sure to include that in his revision. He wrote for about 15 minutes, looking frequently at his textbook (his "old" strategy of getting the information he needs by copying ideas from his reading) and at his graphic plan (his "new" strategy of plugging information into boxes representing paragraphs), and produced this version of the essay:

> Late one night a large women was walking down the street when all of a sudden she felt a large jerk, a boy was trying to take her purse. The purse had every thing in it but a hammer. When the boy hit the women the purse waded so much that the boy fell to the ground and his feet flew up into the air. The women quickly grabbed the boy by his shirt and told the boy to pick up her purse. The women then asked the boy if she lets go will he run away. The boy says yes. She realizes that the boy is all dirty, so she asks him doesn't he have someone at home who will make sure that he gets clean. The boy replies No!. So the women thinks to her self why don't I take this boy home and clean him.
>
> In the story the boy says he didn't mean to hit the women but I think the boy is lying to the women. Also I think all the boy wants to do is get free so he would probably lie if he could get free. The women says I see that your face is dirty and she is going to wash his face makes her sound like that she cares a lot this boy.
>
> I think the boy will probably go live with the women and learn what right is from wrong. But I think the women will send this boy to school if he is not in school and make him learn so that he can get an education so that he can take care of himself when he gets older and not steal. I think the women will also clean the boy up but at the same time teach him and care for him so that he dosen't feel like he needs to steal and also give him food and shelter and clothing if he dosen't have shelter or clothing. It dosen't sound like he has to look forward

for very much when he wakes up every morning.
I also think the women will teach the boy not
to try to lie.

Jason's revised essay shows the effects of combining his old and new writing strategies. The first paragraph shows a considerable amount of reproducing information from the story, the old strategy. Clearly, though, the next two paragraphs show much less of the dependence on copying from the story and more of Jason's own thinking about events and characters. Having spaces to do his own thinking encouraged him to do more of it, as if the planning "boxes" he drew in preparation for containing his ideas somehow make it easier to explore the ideas. The revision also shows that he is beginning to frame his ideas in terms of a conventional text pattern, the hierarchical arrangement of main idea and clarifying information typical of most academic writing.

With decreasing amounts of help from us in the next several papers Jason wrote, we reinforced the strategy he learned by working the pattern of main idea and clarifying information—or leading and following sentences—into his writing. Jason created a rather sophisticated method of planning using the notion of nested boxes, and this method seemed to work well for him, probably because writing his essays became largely a matter of generating the details of content for the boxes of "leading" and "following" ideas. The planning and structuring of ideas came under better control than before Jason learned to plan his writing through the visual representation of text strategy. Jason also discovered that he could write the parts of the essays in any order, filling in the content of any box he wanted to work on without worrying about the others. This method of planning, in its flexibility and recursiveness, has clear advantages over conventional outlining.

Balancing Acquisition and Learning

Our work with Jason illustrates the meaning of the two general principles regarding the development of new skills discussed earlier:

1. The acquisition of increased ability can be assisted by the learning of strategies for managing performance.
2. Strategies for managing performance are best learned in social contexts which support both acquisition and learning.

Our work with Jason was in accord with these principles. Jason learned a new writing strategy, one that clearly helped him manage his performance, and he learned it in a supportive social context, one that let him identify the difficulty he was having and then helped him overcome it. We allowed for the acquisition of writing skills by building on an apparent strength (visual learning), on an ability or strategy Jason expressed an interest in learning (how to organize, and signal the organization of, your thinking while writing), and on a strategy he was already using (getting some of his ideas for writing about reading by copying from the reading itself). Our instruction was also aimed toward new learning, however, in that we identified the strategy (graphic organization of text) to be used in managing the performance of reorganizing Jason's writing. That the social context was crucial to this combination of acquisition and learning is indicated by the conversations we had with Jason during writing conferences. These conversations helped him to rethink his essay, reorganizing and adding to it, and, more generally, they helped him understand that paragraphs can be thought of as bordered by imagined "boxes" representing conceptual spaces to store related ideas, one of which "leads" the others. We used modeling in two ways, by presenting Jason with model paragraphs and by demonstrating one of the ways writers think about paragraph and text structure, through visual representation. Clearly, we were behaving like teachers and providing useful instruction, but we were careful to avoid doing the thinking about paragraph structure for Jason. We gave him an opportunity—the same opportunity that skilled writers generally have had—to arrive at useful "writer's knowledge" through intuition and inference garnered from writing practice. This is the role of acquisition again, as when we let him come up with his own labels for topic sentences and clarifying information: the first sentence "leads" the paragraph and the other sentences "follow the leader." When Jason expressed his ideas about indenting, keeping paragraphs the same length, and using leading and following sentences, he was telling us that he was thinking successfully about managing a frequently occurring type of school writing in which students are asked to summarize a text and then add their own ideas. The resultant working knowledge of paragraph structure helped him to succeed where his experiment with quotation marks had failed. Prompted by our modeling and guidance, Jason learned the strategy for graphically representing the shape and function of paragraphs, and that strategy became the key to his acquisition, by himself, of a generalizable mental representation of paragraph structure. With repeated practice, the strategy for organizing his thinking into paragraphs will serve him well whenever he needs to write to express challenging new ideas.

Helping students (instruction) to construct personally meaningful writer's knowledge (acquisition) through insights gleaned from goal-directed, successful practice (learning) is what makes strategy instruction valuable. Instruction leads acquisition and learning, but, more important, they all work together in a supportive social context. This combination is crucial because writing development is a hybrid; it combines development in the sense of acquisition with development in the sense of learning from instruction and social interaction. None of us has to invent the written language system, nor do we simply have to master its conventions. Rather, we each acquire and learn writing abilities as we use written language to serve our constructive and communicative purposes. That is my interpretation of what happened as Jason visually acquired an organizing device and simultaneously learned about paragraphing conventions. He, quite literally, got his thoughts together by matching personal insights with a socially shared way of representing and communicating personal knowledge. Strategic thinking aimed toward managing performance in writing helps writers overcome difficulties they are experiencing by uniting expressive insights and textual conventions. Teaching such thinking and appropriate strategies is best thought of as co-constructing strategic learning with students, as I show in the next chapter.

Chapter Three

Teaching Writing Strategies

The purpose of strategic writing instruction is to teach writers to think strategically about writing so they will look for and use strategies for controlling their writing processes. I don't think it's wise to stop there, however, because that statement tends to view strategies as cognitive rather than sociocognitive. Furthermore, the statement might be interpreted as suggesting that helping struggling writers is simply a matter of *giving* them strategies to guide their writing processes. In this chapter I want to expand our understanding of the purpose of strategic writing instruction so that it includes more than teaching strategies in the sense of giving or transmitting them to others. I want to make a case for co-constructing strategies with students.

Strategic behavior is purposeful and takes place in social contexts. Indeed, strategic behavior is purposeful *because* it takes place in social contexts. Writing, like language in general, unites the cognitive and the social (Cazden, 1988), and strategies for controlling writing processes are without genuine purpose unless the social dimensions of language and learning are included. In an example[1] I introduce now and discuss in detail later in this

---

[1]This example is an expansion of a case I presented in Collins and Collins (1996). Copyright 1996 by the National Council of Teachers of English. Used with permission.

chapter, a learning-disabled ninth-grader I'll call Brandon produced the following response to an assignment in English class that required him to present his opinion on the question, "Do you think professional athletes get paid too much or too little for their jobs?":

> Salaries, do you think someone who works 3 hours a week for 16 week desreve $2.6 million dollars. The person works 48 hours total and earns each hour $54,166,67. No one should earn that much money. Another person who makes too much for not enough work. Kevin Gogan just signed a contract for $3.6 million dollars for 3 years. No one dervise to earn that much money espically when people who work twice as hard don't make even close to that much money. I think something is wrong her.

Brandon's sentences seem undeveloped and disconnected, as if he is concentrating on his subject and writing down related ideas without telling us how they are related. It appears as if he has put his main idea in the middle of a circle and then surrounded it with other circles each containing associated ideas, as Figure 3.1 illustrates.

Brandon did not actually draw "Salaries" in a middle circle and surround it with his other ideas. Perhaps not doing so contributed to his ideas being loosely associated rather than clearly connected in his paragraph. The expression of the ideas ranges from one word in the case of "Salaries" to several sentences in the case of each of the two examples. Of course, we can say that the writing process is composed of steps, and that after Brandon writes a draft to brainstorm ideas, he should next be taught a strategy for organizing his ideas coherently, and so on. At best, such serially linked instruction seems questionable because it teaches students to do as they are told at each step of a process without ever controlling the process as a whole. Because the goal of strategy instruction is self-regulated performance, it seems more efficient to ask Brandon to think of writing as coherent from the start.

Indeed, one of the most basic purposes of writing is to bring an appropriate degree of coherence, as required for an intended

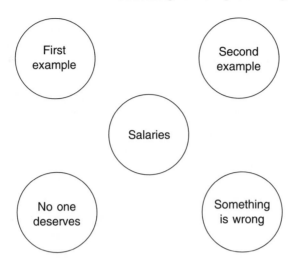

FIGURE 3.1. Associated ideas in Brandon's paragraph.

audience, to expressive ideas. Each of the steps in the writing process, and the process as a whole, can be thought of as involving the unification of an expressive intention with a social instrument for constructing and communicating meaning. Brandon's opinion on the salaries of professional athletes, in other words, will be clear when his writing clearly establishes and represents his opinion. We write to realize our thoughts in social and conventional terms. This is true of writing because it is true of language; language always unites personal and social meanings. Bakhtin (1975/1981) makes the point that this process of unification is also how we learn language:

> The word in language is half someone else's. It becomes "one's own" only when the speaker populates it with his own intention, his own accent, when he appropriates the word adapting it to his own semantic and expressive intention. Prior to this moment of appropriation, the word does not exist in a neutral and impersonal language (it is not, after all, out of a dictionary that a speaker gets his words!) but rather it exists in other people's mouths, in other people's contexts, serving other people's intentions: it is from there that one must take the word and make it one's own. (p. 294)

If we substitute *strategy* for *word* in that excerpt, we begin to understand the way strategic writing instruction works in a sociocognitive framework. Strategies can be borrowed and used at each step of the writing process, but it is taking ownership of the strategy, making it serve one's own semantic and expressive intentions, that makes it strategic. Without that appropriation the strategy is an empty formula, unreliable as a guide for constructing one's own meaning in writing.[2] The irony in "giving" a strategy to a student is that the strategy may remain the teacher's because it is the teacher who decides the strategy is needed and when and how to use it. The strategy remains someone else's and serves his or her purposes, or, at best, the strategy becomes a hit-or-miss guide to achieving the student's own purposes. This is why I recommend an instructional process with a double focus on the difficulties struggling writers are experiencing and on the expressive and communicative objectives latent in their written efforts. This double focus creates a sociocognitive framework which allows for the co-construction of learning strategies by teachers and students by avoiding any attempt to simply give strategies to struggling writers, or to otherwise superimpose our strategies on their writing efforts, because it insists that we identify the strategies they are using as a basis for suggesting new strategies for them to try.

The fact that writing strategies are learned best in sociocognitive contexts is not always obvious in the literature on writing strategies. Much of the literature, for example, discusses *cognitive strategies,* or similar constructs such as *thinking strategies* and *learning strategies.* Still, from the very beginning, research on writing strategies had a recognizable sociocognitive theme, and that theme became more and more pronounced as research in strategic learning developed. Throughout the research, the main theoretical assumption is that strategic literacy consists of deliberate control over one's own reading and writing processes, and in more recent studies it becomes increasingly clear that strategic literacy is socially formed through purposeful transactions with texts and with other readers and writers.

---

[2]The misuse of strategies as formulas is one of the subjects of the next chapter.

Research on Writing Strategies

Research has much to say about learning strategies, how they are acquired and learned, how their acquisition can be facilitated, and how their learning can be enhanced through explicit teaching (see Weinstein & Mayer, 1986, for an excellent general introduction to the research on learning strategies). Research on literacy strategies is a significant part of the research on learning strategies. The notion of teaching writing by emphasizing writing strategies grew out of a problem-solving perspective on thinking that was supported by studies in cognitive psychology and cognitive science, the latter an interdisciplinary field of research focusing on artificial intelligence in computers and real intelligence in humans. Early research in writing from the problem-solving perspective went along with the traditional notion that the writing process has three stages (prewriting, writing, and rewriting), but it saw them as having psychological correspondence with stages in a more general model of cognitive processing of linguistic information (construction of meaning, transformation of meaning into language and actual production of spoken or written language) each of which has goals and means of achieving them (Anderson, 1985). What was new in the cognitive-science description of the writing process was the view of writing as problem solving.

One of the earliest expressions of the problem-solving perspective on writing was an article by Flower and Hayes (1977). Like Emig (1971), Flower and Hayes asked writers to compose aloud while writing, but they paid particular attention to the ways writers set up and solve problems as they write. They presented a heuristic strategy for analytical writing comprising both traditional rhetorical strategies, such as brainstorming, and problem-solving strategies used by good writers in their research, such as building an "issue tree" after generating ideas rather than outlining before generating ideas. They summarized their findings this way:

> The process then is an iterative one. For each subproblem along the way—whether it is making a logical connection between hazy ideas, or finding a persuasive tone—the writer may draw on a whole repertoire of procedures and heuristic

strategies. Having conscious access to some of these strategies can make the process a lot easier. (p. 461)

Flower and Hayes (1977) close their article with three implications for teaching writing strategies, and it is here that their article strikes a sociocognitive chord. The first implication is that heuristics do not offer a step-by-step formula for producing writing. Rather, heuristics are recursive, flexible, and optional. Several questions are implicit here: How are heuristics learned? How are they flexibly applied to writing processes? How do writers know when to exercise their options for the construction of meaning? The second implication begins to answer these questions by pointing out that writers must experience a new thinking technique to learn it. The experience comes in classroom settings; that is, it consists of social interaction which helps ensure that writers learn to use and apply new techniques. The third implication is that heuristics ask students to view writing as a communication problem to be solved with all the strategies they can command. This gives the sense, early on, that writing is a whole communicative process that can be mastered, not just a collection of individual skills to be practiced in serial fashion.

Continuing research on writing processes from the cognitive-science perspective (e.g., Flower & Hayes, 1980; Rose, 1984; Bereiter & Scardamalia, 1987) used composing-aloud protocols in which writers of varying ages and abilities were asked to speak their thoughts while writing. This research showed that the procedures, or problem-solving strategies, used by expert writers are considerably more varied, elaborate, focused, flexible, and goal-directed than the strategies used by novice writers. The implication for instruction in this research was that the strategies used by expert writers can be identified and subsequently taught to novices, as in Flower's (1985) textbook for college writers. This textbook reflected an understanding of writing as a strategic process: "Writers are constantly giving themselves instructions for how to write and what to do and then monitoring how well their current effort is going" (p. 24). Flower based her identification of strategies on the effective strategies good writers use, such as these for planning what to write:

Brainstorm, jotting down ideas in whatever order they come. (p. 30)

Break the large problem of writing down into smaller problems. (p. 38)

Test mental image of the problem: reader, writer, purpose. (p. 64)

Explain the assignment to yourself. (pp. 66–69)

Make a plan which includes goals, not just topics. (p. 69)

Make a plan to do and to say. (pp. 70–73)

Make your goals operational, more specific. (pp. 73–74)

Reveal your plan to the reader; open with a problem or purpose statement. (pp. 74–75)

This is an admirable list of planning strategies, and it certainly contains many strategies of potential benefit to struggling writers. Later research, however, questioned the argument that the "effective strategies good writers use" can be transferred readily to struggling writers. A dominant metaphor for mind in cognitive science is the computer, and perhaps an underlying assumption that strategies in writing are like procedures in computer programming—routines that perform specific, well-defined tasks and that are transferable to other tasks (Dromey, 1982)—supported the idea that we could identify writing strategies used by successful writers and teach them to struggling writers. Current research prefers to see writing strategies as having to be constructed by writers for themselves, not just transferred from one writer (or teacher or textbook) to another. Flower (1994), for example, takes this position in her recent work by adopting a social–cognitive perspective on writing. This time Flower presents planning as a collaborative act, one in which a writer's plan for a piece is developed and refined in a process of collaborating with a supportive partner:

> Writers are shown how to encourage each other to go beyond information-driven plans "to say" something in order to create rhetorical plans "to do" something in writing (1) by focusing on purposes, key points, audience, and textual conventions, (2) by trying to consolidate those goals, and (3) by reflecting on their thinking. These three moves reflect the long-term goal of collaborative planning: to help both students to de-

velop strategies for constructive planning and to gain more
awareness of their choices. (p. 142)

In the early 1970s the term "metacognition" was coined to
conceptualize a part of cognition that controls other cognitive
functions. Metacognition was described as having two dimensions, knowledge of cognition and regulation of cognition
(Brown, 1980, 1987) and to work with two general kinds of
knowledge—declarative knowledge, or knowledge about ourselves and our performances, and procedural knowledge, knowledge about procedures, or strategies, for achieving goals and
regulating performance. In terms of the computer metaphor for
mind, declarative knowledge is like data stored within the computer's memory, and procedural knowledge is like the programs
that run on computers. In composition, declarative knowledge
supplies the content and conventions for pieces of writing
because it is knowledge stored in memory (information about
the world, about ideas, entities, and relations, including knowledge about writing rules and conventional structures) and knowledge about how to go about getting additional information one
needs (reading for information, etc.). In composition, procedural knowledge supplies the actions, as a series of steps involving the manipulation of declarative knowledge, to accomplish
one's purposes in writing and to plan, monitor, and evaluate
performance.

Since the mid-1980s, the metaphors of mind as computer
and education as transfer of knowledge from teachers to students have given way in the research on writing strategies to two
new metaphors: mind as meaning maker and education as social
construction. These changes reflect a more basic revision of the
way researchers think of strategic human behavior. Paris, Lipson,
and Wixson (1983), for example, point out that it is learners who
are strategic, not strategies or actions removed from contexts.
To make the point that humans are strategic, not their actions,
they offer an analogy comparing a well-timed lob in tennis and
a series of shopping errands accomplished by the design of an
efficient path to a lucky shot and an accidental shopping route.
They coin the term "conditional knowledge" and define it as
knowledge about *when* and *why* to apply various strategies, as in
when to try for a certain level of formality or *why* composing a

piece of writing is necessary. They see the necessity of adding conditional knowledge to declarative and procedural knowledge because it is conditional knowledge that helps orchestrate declarative and procedural knowledge to achieve goals. Control over performance resides in the combination of declarative, procedural, and conditional knowledge. Declarative knowledge gives us information, procedural knowledge gives us strategies for using information to accomplish objectives, and conditional knowledge gives us deliberate intention and design in using strategies. In terms of writing, for example, declarative knowledge provides an awareness of content; procedural knowledge provides ways of remembering, obtaining, and constructing information to achieve communicative purposes; and conditional knowledge tells the writer what conditions call for selecting among options such as syntax, wording, tone, and register. In this formulation, writing strategies consist of both a set of controls (procedures) for accomplishing an end and a clear, intentional sense of when and how to use the controls (conditions). Strategic writing instruction teaches strategies designed to ensure that writers acquire or learn both procedures for controlling their writing and conditions for using the procedures.

The distinction among declarative, procedural, and conditional knowledge can be further illustrated in terms of the examples I used in the last chapter: my saxophone playing and Jason's writing:

Saxophone

Declarative: Knowledge of putting the sax together, what symbols represent which notes, which keys represents which notes, how to produce notes of varying length, that the relative lengths of notes is established by musicians, not by the music on the page.

Procedural: How to depress each key and how long to depress each key, how to establish cadence and rhythm, how to decode and interpret notes while playing.

Conditional: When and what to practice alone and when to play along with someone else, how to listen to a pattern of notes to facilitate its replication, how to use other musicians as models, when to depress each key and when to release it.

Jason's writing

Declarative: General knowledge for writing about one's reading, specific knowledge about writing for a particular situational context such as what a teacher wants, information needed for the content of writing about Langston Hughes's short story "Thank You, Ma'am."

Procedural: How to borrow material from the Hughes text; how to express your own responses, opinions, and interpretations; how to separate those two; how to make a prediction about what will happen in the second half of the story; how to write sentences and paragraphs, capitalize, spell, and punctuate.

Conditional: When to copy from the book, when to paraphrase and summarize, when to insert one's own ideas; how much total writing will be enough, and how much for each part of the task; how much time and effort to put into the task; whether spelling problems will be taken seriously; how neat the finished paper should be; when to ask for help and when to go it alone; when to share the writing.

In both cases, any one of the three types of knowledge is not enough, by itself, to guide performance. All three must be present for control over performance to be effective. The label "metacognition" refers to the mental operations that control patterns of cognitive behavior, but I prefer not to think of metacognition as a separate cognitive function, or as a separate set of skills or operations to be taught to students, but rather as a combination of controls, that is, procedures and conditions, focusing on a particular performance. In this sense, *metacognitive* is a synonym for *strategic*. If you catch yourself daydreaming while reading and tell yourself to begin to pay more attention to the words on the page, for example, you have exercised deliberate control over a literacy process; but by itself, that control is not strategic or metacognitive. Reading performance becomes focused and consciously managed when deliberate control takes the form of a plan for getting the reading done for a particular purpose: the necessity of reading to cover a lot of material in a fixed amount of time to plan a lesson, for example, leads to a plan for calculating the number of pages in the chapters that must be read, allotting a fixed number of pages to each hour available for reading, speeding up the reading to stay on schedule, taking note of main ideas, and so on. Reading is then strategic.

Strategies for Struggling Middle and High School Writers

Sustained research programs focusing on writing strategies for students who have difficulties with writing were conducted mostly at the elementary level, as in the work of Harris and Graham (1992) at the University of Maryland (e.g., *Helping Young Writers Master the Craft: Strategy Instruction and Self-Regulation in the Writing Process*), the work of Englert (1995) and her colleagues at Michigan State University (e.g., "Teaching Written Language Skills," in *Effective Instruction for Students with Learning Difficulties*), and the work of Bereiter and Scardamalia (1987) in Toronto (e.g., *The Psychology of Written Composition*). The main thrust of my work for the past 6 years was to extend the research on writing strategies for struggling writers into secondary schools. During this time my graduate students and I visited schools and worked with teacher-researchers in classrooms where students have difficulties with writing. We tried out strategic methods from other studies and developed strategic methods of our own, always with an eye toward helping struggling writers overcome their difficulties (see, e.g., Collins & Godinho, 1996; Collins & Collins, 1996). The schools we worked in were in urban, suburban, and rural districts; the classrooms included every grade from 5th through 12th; and the students included both general education and special education students with mild disabilities. The bulk of this work was in one-to-one tutorial sessions in writing workshops in classrooms during or after school, but we also worked with whole classes and small groups. Early in the project we settled on studying strategies-based teaching methods because of the many positive reports of strategic literacy instruction in the professional literature. We read everything we could find on strategic literacy and, more generally, on cognitive strategies and learning strategies. Also important in the development of our thinking about strategic writing instruction were ongoing meetings, discussions, and collaborative research projects which comprised the work of our "Strategies Group," an ongoing research colloquium involving my colleagues at the State University of New York at Buffalo: Jack Cawley, Elfreda Blue, and Rene Parmar in special education; Janice Almasi and Laura Klenk in reading education; and Suzanne Miller, Diane Zigo, and Pamela Hartman in English education.

In our meetings with principals and teachers in the schools in which we conducted our studies, we said that we wanted to work with students for whom writing presented serious difficulties, including both regular and special education students. We did not distinguish among types of writing problems, such as reluctance to write, trouble with particular tasks, or underdeveloped literacy skills or abilities. We obtained the necessary permissions, planned with cooperating teachers, and began working in classrooms on days when students were writing in class. We made ourselves available as tutors, and, from our tutoring and with the teachers' help, we identified writers who were having difficulty. We worked with these writers individually on multiple drafts of one or more writing tasks. Following the procedures of Hayes and Flower (1980), we asked some of our writers to compose aloud, speaking as much of their thinking as possible while they wrote in response to tasks given by their teachers. We recorded and transcribed these reports and used them to get insights into the thinking and writing processes of our writers. We found, however, that students frequently interrupted their composing-aloud protocols and became silent when the writing task began to give them serious trouble. Because those moments were the ones we were most interested in, we had to devise other methods of having students voice their thoughts about struggling with writing.

It's not hard to understand why students have difficulty describing trouble spots in their writing processes while composing aloud or through other, more direct, means such as responding to questions about writing problems. Being asked to describe a difficulty one is having is a little like being asked where a lost item was last seen; if a student can describe a writing problem, chances are it's not a serious problem, just as remembering where a lost item was last seen might mean it's probably not lost at all. Also, if a student is having a serious problem thinking about the content or form of writing, he or she has less cognitive energy or motivation for voicing a description of the problem. Composing aloud did offer some insights into our writers' thinking, but our main conclusion from the think-aloud protocols was that students are usually not likely to talk about writing problems while actually writing.

We settled instead on telling students that we were especially interested in what makes writing hard at times, and we asked them to write and to ask us for help whenever they had questions or when they felt they had come to a difficult part of their writing. We found that this technique worked quite well in revealing what students considered difficult and in encouraging them to voice any doubts, questions, concerns, or puzzlements they might experience while writing. The "ask for help" technique allowed us to talk with students about their difficulties with writing, to discover underlying problems and potential strengths, and to suggest a strategic approach or a particular strategy for dealing with the difficulties. Jason's question about quotation marks in Chapter 2 is an example of our investigative technique in use. Knowing we were interested in questions he might have about writing, Jason pointed to the end of one of the sentences in quotation marks interspersed throughout his essay on the Langston Hughes short story and asked, "Should that be a quote right there?" Similarly, knowing that Jason is sharing a question that, to him, indicates an important trouble spot, we wanted to know how to interpret his question. What trouble was he really having? What writing problem was he trying to solve by tentatively using quotation marks? Such questions prompted us to ask him why he used quotation marks, which in turn led to his answer, "because I was writing for myself." It became clear after a little further discussion that Jason was not wondering how to use quotation marks as much as he was trying to structurally and visually separate his own opinion from his summary of the Hughes story. He sensed that summary and opinion should be separated somehow in his writing, and he was checking the appropriateness of achieving the separation by setting off his own remarks with quotation marks. This is what led us to work with him on a strategy for separating ideas by visualizing paragraphs as categories of sentences rather than by separating individual sentences with visual boundaries such as quotation marks. Our research method thus did exactly what we wanted: It focused our attention, and that of students and teachers working with us, on writing difficulties and strategies to overcome them. The method, furthermore, offered a bonus for participants because we found ourselves together developing a "strategic habit of mind." The more we talked with classroom teachers and their students about writing in terms of problems and strategies, the better we all understood writing as a strategic problem-solving activity.

As the example of our work with Jason suggests, our primary research method of having writers share their struggles with us by asking questions or by requesting help changed the focus of our study from the ways student writers struggle to *the ways students and teachers co-construct an understanding of writing problems and strategic ways of thinking for overcoming them.* Jason's writing struggle was not over difficulties with using quotation marks, and a lesson in using quotation marks, contrary to what his initial question suggested, was not what he needed. When we shifted our research interest from understanding writing difficulties by studying cognitive activity involved in writing to achieving an understanding of writing difficulties by studying the dialogue between students and teachers, we sharpened our ability to understand what problems and difficulties really trouble student writers. At that point our interest in writing strategies shifted from a cognitive base to a sociocognitive one. This, in turn, caused us to change the unit of analysis in our research from individual writing processes in classroom settings, wherein we considered process and instruction as interactive but separate, to the learning–teaching process, which we considered to be a unified whole in both schooling and research.

A unified focus on how teaching and learning work together to build understanding of learning difficulties and strategies for overcoming them, in short, was the heart of the research method we used. In our decision *not* to separate teaching and learning, to instead study how they combine together and how they work in tandem, I am reminded of Vygotsky's (1934/1986) comments on avoiding the separation of water into its constituent elements to study the question of why water extinguishes fire—we would only be further puzzled by the realization that oxygen sustains fire and hydrogen burns. "Nothing is left to the investigator," Vygotsky (1934/1986) adds, "but to search out the mechanical interaction of the two elements in the hope of reconstructing, in a purely speculative way, the vanished properties of the whole" (p. 4).

Our decisions to study the whole teaching–learning process and to make a social process, rather than a psychological one, the heart of our research method is entirely consistent with developments in theory and research in writing and writing strategies over the course of the past 20 years. In her study of response to student writing, for example, Freedman (1987) takes a position similar to ours when she describes responding to student writing as a process of engaging in collaborative problem solving, as "*jointly accomplished* teaching and learning" (p. 9, emphasis added). When a child writes a story and a reader asks for more information, Freedman points out, the child and reader are collaboratively engaged in a single meaning-making process even though they play separate roles. Further, the child is encouraged to say more about some aspect of the story, begins to internalize an understanding of the needs of readers, and thus begins to learn how to achieve fuller meanings independent of response from readers. This internalization of an initially collaborative process further illustrates the social formation of a strategic habit of mind. Freedman refers to a variety of ways to characterize collaborative acts involving writers and respondents. She uses Vygotsky's (1978) metaphor of a zone of proximal development, a range of ability connecting what students can do alone and what they can do with the help of adults or more talented peers, to describe how collaboration with teachers helps move writers in the direction of potential development. The support teachers provide in the collaborative writing-responding act, Freedman adds, can be described as scaffolding (Bruner, 1983; Cazden, 1988; Hogan & Pressley, 1997), a metaphor for the tools experienced language users provide for novices; as reciprocal teaching (Palincsar & Brown, 1984) in which tutors provide support and gradually release control to readers; and as procedural facilitation (Bereiter & Scardamalia, 1987) in which instruction assists writers by giving access to procedures designed to make cognitive processes involved in writing more manageable. Freedman (1987) points out that collaborative problem solving involves these varieties of support, but her research on the response to student writing practices of excellent English teachers focuses on co-constructive activities between students and teachers; in fact, she bases her monograph on the theory that "the achievement of cognitive gain depends on the substance of social interactions" (p. 8).

Similarly, the co-construction of strategic thinking and writing strategies is the main component of strategic writing instruction. Our research taught us that it is best *not* to think of writing strategies as cognitive processes provided by teachers in an effort to assist student writers. Strategies, to be effective in helping to overcome writing difficulties, must be understood and used by students in the midst of their struggles to express themselves in writing, and the best role for teachers and peers is to assist in the achievement of that understanding and use. Another way of making the same point is to say that there must be a cognitive match between old and new strategies students bring to bear on the writing problem. The role of the teacher is to aid in the discovery and use of an appropriate strategy by studying the difficulty the writer is having (including the use of existing or "old" strategies) and by co-constructing with the writer a strategic way out of the difficulty (including the discovery and use of a "new" strategy which connects with or transforms rather than simply displaces the old one).[3] This, as in Freedman's (1987) more general discussion of writing and responding, is best thought of as a process of *joint problem solving*. To borrow again from Vygotsky (1934/1986): writing strategies cannot be put on like a ready-made garment. Writing strategies for struggling writers must be tailored to fit their struggles, and the teacher's role in strategic writing instruction, therefore, is more than finding a bolt of cloth and a pattern. The teacher's role includes the most crucial step of working with the student to co-construct a custom fit of strategy to struggle. When that step is missing,

---

[3]I explain the importance of conceiving of new strategies as entailing old ones in Chapter 5.

strategies take on the character of formulas—hollow, mechanistic, teacher-dominated, hit-or-miss—as I show in Chapter 4.

Strategies cannot be transferred ready-made from teachers to students. In her introduction to a volume of essays on knowing, learning, and instruction Resnick (1989) points out that the traditional view of education as the direct transfer of knowledge from teachers to students has given way in the past three decades to a constructivist perspective which holds that students construct knowledge for themselves. Learning is an active and constructive process, one that occurs not by recording information but rather by interpreting it, and one in which the learner's mental activity is at the heart of the teaching–learning process. This does not mean, Resnick adds, that learners can be left to discover all knowledge for themselves. Instruction must provide information for knowledge construction, and it must engage and support knowledge construction processes, even when learners doubt their capacity or right to do independent thinking. And, "where necessary, instruction must also directly teach knowledge construction strategies" (Resnick, 1989, p. 2).

That last sentence might seem to contradict the constructivist perspective on learning and the co-constructivist pedagogical stance I've just recommended. Struggling writers are, indeed, good candidates for direct strategy instruction. A strategy is a plan of action for achieving a particular goal, and writing strategies are cognitive operations employed to manage performance in establishing and working toward goals involved in writing tasks. The best writers, like the best learners in general, are the ones who use cognitive and metacognitive strategies to facilitate their performance. With struggling writers, especially those whose performance indicates they may not be using appropriate strategies to facilitate writing performance, the tendency is to jump in and help by directly teaching strategies. Notice, however, that *directly teaching* does not mean *teaching directively*. Strategy instruction should be direct in the sense of being explicit, but the explicit teaching of writing strategies can still be highly collaborative if we focus attention on ways of constructing writing strategies but don't take over the knowledge construction process itself.

And it's a good idea to make strategy instruction both explicit and collaborative because the social context of strategy instruction is extremely important. Writing strategies are inwardly situated controls. In other words, they operate from within a person but are acquired or learned socially, most often, at least in our research, when existing literacy strategies are transformed and new ones adopted through meaningful interaction between writers and audiences. Strategies, in other words, are not acquired or learned in a vacuum but, rather, in psychological and social contexts. Understanding of writing strategies (declarative knowledge) can perhaps be transmitted from teachers to students, but the active and effective use of writing strategies (procedural and conditional knowledge) must be created during the writing–responding–revising process. Strategic control does not automatically result from exposure to a long list of available strategies. Rather, control over writing strategies involves co-construction of the strategies by students in collaboration with teachers or peers because thinking strategically about literacy is an emergent habit of mind that is learned socially, in interaction with texts and other readers and writers. Co-construction and collaboration are ways of helping students recognize the merits of strategic thinking and ways of helping them make strategies fit their own ways of thinking about the writing problem at hand so that, when necessary, they can look for and grasp new strategies and use them purposefully.

In a fuller treatment of the apparent contradiction between strategy instruction and constructivist educational views, Pressley, Harris, and Marks (1992) reach a conclusion similar to mine. They find that the only important difference between good strategy instruction and the generally accepted tenets of constructivist pedagogy is in the degree of explicitness strategy instructors bring to what is to be learned. They define strategies as "goal-directed, cognitive operations employed to facilitate performance" (p. 4), but they add that strategies should not be taught in isolation from meaningful contexts. Rather, strategy instruction should recognize connections between strategies and contexts in which they are used. It is the interaction between strategies and the contexts in which they are used that connects strategy instruction with constructivist teaching. After Moshman (1982), Pressley et al. (1992) distinguish among three types of constructivist teaching: endogenous constructivism, where knowledge construction is entirely a matter of student exploration and discovery; exogenous constructivism, where knowledge construction is largely supported by teacher modeling and explanation; and dialectical constructivism, a middle ground between the other two which emphasizes scaffolding in the form of teacher assistance as needed to work toward independent student performance. They align themselves, as do most constructivist educators, myself included, with the dialectical position and summarize their position this way:

> Good strategy instruction does not involve an inflexible authority figure transmitting fixed, rigid cognitive rules to students in a dispassionate, almost scripted manner. A hallmark of good strategy teaching is adapting to the preparation level of students. Thus strategy teachers usually have initial conceptions about the procedures they want their students to acquire. Good teachers understand, however, that strategic procedures can be operationalized in many ways and that particular components can be carried out in different fashions by different students. Good strategy teaching consists much more of exploring with students these ranges of possibilities, rather than attempting to convey a specific procedural sequence. (p. 26)

In a recent conference presentation Pressley (1996) uses the metaphor of *transaction* in exactly the way I am using *co-construction,* to indicate a sharing and negotiating that goes on between teachers and students as strategies are constructed rather than transmitted. That similarity, furthermore, reflects a larger one: the subject of Pressley's talk is balancing skills and whole-language approaches in reading instruction, just as the subject of this book is balancing skills and process approaches in writing instruction.

Two Main Strands of Strategy-Based Writing Instruction

Strategic writing instruction includes two main strands of strategy-based teaching. One is a general problem-solving focus I've been calling the social formation of a strategic habit of mind. This consists of learning to think strategically about writing and writing difficulties by repeatedly pausing while writing; holding the generation of ideas and words in abeyance; and reflecting on how the writing, or some particular aspect of it, is going. Protocol studies reveal that good writers alternate constantly between writing and reflecting on their writing, and they also show that much of the reflecting consists of planning (Flower & Hayes, 1977, 1980; Bereiter & Scardamalia, 1987). In our studies, asking struggling writers to recognize when they are having trouble with writing and to talk with us about their difficulties encouraged strategic thinking because describing a difficulty and asking what can be done about it is an instance of pausing and planning while writing and the beginning of forming a reflective and strategic habit of mind about one's writing. Teachers cooperating with us, furthermore, frequently told us about other ways (other than pausing over difficulties) of encouraging reflection during the writing process. Teacher-researcher Cathy Fairbend, for example, has her eighth-graders write a paragraph in the top one-third of a page and then follow these directions which are printed in the middle of the page:

> STOP: *REREAD* what you have written and write two questions about your paragraph
>
> 1.
> 2.
>
> Now see if your two questions can help you to rewrite and improve your paragraph.

Students then revise in the bottom third of the page. Clearly, this exercise provides practice in drafting, pausing to think about what's been written, and then changing the writing accordingly.

In our studies the social formation of a strategic habit of mind emerged from repeated opportunities to think strategically about writing and writing difficulties. Once it begins to operate, a strategic habit of mind tends to establish a foundation, and an incentive, for a general problem-solving focus in literacy processes. Frequently, for example, we overheard students in our studies making such statements to each other as, "Man, you need a strategy," or, "The strategy I'd try is. . . . " We believe such statements reveal an emerging strategic habit of mind about writing, a habit we take to be extremely important because without it we would each have to carry around a large quantity of individual strategies to deal with problems we encounter while reading and writing. Forming a strategic habit of mind lessens the burden by allowing us to pause and look for or construct strategies at the point of need, to invent strategies "on the fly" as we encounter problems.[4]

Developing the strategic mind-set happens in conjunction with writing in accordance with the second strand of strategy-based teaching. This second strand focuses on the identification and use of particular writing strategies. In two recent coauthored articles (Collins & Godinho, 1996; Collins & Collins, 1996) we described this strand of strategic writing instruction as having four steps:

1. Identifying a strategy worth teaching.
2. Introducing the strategy by modeling it.
3. Helping students to try the strategy out with workshop-style teacher guidance.
4. Helping students work toward independent mastery of the strategy through repeated practice and reinforcement.

I clarify and exemplify these four steps by returning to Brandon's paragraph discussed earlier in this chapter[5]:

> Salaries, do you think someone who works 3 hours a week for 16 week desreve $2.6 million dollars. The person works 48 hours total and earns each hour $54,166,67. No one should earn that much

---

[4]My colleagues Jack Cawley and Rene Parmar express a similar idea by noting that "we want students to be problem solvers, not to just solve problems."

[5]To the original (Collins & Collins, 1996), this version adds excerpts from actual student–teacher dialogue during one of the writing conferences. My purpose in sharing the dialogue is to add insight into the process of shared strategy construction during the four-step strategic writing instruction process. In this manner, the example shows both how a writing strategy was developed and practiced and how it was co-constructed by a teacher and student working in partnership.

money. Another person who makes too much for
not enough work. Kevin Gogan just signed a
contract for $3.6 million dollars for 3 years.
No one dervise to earn that much money espically
when people who work twice as hard don't make
even close to that much money. I think something
is wrong her.

Brandon told me that he had worked hard on this piece, and
he showed me two newspaper articles from which he took his
information on professional athletes' salaries for his examples.
He clearly wanted me to know that he had worked diligently on
the piece and not just dashed it off. As we talked about his effort,
he confided that his teachers sometimes thought he was a lazy
writer—in his words, "one who writes in a hurry" and "doesn't
try very hard"—but he insisted that he really does spend a lot of
time on his writing assignments. Perhaps such weaknesses as
those apparent in Brandon's response to the "Salaries" task—the
lack of both idea development and a discernible pattern of logic,
for example—make him appear lazy, as if he is content with
hurriedly abbreviating his ideas rather than spelling them out
fully and logically.

The absence of explicit logic is what I decided to make the
focus of strategy instruction with Brandon. The first step is
"Identifying a strategy worth teaching," and I made the identification by noticing that the organization of Brandon's piece is
not obvious to readers. There is a hint of latent logic, and we
can make it visible by rearranging the circles from Figure 3.1 to
make the pattern in Figure 3.2.

The circles still float unattached to each other in the new
figure, just as they did in the previous one, and it is unclear
therefore exactly how Brandon gets from "Salaries" to "Something is wrong." It seemed appropriate to start Step 1 of strategy
instruction by working with Brandon on writing a thesis statement for organizing and connecting the paragraph, and this is
what I tried at first. Throughout our next two conferences, which
lasted 5 or 10 minutes each, we talked about thesis statements
and supporting ideas. Brandon seemed to have no trouble
grasping the notion that paragraphs and compositions have
central, controlling ideas and that main ideas must be developed
by means of supporting, more specific ideas. He readily agreed

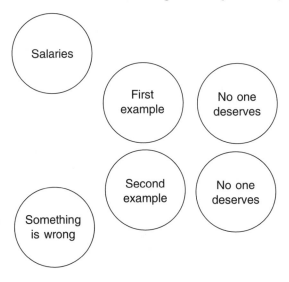

FIGURE 3.2. Structure of Brandon's paragraph.

that these specific ideas must be carefully chosen and organized in a logical way, and he agreed that their relation to each other and to the central idea must be made clear. He had trouble, however, remembering what was said during our conferences:

JLC: Yesterday Brandon wasn't feeling well so he didn't come. So the big question is, after two days, does he remember what we talked about?

B: Oh, yeah, your first sentence is, um, your first sentence should be your, somethin' uh, I don't know.

JLC: You don't remember what we called it?

B: No. I'm trying to think of that.

A strategy is not much good if it can't be remembered. I decided that I had been giving Brandon declarative information rather than a procedure and conditions for using it. Clearly, we needed another way of getting an appropriate pattern of organization into Brandon's writing. I wondered how composition teachers discussed patterns of logic before the notions of thesis statement and topic sentence were invented. To that end, I consulted the oldest composition text I could find, Greenough and Hersey's *English Composition* (1923), where I discovered repeated references to visual means of conceptualizing organization:

> The same reason that makes pictures, maps, and charts vastly more effective than text for certain purposes makes an outline plan the best test of the relative order and weight of the material. For a plan is a kind of picture, and a very vivid one so far as the order of points and the matter of coordination and subordination are concerned. (p. 32)

> One means of helping [the reader] keep his bearings is to give him at the beginning a bird's eye view of the country through which he is to travel. (p. 40)

With these ideas in mind, especially with the idea of visually representing a composition as a trail through the territory covered by a topic, I decided that Brandon might benefit from having the language and declarative knowledge of writing class— topic sentence, thesis statement, coherence and cohesion between ideas, and so on—clarified through graphic means. I still focused on the problem of a lack of logical connectedness in Brandon's writing. In the "Salaries" assignment, Brandon has a topic, two examples, and a conclusion, but the ideas seem disconnected or, at best, related by association or juxtaposition rather than by a discernible pattern of logic. I decided to work on a strategy for conceptualizing logically connected writing by visually representing the pattern of logic in a piece of writing. This was my second try at Step 1, Identifying a strategy worth teaching. By changing from a "topic sentence and supporting information" strategy to a "visualizing patterns of relatedness" strategy, I focused more on procedural and conditional knowledge (how and when to connect ideas) than on declarative knowledge (information about connectedness in writing).

Next, I began Step 2, "Introducing the strategy by modeling it." Together with Brandon, I coauthored another response to the "Salaries" topic. By coauthoring I modeled both how a writer works and how a coherent paragraph is put together. The coauthoring took about 5 minutes and consisted of Brandon dictating what he wanted to say while I wrote down his ideas in a more logical way than in his first draft. I composed aloud as I wrote, repeating what Brandon said and transforming his words into a well-connected paragraph:

> I think professional athletes get paid too much for their work. In the Monday, April 18, *Buffalo News,* for example, we learned that a Houston Oilers football player named Sean Jones gets paid 2.6 million dollars for each season. I have heard of Sean Jones, but I don't think he deserves that much money for performing three hours a week for 16 weeks out of the year. Many people work harder than he does for a lot less money. I don't think football players work hard enough to receive such outrageously high salaries. Work has lost its meaning when a nurse or a bricklayer or even a doctor get so much less than a man whose work is child's play.

In modeling the construction of a coherent paragraph, I avoided the temptation to lecture Brandon about what I was doing, how I was connecting one idea to another to establish logic and coherence across ideas in the paragraph. Instead, I modeled how I sometimes write by transforming inchoate thoughts into explicit and connected prose by making a paragraph on paper resemble an image or model of the paragraph in my mind, rather like driving a car according to a mental image of a frequently traveled series of roads to get to an intended destination. Because I don't lecture myself on coherence while I write, I didn't lecture Brandon either. I just modeled good writing and the thinking about content and logic writers do to produce it.

Next, we went on to Step 3, "Helping students to try the strategy out with workshop-style teacher guidance." Here I wanted to help Brandon imagine connections among ideas in our coauthored paragraph, just as I imagined them while composing the paragraph. We used a drawing program on a microcomputer to highlight ideas and connections across them. We first highlighted the main idea in the revised "Salaries" paragraph. We did this by drawing a box around the main idea (see Figure 3.3).

After we collaboratively selected and marked the main idea, I asked Brandon to draw arrows from words referring back to

I think professional athletes get paid too much for
their work.

In the Monday, April 18, Buffalo News, for example,
we learned that a Houston Oilers football player
named Sean Jones gets paid 2.6 million dollars for
each season. I have heard of Sean Jones, but I don't
think he deserves that much money for performing
three hours a week for 16 weeks out of the year.
Many people work harder than he does for a lot less
money. I don't think football players work hard
enough to receive such outrageously high salaries.
Work has lost its meaning when a nurse or a
bricklayer or even a doctor get so much less than
a man whose work is child's play.

FIGURE 3.3. Framing of main idea in revised essay.

the main idea in each of the subsequent sentences. We worked
together on one such sentence, as indicated in Figure 3.4.

Brandon then took over the drawing of arrows for the
connections between each of the other sentences and the main
idea as we discussed patterns of relatedness across each of the
sentences in the paragraph. Thus, in Step 3 we progressed from
having me provide much help to Brandon to having him work
alone. Here's an excerpt from our writing conference:

I think professional athletes get paid too much
for their work.

In the Monday, April 18, Buffalo News, for example,
we learned that a Houston Oilers football player
named Sean Jones gets paid 2.6 million dollars for
each season. I have heard of Sean Jones, but I don't
think he deserves that much money for performing
three hours a week for 16 weeks out of the year.
Many people work harder than he does for a lot less
money. I don't think football players work hard
enough to receive such outrageously high salaries.
Work has lost its meaning when a nurse or a
bricklayer or even a doctor get so much less than
a man whose work is child's play.

FIGURE 3.4. Connections between main idea and second sentence in the
revised essay.

JLC: This sentence "Many people work harder than he does." Who is "he"?

B: Oh, Sean Jones.

JLC: Where's Sean Jones?

B: Up there.

JLC: Now where does this "Sean Jones sentence" point to? "I have heard of Sean Jones." What does that point to?

B: The one above it.

JLC: The one above it. Where does the one above it point to?

B: Mmmmmm, it doesn't point to anything.

JLC: Yeah. It points.

B: Oh, it points to the one above it.

JLC: To the first sentence, you see. You see what we're saying?

B: You're going up a ladder and then up at the top.

JLC: Yeah.

B: The top of it. That's where all the action is.

JLC: I like that. It's like you're going up a ladder, and at the top is where all the action is, it's where the main idea is. The reason this works as a good piece of writing, is everything is focused, you see?

B: Mmm hmm. It leads to something up, else above it.

While he was drawing arrows, Brandon seemed to grasp the idea of logically connecting sentences because he talked about going up to the top sentence and about referring back to it, and he talked about basing everything else on the top sentence. I take this to be evidence of our co-constructing an understanding of logical coherence in writing. We did that, however, in Brandon's own terms, not mine. His most frequent label for the main idea was simply "top sentence." I suggested to Brandon that he think of connecting sentences as "drawing a map," and Brandon said, "Yeah, X marks the spot and everything leads to X." Brandon also said that the top layer of the computer diagram, the layer showing all the arrows connecting all the sentences as in Figure 3.5, reminded him of the game of "Chutes and

Ladders," and he talked about going up to the top sentence and basing everything else on the top sentence as "the ladder idea, at the top of all the action, where everything is based from."

Of course, explicitly marking patterns of reference is something we can do only after we write, and Brandon still had to work on using a visual representation of a main idea and patterns of relatedness with other ideas as a useful strategy while producing writing. In an extra-credit project for his social studies teacher, Brandon had to write summaries and reactions for 10 news articles, and this project provided the perfect opportunity to get to Step 4, "Helping students work toward independent mastery of the strategy through repeated practice and reinforcement," by repeatedly practicing and reinforcing the strategy of thinking about an "arrow ladder" or a map of a route between ideas as an aid to writing so that ideas are connected with a discernible pattern of logic and not just listed or juxtaposed. With decreasing assistance from me, Brandon wrote 10 two-paragraph news summaries with the diagram of the "Patterns of Logic" strategy, shown in Figure 3.5, in front of him.

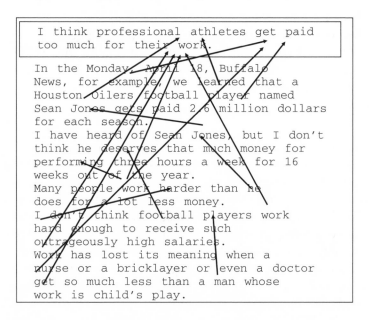

FIGURE 3.5. Final diagram of patterns of logic in revised "Salaries" essay.

The following example of Brandon's news summaries, written and revised and edited by him with minimal help (but with some borrowing of content from the news article he's writing about), speaks to the success of the strategy:

> This is a short article about business opportunities for Americans in South Africa. It reports that the economic climate in South Africa is quickly improving after years of sanctions. Business opportunities are especially strong for African-American-owned firms because South Africa offers an untapped market of 45 million consumers. Two major black-owned companies, a manufacturer of hair-care products and an investment-management firm have already started doing business there. Many hundreds of small companies and entrepreneurs and consultants are also doing business there.
>
> In my opinion business opportunities for Americans in South Africa are a very positive sign. Both Americans and South Africans benefit from the involvement of American business in South Africa. American business people, especially African Americans, have a new market for their goods and services, South Africans have new products and services to improve their lives. This favorable business climate will help to stabilize the new political structure in South Africa.

General Guidelines for Strategic Writing Instruction

In both its strands—the general strategic mind-set and specific four-step strategy-based teaching—strategic writing instruction works particularly well when strategies for controlling writing processes are considered and constructed at the point of need, such as when students write in class. It is possible, of course, for teachers to lead whole classes and small groups through strategic writing lessons, and I discuss ways of doing that in the next chapter. The individual teacher–student writing conference, however, optimizes conditions for discovering and co-constructing writing strategies for students who are having the most difficulty with particular writing tasks. A 10-minute conference, or even a longer one, is time well spent if it allows a student to break through to a new level of control over particular aspects of writing processes. The possibility of individualized instruction while students are in the middle of their writing processes may be one reason why in-class writing, as in writing-workshop classrooms, is a chief characteristic of highly effective writing instruction (Freedman, 1987). The best time to discover or teach strategies for managing writing is when students are actively engaged with writing, such as when they are in the midst of working through the recursive steps involved in constructing particular pieces of writing in a writing-workshop environment. What teachers say about writing is less likely to resemble empty information if it is immediately applicable to the writing students are actually doing. And if what teachers say is immediately applicable to helping struggling writers with difficulties they are actually grappling with, then it is even more useful because that is when students are most likely to take seriously what we say and to work with us to construct a meaningful writing strategy out of it.

The example of my instructional intervention in Brandon's writing processes illustrates the four general steps in strategic writing instruction, and it also illustrates the recursiveness of the steps. The first step is "Identifying a strategy worth teaching," and in Brandon's case we cycled through that step twice. My first attempt at identifying a useful strategy focused on teaching thesis statements and supporting ideas. Brandon didn't benefit much from that, so I searched for another way to teach logical connectedness and organization, and I hit upon using a visual means of representing logic and cohesion across sentences. In fact, it was my work with Brandon which aroused my general interest in visual strategies for writing as was shown, for example, in the case of Jason in Chapter 2. The second step is "introducing the strategy by modeling it," and in Brandon's case this took the form of our coauthoring a revised version of the essay during which I thought aloud about connecting ideas in the revised paragraph. This step led to the third one, "Helping students try out the strategy with workshop-style teacher guidance" where I provided decreasing amounts of help as Brandon drew arrows representing patterns of logic across and among the sentences in the revised paragraph. Finally in Step 4, "Helping students work toward independent mastery of the strategy through repeated practice and reinforcement," Brandon wrote 10 additional short essays with the diagram of arrows representing patterns of coherence in front of him. He completed these essays with decreasing amounts of help from me. In fact, for the final three or four pieces he was working independently on the content and form of his writing.

Recall that it was Brandon who identified a need, or point of struggle, in his writing. In spite of his hard work, he felt his teachers sometimes still thought of him as a lazy writer. My initial guess was that something about his writing, perhaps its abbreviated quality, was giving his teachers that impression. My more considered decision is that his writing process, as represented by plugging ideas into isolated "circles," contributed most to his difficulty. This doesn't mean that we should advise Brandon to plan more carefully or to be more specific or to work harder—three kinds of advice he had received from past teachers. Instead, I recommend co-constructing strategies that work to give him control over his writing processes. This teaches him the strategies he needs for the writing he wants to do in addition to helping him develop a strategic habit of mind about his writing and writing in general.

Chapter   Four

Writing Strategies Are Not Formulas (But Formulas Can Be Used Strategically)

The purpose of strategic writing instruction is to teach writers to use appropriate cognitive plans to guide and control their writing processes. So far my examples of strategy-based instruction focused on teaching single strategies to one student at a time because I wanted to highlight both the teaching methods and the necessity of matching strategies to individual styles and struggles. We know, however, that improvement in literacy skills requires more than instruction in single strategies (Brown, Pressley, Van Meter, & Schuder, 1996; Palincsar & Brown, 1984) and that effective teachers provide qualitatively similar instruction for students of all abilities but provide additional support for weaker students (Pressley, Rankin, & Yokoi, 1996). The realities of classroom life, furthermore, require that teachers work with many students at once. These considerations raise the question of how to use strategic writing instruction with 25 or 30 or more students of varying ability. If the secret to success with strategic writing instruction is the co-construction of writing strategies, how can teachers do that with classrooms full of kids?

Invariably when I talk with teachers about strategy-based writing instruction I get a question like that one about class size and teacher workload. It might go something like this: Strategy instruction sounds wonderful, but how can I use it with 150 students? The number varies, usually within a range between 100 and 180, but the meaning of the question is always the same. Teachers are really asking how instruction can be individualized when there are so many individuals to teach. This is not an uncommon or unreasonable concern; in Freedman's (1987) national survey of response to writing practices, teachers made the seemingly contradictory claims that students must receive individualized instruction (p. 91) and that class size prevents the allocation of sufficient time for individual conferences (p. 61).

Strategy-based instruction does require varying amounts of individualization, at least in the form of teaching multiple strategies adjusted to varying abilities, but the real secret to teaching writing strategies in a sociocognitive framework is to socialize instruction, not individualize it. The underlying theory is that students learn to use strategies in school the same way that they learn to use them in other settings: by participating in meaning-making communities or partnerships. Students engage in public conversations which become internalized as strategies to guide and regulate reading and writing performance (Englert & Mariage, 1996b) through their participation in meaning-making communities. The co-construction of learning strategies between a teacher and student is just one component, albeit a very important one, of a larger set of interactions involving the internalization and transformation of social talk to produce self-regulatory learning strategies.

I want to address the class size question I introduced earlier, because I know teachers take that question very seriously, owing to the fact that schools embed the problem of helping struggling writers within the institutional necessity of teaching many students at once. I am familiar with the research on class size in English,[1] and I realize that what we know with any degree of

---

[1]For an excellent, brief and highly readable introduction to the issues in research on class size in English classes, see Smith and NCTE Task Force on Class Size and Workload in Secondary English Instruction (1986). For a general overview of research on class size, see Finn and Voelkl (1994).

confidence can be summarized briefly: Classes ranging from 13 to 17 compared with classes ranging from 22 to 25 show statistically significant advantages in achievement at the early elementary level (K–3), and that minorities benefit significantly more than nonminorities (Finn & Achilles, 1990) from reduced class sizes. Given the importance of communities of learning summarized in the preceding paragraph, class size research in the lower grades suggests that it might be the case that smaller classes make it easier for students to participate as members of communities of meaning makers. In the upper grades or in particular subjects, however, we don't know much about the effects of small classes, and we haven't investigated at all the benefits of focusing teacher preparation on small-class settings (Finn & Voelkl, 1994). In spite of the limited research, my interpretation of what we know about class size and achievement is that there is enough evidence that something positive happens when class sizes are reduced to support the belief that *large class sizes should not automatically determine or limit what teachers do.* Regardless of class size, teachers should look for ways to set up communities of learners and to help students become participating members in the language interaction within those communities. Simply stated, my answer to the question I presented earlier—Strategy instruction sounds wonderful, but how can I use it with 150 students?—is by forming meaningful communities of learners.

It is possible, for example, to explain and model writing strategies for a whole class as a community. Once a strategy is introduced to a classroom full of writers, it can be practiced within smaller groups. If just hearing about strategies is not enough, if strategies must be constructed by being used meaningfully within the dynamics of socialized problem-solving processes, what is the role of the teacher in these learning communities? The answer is to scaffold individual learning. In cases in which acquisition is sufficient for all students in a classroom to catch on quickly to a new writing strategy, instruction may stop at explaining and modeling. Students then go on to adapt and install the strategy independently in their writing processes as they write. Such classrooms are rare, however, and probably involve writers who are already quite skilled. In the much more common classroom in which learning must take over where acquisition leaves off, strategic writing instruction should include the scaffolded use of strategies within community-supported individual writing processes. Even in a sociocognitive framework, even at the height of collaborative and cooperative group processes, learning is an individual achievement (Collins, 1991), and scaffolding is a way to support that achievement.

In our research we identified time and focused, scaffolded practice as main factors in the processes individuals use to internalize writing strategies in social settings. Struggling writers need more time and practice than successful writers, and some struggling writers need more time and practice than others. This is where workshop-style instruction and writing conferences certainly help. Within the writing-workshop framework, a teaching strategy that has worked well for effective teachers in our research classrooms is to begin the workshop with a sequence of writing tasks in mind. If the workshop is to last 6 weeks, for example, teachers might plan a sequence of five or six related reading and writing tasks. They expect the quickest students to get through all or most of the tasks, and they expect the slower students to manage only two or three. Without exception, however, effective teachers we observed also expect that *the quality of the work will not vary significantly across students.* Their assumption is that it is better to do a few tasks successfully, especially for struggling writers, than to attempt many without ever experiencing a substantial degree of success. (How many struggling writers have never produced an "A" paper? How is that lack of achievement and recognition connected to their continuing struggles and to their identities as writers?) A pre-planned sequence of tasks, therefore, clearly benefits struggling writers, permitting each to work at his or her own speed and to receive the necessary amount of support from teachers and peers.

In a writing workshop in a ninth-grade inclusion classroom, for example, teacher-researcher Garland Godinho uses assignment grids to organize sequences of literacy tasks around the study of particular works. Her ninth-grade curriculum also requires the learning of literary terminology, learning about the subject or content of literary works, and learning different kinds of writing, such as persuasive, expository, narrative, and creative. She integrates these curricular requirements by setting up a

	Plot	Setting	Character	Culture
Description		Desert life	Shabanu	
Comparison contrast		Desert and Amherst		Choose 3 customs and compare to 3 U.S. customs
Summary	Main events of selected chapters		Summarize a character or conflict	
Persuasion explanation	Foreshadowing Suspense Climax Conflict		Give advice to Shabanu Conflict	
Narrative	New ending		Shabanu remembers Guluband	Imagine yourself in the Middle East

FIGURE 4.1. Sample assignment grid.

rubric or grid for organizing student work. On the horizontal axis in the example in Figure 4.1 are categories of ideas relevant to studying *Shabanu: Daughter of the Wind,* a novel by Suzanne Fisher Staples.[2] On the vertical axis are the different modes of writing. The grid permits Garland to think about sequences of learning experiences to help her students complete the writing tasks. It also helps her think about the composition and literary-response skills she wants to teach and the strategic planning steps needed to produce quality pieces of writing, as I show later in this chapter.

Freedman (1987), similarly, shows that sequences of writing assignments are characteristic of the excellent teachers of writing in the ethnographic portion of her study of response to writing. Their assignments come in blocks of three, with the third being a culmination of the first two, as in this example from English teacher Art Peterson:

[2]This example is from Collins and Godinho (1996). Copyright 1996 by Lawrence Erlbaum Associates. Used with permission.

1. Character Study of a friend or acquaintance
2. Character Study of a Well-Known Contemporary Figure
3. Character Sketch of a Figure from *Great Expectations* (Freedman, 1987, pp. 201–203)

A sequence of tasks keeps the quicker learners in a classroom working with limited teacher assistance from one task to another while teachers work more intensively on scaffolding the work of the others. Scaffolding is a metaphor for guiding and supporting students, and in strategic writing instruction teachers provide diminishing amounts of scaffolding across several tasks to support the learning of strategies by students. "Scaffolding" is another term for the networking and mentoring I referred to in Chapter 1: "The expert intervenes with a supportive tool as the learner needs the help" (Freedman, 1987, p. 8). A supportive tool can be a thinking or learning strategy, or a textual format within which students can frame their remarks (Applebee, 1984). The examples of Jason (Chapter 2) and Brandon (Chapter 3) learning to control patterns of logic in their writing show supportive tools in the form of both strategies and textual formats used as strategies, and I provide other examples later in this chapter.

Individualized Learning of Writing Strategies

The goal of strategy instruction is self-regulated performance by individuals, but acquiring and learning strategies are accomplished socially, through explicit instruction and transactions with texts and with other writers and readers within communities of meaning makers. Schuder (1993) offers a useful functional definition of learning strategies:

> *Learning strategies are the principal operators in conscious executive control functions (e.g., planning, monitoring, problem solving) used as needed by learners to help manage the deployment of whatever skills, knowledge and disposition to learn they have in specific learning situations.* (p. 186, emphasis in original)

This definition emphasizes, again, that it is not only strategies but also their functions that matters. Explicit instruction and teacher–learner–text transactions can combine whole-class and small-group activities, but the activities should scaffold individual learning of strategies and their functions within writing processes. In this manner, individual students take ownership of strategies by co-constructing them transactionally and working toward independent uses of the strategies.

The excerpts from our case study of Brandon in Chapter 3 show how strategic literacy is socially formed through purposeful transactions with texts and with other readers and writers. We worked with Brandon for about a year, including 6 weeks during the summer between his 9th and 10th grades. During this year we came to know a great deal about his literacy processes and about the struggles he encounters while reading and writing. Like Jason in Chapter 2, Brandon showed evidence of relying on a visual mode of learning, and like many struggling writers in our studies, he had the most trouble while writing about his reading. He also seemed to depend on some of the forms of spoken language during both reading and writing, such as when he sounded out difficult words while reading aloud or when he attempted to spell difficult words by analogy with similar sounding words. The strategies we co-constructed with Brandon, however, did not try to break him of his reliance on visual learning and spoken language. Instead, we saw those as strengths tied to cognitive and cultural influences and therefore as default strategies or places to begin helping Brandon to construct literacy strategies that would work for him.

With each of the writers who were the focus of full case studies in our research we assembled a cumulative list of successful reading and writing strategies. Brandon's list of strategies shows the variety and individual nature of the learning tools we constructed with him, worded here in exactly the way they were recorded in Brandon's writing folder near the end of the year we worked with him:

Strategies for Writing

1. *Do multiple readings.* Almost all of your writing in school is about reading you've done. The multiple readings strategy means reading parts of the material more than once. Good readers always do multiple readings. Do your

writing with the pages you're reading open in front of you and keep referring to them while you write.

2. *Take notes on what the reading says.* Don't try to write about your reading from memory, especially with difficult reading material. Taking notes helps you figure out what the reading says. Do some reading and notetaking before you write, to help you plan the writing, and do some more whenever you need to figure out another part of the reading.

3. *Stop and think: Why am I writing? Who will read this?* This strategy establishes a purpose and audience for your writing. It helps you get clear on what [Brandon's English and social studies teachers] want and how to fit your ideas in with their expectations.

4. *Predict what the writing will look like.* Imagine the final appearance of the piece of writing you're working on. How many pages? Does it have a title? What paragraphs or parts or sections are needed and what do they each accomplish?

5. *If you have trouble getting started, use other writings as a model.* Make the new piece of writing look like an old one that you know is similar and successful.

6. *Use ideas from the reading and express them in your own words.* It is not cheating to paraphrase ideas from your reading; in fact that's a good way to make the ideas your own.

7. *Top sentence.* Remember the ladder of ideas. Think about what you have written so far and check your first sentence, the one at the top of your writing. If you think of a map of ideas, does *X* mark the spot? Remember, too, that you can change the top sentence as you write and figure out what you really want to say.

8. *Connect your sentences.* Read your writing to see if your sentences create a "ladder" of related ideas by leading back up to the top sentence. Rewrite sentences or add some others to make connections.

9. *Edit for problems.* Here remember to use your lists of spelling problems, homonyms, and words you find difficult. Watch for general words such as *thing* and *everything,* vague pronouns such as *they,* and informal expres-

sions such as *that's incredible* and change them to words that carry more precise meanings.

This list of strategies comprises the metacognitive controls we recommended for Brandon, and it also illustrates the multiple strategies approach we used with writers throughout our research. Keeping the list available in Brandon's writing folder helped him keep the list of strategies in mind while writing and conversing with other writers. Clearly, this particular list of strategies, in its specificity and in its wording, is intended for use by Brandon only. The multiple-readings strategy, for example, would have been less appropriate for Jason (Chapter 2). Part of Jason's struggle in writing about his reading was an apparent overdependence on copying from texts he was writing about, and the multiple-readings strategy—especially worded the way we worked it out with Brandon: "Do your writing with the pages you're reading open in front of you and keep referring to them while you write"—might have encouraged Jason to do even more copying. The strategy of using other writings as models, similarly, proved helpful for Jason, but we had to word it differently on his list so as not to encourage his overdependence on copying from texts. Other writers can benefit from some of the advice contained in Brandon's list of writing strategies, such as using note taking as an aid to understanding or pausing to think about purpose and audience or to check for coherence, but only Brandon can make sense of the full list as a set of writing strategies to keep in mind while writing in school. The ladder metaphor exemplifies that point. Recall that the ladder was Brandon's label for what I called a strategy for "conceptualizing logically connected writing by visually representing the pattern of logic in a piece of writing." That technical label, and others I used to discuss it such as "explicitly marking patterns of reference" and "using a visual representation of a main idea and patterns of relatedness with other ideas" would have perhaps generalized better to other writers but would have been too much for Brandon to make sense of. Such technical wordings would have risked turning procedural and conditional knowledge into declarative knowledge, making our advice on how to think about writing sound to Brandon like another list of informational items to be learned in school. It is best to use

Brandon's terms and meanings for his writing strategies, as when we added meeting his English and social studies teachers' expectations to the purpose and audience strategy to accommodate Brandon's constant worry about what his teachers would think of his writing. Indeed, that is what individualized learning through transactional co-construction of strategies means—constructing learning strategies in personally meaningful terms through shared transactions with texts, with other writers, and with teachers.

When Strategies Are Reduced to Formulas

Given large class sizes, especially large numbers of struggling writers, it is tempting for teachers to resort to teaching strategic knowledge as a body of information. From that perspective, however, writing strategies can become fixed and nonnegotiable, as if they were universally applicable cognitive and scribal activities. When that happens, strategic instruction amounts to teaching self-regulation of language processes by formulas instead of by strategies. The following case illustrates how an excellent and caring teacher can resort to providing formulas instead of thinking strategies to get his students through a major examination.

This case involves an English teacher I'll call Samuel who taught two summer classes of ninth-grade students who had failed the "June Exam," a comprehensive, citywide English test in a city in upstate New York. For Samuel's students, the "June Exam" had become the "August Exam," and his purpose in summer school was to get his students ready to take the test again.

The exam was composed of three parts. Part One consisted of a test of skills such as listening, vocabulary, grammar and usage, spelling, and reading comprehension; Part Two was a literature question; and Part Three presented a composition question. Samuel spent much of the class time getting his students ready for the literature question because he believed that part of the exam presented the most difficulty for his students: "What really kills them is the literature. The literature annihilates them."

Because the school district didn't provide textbooks for his students, Samuel decided to bring his own literary selections to class. He read several stories aloud and then used them to discuss literature questions from past exams. He shared one such question with me:

> Write a well-organized essay of at least 200–250 words on either A or B.
>
> A. Authors often use literature to express a point of view about an idea such as courage, honor, love, friendship, passion, hatred or revenge. From the full-length plays, novels, biographies, essays or poems you've read in class this year, choose two selections and discuss each author's viewpoint. For each, give the author, title, and type of literature. Discuss the point of view presented by the author. Support your answer with examples from the selection. Tell why you would agree or disagree with the writer's viewpoint.
>
> B. Literary characters often possess personalities that seem very attractive (friendly, outgoing, self-confident, etc.). From the literature you've read in class this year, choose two selections which have characters with attractive personalities. For each, give the author, title, and type of literature. Name the character and the type of personality the character seems to possess. Tell why you think the character's personality is attractive. Use specific references to support your opinion.

Samuel first asked his students to concentrate on the question itself, to read the question and try to understand it by rephrasing the question in their own words. He also asked them to respond to questions such as these: What do the examiners want from you in Part A? What is "point of view"? Do you have a point of view? He led discussions of students' points of view on topics of interest to them.

Samuel then asked his students to write, but they reproduced a story in their writing instead of discussing point of view. Without exception, they wrote summaries of one of the stories he read. He told them providing a plot summary in response to the test question was inappropriate:

> "I would give them examples. If you were invited to your brother's wedding, would you go in sneakers, tank top and

shorts? Would you be doing as he would like you to do? No. Alright, let's do it as they would like us to do it. Let's use what we know about the story and make it work."

When he asked them to tell what they knew about the story, however, Samuel saw that his students couldn't get started. He had them look closely at the test question to get them to use information in the question to get started writing a response. He modeled that strategy for them:

"Try this out; this is what they give you, and you can start your writing this way. 'Authors often use literature to express a point of view about an idea such as courage, honor, love, friendship, passion, hatred or revenge.' We wrote that down on the board, and they wrote it down in their notebooks. I said, 'All right, considering the literature we read, which of those strong feelings can we key on?' One of the ones we keyed on was about courage. We had read a story called 'The Sniper.' They would come up with, 'In this paragraph we are going to talk about courage.' I'd ask, 'and what are we going to say about courage? Look at the question. What does it want you to say?' And then they would give me the necessary answers that would address the question. So while they were giving me this information, I would be writing it on the board."

Throughout this discussion, Samuel made sure students did what the examiners wanted them to do. He had them give title and author and type of literature, and he made sure they understood what those terms meant. He modeled how to make main points and how to find supporting evidence in the story. In this manner, Samuel hoped his students would acquire the ability to get started writing and the organizational skills they needed to respond to the test question instead of providing what he called "repetitions of text, [as in] 'this story is about two guys shooting at each other across a street on rooftops.' "

Samuel reported that some of his students did learn that they had to address the test question and not just repeat the story. Others, however, adopted a different strategy. They re-wrote their practice essays during the examination:

"The August exam might have asked them to address a problem that they saw, that a character encountered. Their response would be, 'In some stories characters show courage, and hatred and these other things.' And rather than address the issue or problem, they would discuss the courage that a character demonstrated."

The method of structuring a response to the test question which Samuel had hoped would generalize from practice in class to the new test situation didn't generalize for some of his students. Many of the students reproduced the essays they practiced with in class instead of addressing the new test question on the August exam. Samuel sees this as a problem with understanding the question:

"As far as what this lesson offers, it offers basically an organizational crutch. While some of them can pick up on organizational methods and the need to organize your thoughts in some kind of order, the majority of the kids had difficulty in dealing with the text and since they couldn't understand what the question wanted from them, they went back to what they knew had worked before. 'This is what my teacher said worked here and when I did this for this other question, I got good here; I improved here. I have to get out of summer school and go to 10th grade. So, I'll do it; I'll use this. I know this.' I had great essays, but they just did not address the issue, didn't address the topic. And I feel that was because the kids just couldn't get near it."

Samuel's analysis of his lesson appears to be an accurate one. The lesson does indeed offer an organizational crutch, a formula for responding to a particular test question. The formula consists of finding a pattern for structuring an answer to a test question in the question itself. The pattern of organization he and his students found in practice, however, was meant to be reinterpreted in light of a new question, not just transplanted or superimposed on the students' writing during the test. Instead, some of the students misunderstood his directions and used the content they had practiced with in class instead of the content asked for by the test. The lesson didn't provide an opportunity for students to discover how to match content and form for themselves. Instead, the lesson, and consequently the test situation, was at odds with the thinking and writing the students were doing. Samuel initially read the stories to his students, and they wrote plot summaries. He told them plot summaries were not acceptable responses to the test question and then taught a lesson on appropriateness of response, on giving examiners what they want. Students from that point on did little writing between the practice test and the real one; in fact, the only writing students did during that time was copying from the board. The rest of the class time was spent listening to Samuel and providing answers to his questions in discussion format as he modeled how to produce an appropriate response to a test question. Knowing that the test question would provide an outline or structure for its own answer, Samuel tried through demonstration and discussion to model using that structure to respond to the real test question. The students never did practice individually generating and organizing content for writing from literature study, and therefore some of them did not take ownership of a strategy for responding to the literature question. Their reading consisted of listening to Samuel's reading; their notes consisted of copying his notes. As a result, their strategy remained his formula. It doesn't seem surprising that the lesson misfired for some of the students because Samuel was trusting acquisition where learning was necessary. What some students acquired, however, was a sense, or perhaps a wish, that an essay can be reproduced or "transplanted" to get through a tough test. In this case, organizational strategies imposed by a teacher from outside the discovery of content for writing gave control over matching content and organization, experience, and heuristic to the teacher. Students' attempts to go back to the content of the practice lesson may have been motivated by a desire to gain control over content by going back to the teacher's content to connect with the teacher's "organizational crutch." Given the constraints of an almost impossible teaching situation—the necessity of preparing two classes of ninth-grade struggling writers with records of recent failure for an imminent literature examination, for which preparation they have no literature textbooks—Samuel's approach is to teach a "quick fix" formula to everyone in his classes in the hope that students will be able to use it during the test. But classes don't learn. Individuals do.

A focus strictly on teaching whole classes inhibits strategies-based writing instruction. The co-construction of learning strategies is blocked by the traditional, transmissionist dispensing of knowledge from a single teacher to many students. Such teaching can turn strategies into tricks or formulas through what Livingston (1996) calls a "strategies only" approach. This approach involves teaching problem solving declaratively, but not procedurally and conditionally, making it unlikely that the students will use their knowledge outside of the immediate instructional context. This strategy also resembles the "laissez-faire" strategies approach (Pressley, Borkowski, & O'Sullivan, 1985) because its chief characteristic is a tendency for teachers to maintain control over what will be learned and practiced, so that students are not actively engaged within learning communities in deciding which strategies to use and how and when to use them.

Problem Solving as Algorithm and as Strategy

Teaching strategies as a body of declarative and procedural information, or as a fixed and universally applicable series of activities, is teaching language processes as if they were formulas for solving problems or accomplishing ends. This is an algorithmic understanding of problem solving, a label I borrow from mathematics and computer science, where an algorithm is a set procedure, a kind of recipe, for finding a solution to a problem in a fixed series of steps. Algorithm-based problem-solving processes have their obvious uses, but we shouldn't try to substitute them for strategy-based problem solving.

I'll clarify the distinction between problem solving as algorithm and as strategy by presenting an example of each. In both cases the example is a math problem. The first problem is rather simple and straightforward:

Mary is 24. She is twice as old as Jane. How old is Jane?

What makes this example simple and straightforward is the fact that we all have a readily available means, an algorithm, for solving it. When I use this problem and the next in workshops with teachers, they often report that they solved it even before finishing their reading of the problem. Knowing that one person's age, 24, is twice another person's age tends to automatically call out "12," even before the second person's age is asked for. Indeed, the problem is so easily solved, we might not even realize that we are using an algorithm to solve it. The correct answer, however, is not achieved by guessing or by some other unsystematic means, such as by trying and eliminating all ages lower than 24 until 12 is shown to fit. The important clue is "twice as old" because it tells us to divide Mary's age by two to arrive at Jane's age. By simply applying the procedure "divide the older person's age (24) by the given factor (2) to arrive at the younger person's age," we solve the problem.

The second example is not so simple and straightforward:

Mary is 24. She is twice as old as Jane was when Mary was Jane's age. How old is Jane?

If this example is more difficult than the first, it is because this time we don't have a readily available algorithm to assist with working toward a solution. In fact, teachers sometimes report that the algorithm in the first example ("divide the older person's age by the given factor to arrive at the younger person's age") gets in the way of solving the second problem. This time the clue "twice as old" can be misleading. In fact, some teachers have insisted the correct answer to the second problem is 12 even after they've been told it's wrong, probably because the "twice as old" algorithm is the only one available.

For those of us who don't have ready an appropriate algorithm, arriving at a solution for the second problem requires processes other than algorithmic ones. These can include strategic processes. The reconstructed record of the process used by one English teacher, Garland Godinho, to solve the second problem illustrates strategic problem solving:

"I did not come to answer or solve this problem in a conventional way. I tried to, by way of setting up ratios and exploring the outer recesses of my mind for the memory (or even partial memory) of a formula that might work in leading me to the Answer. These are some scratchings of my search:

Present		Past
M:J	=	M:J
$24:X$	=	$X:12$
X	=	X^2
$2X$	=	$24/12$
$2X$	=	2
X	=	1

"After not too much consternation, I was able to assert that JANE WAS 12 WHEN MARY (24) WAS JANE'S AGE. I had to keep reading the second half of the problem over and over. The only way I can think of to describe why, is that I kept 'losing it.' I kept losing the line of direction of the problem. I read it to myself, I read it out loud, I read it to the person sitting next to me.

"I can't fully explain how I got the answer of 18, but when I did get it, I was *absolutely* sure it was correct. I seemed to have gotten a visual image of the problematic situation in my mind. The visual image told me that the number of years between 12 and Jane's age and 24 and Jane's age HAD TO BE EQUAL. So I was able, then, to calculate the equal distance as 6 years and the age to be 18."

Garland is right; the correct answer is 18. Her success comes from the insight or intuition that the ages of Jane and Mary are related, which she turns into a problem-solving strategy built on the proposition that the ages are connected in a regular way. This is achieved by reading the problem over and over—silently, out loud, and to another person—and by visualizing the relation between Jane's and Mary's ages. As long as Garland tried to solve the problem with a formula, she was solving for Jane's age presumably by using the "twice as old" algorithm. Through multiple readings, talking, and visualization, she was able to switch to the more profitable strategy of solving for the relationship between Jane's and Mary's ages.

The type of discovery process Garland used is sometimes called a heuristic procedure. In using language, we don't learn algorithms and then wait for well-defined problems to solve; such a procedure is more descriptive of what computers do. Human problem solving is based on past experience and heuristics, that is, on rules or strategies or designs for discovering patterns of relatedness in experience. In human problem solving, cognitive processing applies heuristics to a knowledge base, both of which are developed through acquisition and learning over time. Notice, again, that human problem solving is a social process. Building a knowledge base from experience, selecting from a knowledge base of stored experience, matching knowledge with heuristics, and gaining access to new meanings by discovering new patterns of relatedness as problem situations demand all take place in social settings, as illustrated by Garland's transactional problem-solving processes.

Algorithmic problem-solving strategies are more suited to computers than to writers. Computers apply finite numbers of algorithms to finite quantities of data; their work is limited to data and algorithms stored in their electronic memories. For human problem solving, knowledge can be selected from a knowledge base of stored experience or obtained or constructed during the problem-solving process, and knowledge is then matched with appropriate heuristics, which are also remembered from experience or obtained or constructed in process, as was Garland's realization that Jane's and Mary's ages had to be related by a constant difference.

For the same reason it works well with computers, algorithm-based problem solving is limited for humans. Computers manipulate symbols entirely through syntax; the symbols are zeroes and ones, but they have no meaning, not even as numbers (Searle, 1984). Human-language processes, on the other hand, are fundamentally semantic. They involve words and syntax, but they are primarily acts of meaning making and imagination, of constructing frames and images and words and moving them about in our heads in new arrangements (Bronowski, 1990, p. 204). Strategies necessary for working with language cannot be sufficiently acquired or learned strictly as formulas because they must serve the language user's own semantic and expressive intentions. This is the key difference between passive and active learning. Bereiter and Scardamalia (1987) use the term "intentional learning" to refer to self-regulated, purposive meaning making, and they contrast it with passive learning:

> Contemporary school practices of all kinds seem to encourage [a] more passive kind of cognition. One set of school practices favors passivity by continually telling students what to do. The opposing set of practices favors passivity by encouraging students to follow their spontaneous interests and impulses. Largely absent, scarcely even contemplated, are school practices that encourage students to assume responsibility for what becomes of their minds. (p. 361)

Learning a Strategy for Learning from Writing

The best way to teach strategies so that they serve an individual writer's intentions is to make strategies available to assist in the construction of meaning during students' writing processes. I illustrate a method of doing that by describing a lesson on writing as a mode of learning taught by one of the English teachers in our research, Jeannine Rugani. As a final project after reading *The Catcher in the Rye* in ninth-grade English, Jeannine led a class discussion of issues involved in deciding whether the book should be banned. She then asked her students to write in response to the following task:

> "Write a well-composed essay of about 200 words answering the question, should *The Catcher in the Rye* be banned?
>
> "Include an opening and closing paragraph and use points we discussed in class to support your argument for or against censoring the novel. You may choose to address an audience comprised of adults or your classmates."

In writing their first drafts many of Jeannine's students simply took a position on the censorship question and then repeated some of what had been said during class discussion. Jeannine realized that this was what her assignment asked for, but she noticed that her stronger writers, about one-third of the class of 20, worked to recast and elaborate on ideas from discussion, to add ideas of their own, and to embed their ideas within a coherent argument for or against censorship of the novel. Relatively weaker writers, the other two-thirds, settled for listing ideas from discussion. This difference between stronger and weaker writers fits the distinction between knowledge transforming and knowledge telling (Bereiter & Scardamalia, 1987).[3] Jeannine's weaker writers were for the most part using writing to tell what they had studied about censorship and *The Catcher in the Rye* rather than using writing to transform their knowledge into an original and well-reasoned argument, as the stronger writers did.

One symptom of repeating knowledge instead of transforming it was evident in the endings of their first drafts. Most of the weaker writers apparently either ignored or had trouble with the requirement to include a closing paragraph, and others used what Freedman (1987) called a "formulaic tie back to the first paragraph" (p. 149) in place of a well-developed conclusion. Either way, their essays seemed to abruptly end at the point where they ran out of ideas to "copy" from class discussion. Jeannine decided to teach a strategy to help her students transform ideas from reading and discussion by rewriting their first drafts so that they build toward convincing concluding paragraphs. She designed and taught a strategy for constructing a conclusion by learning from one's own writing. The strategy helped students begin to transform their thinking about class discussion, as indicated by the following example of first and second drafts from one of the students, a girl whom Jeannine describes as a struggling reader and writer:

First Draft

I think that the Book the *Catcher in the Rye* should not be banned. I will explain why I feel this way.

The *Catcher in the Rye* there was unabriate language and some crazy things in the book, but that is no reson to banne a book.

You can walk down the hall for 5 minutes and hear worst language and a lot more of it that you whould hear in the book.

[3] In Chapter 5 I take a closer look at this distinction and show how it relates to strategic writing instruction by describing several default strategies characteristic of struggling writers in our studies.

If people think it is bad enough to banned the they would have to banned T.V. Any person enculding young kids can turn on the T.V. and watch the canels and will hear and see the same stuff that is in this book. A kid can't go and pick up a book either Because the can't Read or they don't want to read it then they can if they want to.

Second Draft

I think the book *The Catcher in the Rye* should not be banned. In this essay I will explain why I feel this way.

In *The Catcher in the Rye* there was inappropriate language and some other crazy things, but that is no reason to ban a book.

You can walk down the hall in school for five minutes, and hear worse language than you would hear in the book.

If people think it is bad enough to ban then they would have to ban many television shows, also. Any person encluding young kids can turn on the t.v., watch it , hear it and see the same kind of stuff that is in the book. Kids most likely are not going to pick up a book like this either because they can't Read or they don't want to read it.

Basically if people want to read it then they can if they want to.

Some people showing the unage drinking and will influence other kids that are underaged to drink. Kids will drink if the want to, it is their chocie. One book is not going to effect any one.

The book also gives another look on a teenage life. To my opinion this book make me feel like I would never want to be this way. The book also relates to teenagers.

Again I am saying vulgarity is common daily, drinking and smoking is one persons chocie no one can make them do this, and a rated R movie is ten times worse than this book.

The reasons I have just explained to you, I hope I have perswaded you to have the same opinion I do. The book *The Catcher in the Rye* should not be banned. If you ban this book you

are taking a book from other who are wanting
to read a very creative and well writien piece.

The first draft of this writer's essay illustrates a problem
Jeannine called "ending instead of concluding." The second
draft still has its problems and needs more work, but it is obvious
that the writer is trying to add to, elaborate on, and connect her
ideas so that they lead to a convincing conclusion. The first draft
really has only one idea, the ubiquity of vulgarity, to support not
banning the book, an idea that came straight from class discussion. It is possible that at the end of the first draft the writer
was striving for a new idea of her own ("A kid can't go and pick
up a book either Because the can't Read or they don't want to
read it then they can if they want to."), but the idea hasn't been
represented sufficiently in the text. The second draft says a little
more about the ideas from class discussion and clarifies the "kid
can't read" idea from the first draft by explaining that young
kids won't be spoiled by the book because they can't read it. The
second draft also adds new ideas on teenage life and tries to
connect them to each other and to a conclusion.

Most of the other writers in the class made similar changes
in the direction of transforming their ideas though writing.
Jeannine encouraged these revision processes by working on the
knowledge-telling problem through a strategies-based lesson on
writing conclusions as the logical outcome of a piece of writing.
With assistance from members of a graduate course, Jeannine
defined the conclusions strategy in terms that emphasized learning from writing. Jeannine was able to fit this strategy into our
general four-step model for teaching learning strategies:

1. *Identify a writing strategy worth teaching.* Jeannine called
the writing strategy *concluding as an act of learning* because she
wanted students to think of writing a conclusion as an act of
reviewing, adding to and learning from their own writing.

2. *Introduce students to the writing strategy by modeling it.*
Jeannine modeled how to think about a conclusion as an act of
learning from one's own writing.

3. *Help students try out the writing strategy with workshop-style
teacher guidance.* Jeannine had her students revise their essays to

get beyond class discussion and to strengthen the way they worked toward conclusions, and she scaffolded their learning during this step.

4. *Help students work toward independent mastery of the writing strategy through repeated practice and reinforcement.* The repetition and reinforcement came during subsequent assignments.

The actual teaching of the *concluding as an act of learning* strategy followed a plan which corresponded to the four-step model just described. Jeannine constructed the plan with the assistance of members of our graduate seminar, and this is how she carried it out:

1. Jeannine passed back the first drafts and talked about conclusions. She said that one way to write a strong conclusion is to think of the conclusion as your chance to decide what you are learning while writing an essay. She asked students to review what they had written about censorship and *The Catcher in the Rye*: Members of our graduate seminar suggested asking questions such as, "What do your ideas add up to?" We also suggested a shopping-cart metaphor: "Think of writing this piece as a little like shopping in a supermarket. You've read the book, we've talked about reasons on both sides of the censorship argument, and you've selected ideas from your thoughts on the reading and the discussion. While you were writing, you were selecting ideas and putting them in your shopping cart. Now you're at the checkout counter and you're taking ideas out of the cart and seeing what they add up to. This is what writing a conclusion is like because it involves reexamining your ideas and determining their total value."

2. Jeannine used an article on banning books from *Good Housekeeping* to model the thinking that goes into thinking about conclusions while writing. She read the last two paragraphs aloud and asked the students what the article was about. They were surprised by her question because they didn't have copies of the article to refer to. She reread the last two paragraphs, and this time students responded to her question by identifying ways to combat book banning. She then read the title of the article and praised the class for figuring out what it was about. Notice here that Jeannine could have modeled writing a conclusion by

presenting ideas and then constructing a conclusion from them. Instead, she gave students a conclusion and modeled how ideas in an essay can be connected to it by having students construct the ideas. This latter approach makes a good deal of sense because building on the weaker writers' tendency to "tell knowledge" by copying or repeating from class discussion was a primary objective of her lesson, and modeling writing a conclusion by presenting ideas and then constructing a conclusion from them may have simply elicited more knowledge telling.

3. Next, students revised their essays using the "concluding as an act of learning" strategy. Jeannine circulated among the writers and provided assistance. In her own words, "They all took the strategy and their writing pretty seriously. (I was impressed—that's rare.)" Students revised their essays in that class and the next. Three students needed more time and were given it.

4. Jeannine helped students work toward independent mastery of the writing strategy through repeated practice and reinforcement during subsequent assignments.

Throughout this lesson, Jeannine adapted strategies instruction to the needs of her students. She first identified a common need for many of her students by observing how they went about incorporating ideas from class discussion into their writing. Then, as they wrote their revisions, she scaffolded individual needs. The strategy she taught through modeling and scaffolding was designed to get students to think constructively about transforming their knowledge instead of just repeating it. The strategy suggested a particular step in the process of thinking during writing by asking students to revise in the direction of making conclusions something they work toward in their writing, not just something they tack on at the end. Nearly all the revised essays moved in this direction, as illustrated by the formal characteristics of first and second drafts in Figure 4.2.

Jeannine adds that her weaker writers benefited from the learning-while-writing strategy, but her stronger writers indicated they needed another strategy. In response to the advice to plan revisions that work toward conclusions, one of the stronger writers said, "I already did that." She reread his conclusion and asked a question she had learned as a college writer, "So what?":

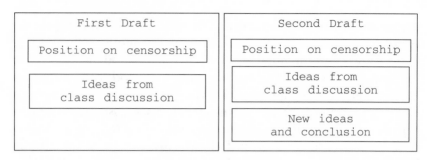

FIGURE 4.2. Structure of first and second drafts of "Censorship" essays.

"I told the student I was speaking with that after I read his essay, I should say, 'So what? Who cares?' and a revised conclusion would answer that for me and convince me to care or to be as interested as he had been when he wrote it. Since there was a spark of comprehension in that student and a few others, I interrupted the class and presented this additional strategy."

Jeannine's teaching shows how a typical writing task, an essay reflecting on the meaning of reading and class discussion, can be turned into a strategic writing lesson and tailored through minilessons for students of differing abilities. She does the teaching without reducing learning strategies to formulas. Notice, also, that the second draft from the weaker writer quoted earlier includes a final paragraph written in accordance with the "So what?" conclusions strategy in the minilesson for stronger writers.

Formulas Can Be Used Strategically

Many composition teachers and researchers put down teacher-supplied or teacher-influenced formats for student writing, such as when Romano (1987) complains about the way his 13-year-old daughter's spontaneity and creativity were apparently stifled by a teacher's five-part structure consisting of topic sentence, three supporting details, and a conclusion. A related version of the same structure is frequently referred to critically as the "five-paragraph theme," which Emig (1971), for example, calls the "Fifty-Star Theme" (p. 97). Certainly teacher-imposed structural requirements may stifle originality by substituting formulas for heuristics. In one classroom I observed, a teacher was preparing 11th- and 12th-graders to retake a state-mandated competency test in writing which they had failed, some more than once, by teaching a formula for the persuasive essay called ORRC (Opinion, Reason, Reason, Conclusion). Every essay I read which had been written in accordance with that formula had the same hollow, mechanical, fill-in-the-blank quality:

My opinion is _____

I have two reasons for my opinion.

My first reason is _____

_____

My second reason is _____

_____

In conclusion, my opinion is _____

Still, I think it is important to recognize that the formulaic quality of such structures resides in the way they are used, not in the structures themselves. *There is nothing inherently formulaic about written structures.* In both the "Samuel" and "ORRC" examples, teachers are teaching to the test and supplying quick fixes for writers who are expected to perform in a highly constrained way. It may be appropriate for them to prescribe certain formats for writing if that helps failed writers pass the test. The formats become formulas, however, when they become goals for writing, as if making thinking and writing fit a prescribed format is what writing is all about.

The five-part structure is, by itself, innocent of any wrongdoing. It is simply an elaboration of a basic three-part structure (introduction, body, and conclusion for expository writing; beginning, middle, and ending for narrative writing) which results from the fact that discourse "runs in a line"—that is the etymological meaning of *discourse* (Collins & Miller, 1986). In fact, Emig's (1971) paragraph criticizing the five-part structure has three parts:

A species of extensive writing that recurs so frequently in student accounts that it deserves special mention is the five-paragraph theme, consisting of one paragraph of introduction ("tell what you are going to say"), three of expansion and example ("say it"), and one of conclusion ("tell what you have said"). This mode is so indigenously American that it might be called the Fifty-Star Theme. In fact, the reader might imagine behind this and the next three paragraphs Kate Smith singing "God Bless America" or the piccolo obligato from "The Stars and Stripes Forever." (p. 97)

That a structure is so frequently used that it seems "indigenous" is an excellent argument for why we ought to teach it in schools, and doing so does not automatically make the structure mechanical and formulaic every time teachers recommend it to students. The formulaic quality does not reside in the structure but, rather, in the way it is used. If it is a pattern to which students must conform without knowing when or why to use the pattern, as in Samuel's teaching of test-taking tricks, it is indeed formulaic. If, on the other hand, the structure provides a meaningful scaffold for writing, meaningful because students know how, when, and why to use it to guide their writing, it is not a formula at all. It is a writing strategy.

Several years ago I decided to use my own writing to test the idea that a format for writing can take on personal meaning and usefulness to work as a strategy. I drew up a five-part plan to use as a scaffold to guide the writing of a chapter (Collins, 1989) I was asked to do on text-analysis software. I discovered that the plan, reproduced in Figure 4.3, made the writing of the chapter surprisingly quick and easy.

Perhaps the fact that I supplied the plan myself was what made it useful. Or, maybe I simply knew the content of the essay well enough so that the five-part plan I chose served only the function of making it easier to decide what goes where. Or, having the plan may have made it easier to hold some of the content in abeyance while I worked on other parts of the piece, or perhaps some combination of all these cognitive processes and others I'm not even aware of were activated by the five-part planning strategy. At any rate, the plan was helpful by contributing to the deliberate control I took over the writing of my essay, and it therefore operated at a higher cognitive level than writing to satisfy a formula.

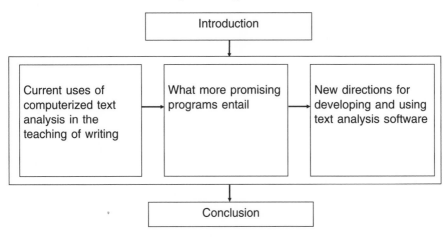

FIGURE 4.3. Five-part plan for "Computerized Text Analysis and the Teaching of Writing."

Even without my five-part diagram I would have written my chapter. What that admission means, however, is not that the format was unnecessary but, rather, that I would have planned the piece some other way. My usual method for short pieces is to plan while repeatedly writing and rewriting an opening paragraph. During such episodes an observer could conclude that I am struggling helplessly: at best, planning below the limen of consciousness; at worst, simply prewriting by putting the writing off as long as possible. What I am really doing, however, is planning the whole piece by trying out ideas to see how they work and to see how well they help me decide what I want to say throughout the piece. I am deliberately trusting myself and my own heuristic designs for writing.

But what about struggling writers who haven't learned how to trust their own designs? Or those who don't have access to designs to shape their writing? Teachers don't need to stay away from recommending designs and structures, three- or five-part or otherwise. What we need to do instead is recommend the strategic use of structures as scaffolds for thinking and writing.

An example from Garland Godinho's ninth-grade inclusion classroom clarifies how a writing structure can be used strategically. The example is from a unit for 21 ninth-grade students who make up a special program called BOSS (Building Opportunities for Student Success). This is an interdisciplinary program involving English and global studies. Heading the program is an instructional team which includes an English teacher (Garland), a global studies teacher, a reading specialist, and a special education teacher. The reading specialist and resource teacher work directly in BOSS classrooms with the students and also have many of the students in reading classes or resource room. They play a big part in modifying the course to meet individual needs and individual education plan requirements. Team members work together to identify what parts of a lesson will be difficult for some students and to decide how to accommodate them. The example uses one of the tasks from the assignment grid for the novel *Shabanu: Daughter of the Wind,* presented earlier in this chapter. Garland worded the actual writing task this way:

> "In a five-paragraph essay describe the conflicts Shabanu experiences in the novel. You can choose from Shabanu in conflict with herself, other people or society. Be sure to explain how each conflict is resolved by the end of the novel. Use examples and text citations to support your ideas."

In conjunction with designing this task, Garland identified strategies to help her students respond to it by analyzing the task to determine what knowledge and skills would be needed to complete it. For the "conflict" task she identified five key knowledge and skill areas: literary conflict and its resolution, conflict in this novel and how to gather examples, how to use quotes in an essay, outlining for expository writing, and creating a thesis statement. For each of these areas, Garland created or borrowed one or more learning strategies to help her students. To assist them in remembering the five types of literary conflict, for example, Garland taught the acronym HANSS and the mnemonic "Hot Apples Need Some Shade":

Hot	A person in conflict with *Him/Herself*
Apples	A person in conflict with *Another Person*
Need	A person in conflict with *Nature*
*SO*me	A person in conflict with *SOciety*
Shade	A person in conflict with the *Supernatural*

To help them identify conflict in the novel, Garland used small-group discussions in which students worked cooperatively to complete a study page.

Conflict

In the novel *Shabanu, Daughter of the Wind* the character Shabanu faces several conflicts.

These conflicts take on a couple of different forms:

1. Shabanu in conflict with _____
2. Shabanu in conflict with _____

List at least five incidents in the novel that deal with these conflicts:

Incident	Characters	Chapter and page
1.		
2.		
3.		
4.		
5.		

Garland next had her students work on completing study sheets she designed to help them plan their essays by generating content and organizing their ideas. Here is an excerpt from one study sheet with a student's work in italics:

Conflict Essay

What is your thesis statement? *One of the major conflicts is Shabanu's resistenel to a socirtys values and gender roles. She want her independence but is pressured to conform by her family.*

    I. INTRODUCTION (1st Paragraph)
        A. Title: *Shabanu daughter of the wind*
        B. Author: *Suzanne Fisher Staples*
        C. Kinds of Conflict: *Shabanu Vs. Society;*
           Shabanu Vs. Another Person

   II. BODY OF ESSAY—All examples and support for
        thesis

(continued)

A. First form of conflict: *Shabanu Vs. Society*
   1. First example:
      a) Why is this conflict? *Wear the chadar*
      b) Is it resolved? *sociaty say all women need to be converd, especially around stranger. She is glad to have it when they meet up with the Bugti's in the desert but she never learns to love it like Phulan does*
      c) Quote: *(include who said it and on what page) For the first time of my life, I pull the chadr over my face and lower my head beneath the gaze of these men* Who said this? *Shabanu* Page *44*
   2. Second example:
      a) Why is this conflict? *Don't want to get married society—no chose you marry who your parents say you'll marry Shabanu—would rather marry who and when she wants*
      b) Is it resolved? *Not resolved but everything suggests she will marry*
      c) Quote: (include who said it and on what page) *I'll never get used to marrying a man old enough to be my grandfather.* Who said this? *Shabanu* Page *192*

The study sheet continued in this manner for a second form of conflict with two examples and then a conclusion.

Students completed the study sheet and then used it to produce a first draft of their essays on conflict in the novel. The difference between Garland's sequence of tasks leading up to the conflict essay and the typical five-paragraph assignment is in the detailed attention to knowledge and strategies used in Garland's sequence of tasks and in the one-on-one conferences she conducts with students as they work on the tasks. The typical multipart formula, such as ORRC described earlier, is really a shortcut, a way of *avoiding* the thinking and hard work that go into writing academic essays. It consists of "plugging in" information rather than constructing it. The problem with shortcuts, of course, is that writers who take them never do catch up to others who learn by thinking through a writing task in its entirety. Garland doesn't expect her writers to use the detailed guides and study sheets and conferences she provides forever; in fact, she expects them to outgrow much of the need for such externally sponsored tools, scaffolds, and strategies long before they leave her classroom. By then, through participation in a literate community, they will have learned inner controls over processes involved in writing to take the place of Garland's external assistance.

Summary

The two teachers whose work I presented in this chapter illustrate two ways of individualizing the learning of writing strategies while teaching whole classes of writers. I selected these two methods of individualization because they appear frequently in our research as preferred ways of teaching formal aspects of writing strategically instead of formulaically, as in Samuel's case. Jeannine's conclusions strategy exemplifies many teachers' preference for letting students produce a first draft and then working with them on strategies for revision and editing. Garland's method illustrates the preference many other teachers show for explicitly guiding student work from the outset. What the two approaches have in common is the recognition that writing involves more than the repetition of content and format; they also recognize that writing is fundamentally about transforming inchoate ideas, images, and associations into sufficiently communicative, logical, or chronological texts. Strategies, in that formulation, are ways of controlling the transformation of private thought into public texts, and teacher assistance leads the learning of strategies through co-construction, a process of internalization of a public, community-based conversation.

Bruner (1986) sees such teacher assistance as reflecting Vygotsky's basic view of conceptual learning as "a collaborative enterprise involving an adult who enters into dialogue with the child in a fashion that provides the child with hints and props that allow [the child] to begin a new climb, guiding the child in next steps before the child is capable of appreciating their significance" (p. 132). He sees this process as one in which students gain the ability to intervene reflectively in the knowledge they encounter. Without this sense of reflective intervention, students are left operating continually from the outside in, as if reiterating someone else's knowledge or formula matters more than transforming and using knowledge. Teaching formats and formulas as if they were ends in themselves is inappropriate because the value of writing formats, like other linguistic conventions and regularities, resides in the contributions they make to constructing and communicating meaning. This is why it is so important to teach formats, conventions, and regularities as strategies. Strategies that permit control of one's own thinking and communicating processes are exactly what struggling writers need, and collaborative, co-constructive methods of teaching them are best because they permit and support reflective self-control.

Chapter   Five

Writing Development
and Default Writing
Strategies

Several times in the first four chapters I referred to Bereiter and Scardamalia's (1987; Scardamalia & Bereiter, 1986) distinction between knowledge telling and knowledge transforming. This distinction offers a useful frame for discussing writing development and the role of strategic writing instruction in fostering development. Knowledge telling and knowledge transforming can be used to describe the writing processes of novice and expert writers and, therefore, they also seem to describe early and late stages on a continuum representing the development of writing abilities. As I show in this chapter, however, writing development is better understood as a recursive process, one in which writers (and here I mean all writers, not just struggling ones) cycle back and forth between knowledge telling and knowledge transforming as they encounter and deal with challenges inherent in writing about certain topics within certain contexts. This means that the distinction between knowledge telling and knowledge transforming can be used not only to describe characteristic models of writing processes at early and late stages of writing development, as in Bereiter and Scardamalia (1987), but also to help us understand how writing development happens as well. Using their terminology, that understanding can be expressed this way: Writing abilities develop when writing tasks are sufficiently challenging to call out knowledge telling and sufficiently manageable to call out knowledge transforming.

In their studies of the cognition of writing, Bereiter and Scardamalia (1987) discovered that writers are involved in two distinct kinds of thinking when they write. One type of thinking is relatively more characteristic of novice writers, who, faced with the difficulties inherent in producing discourse without a conversational partner, turn to a simplifying strategy. The other type of thinking is characteristic of expert writers and consists not of refining or mastering the simple strategy but, rather, of subordinating the simple strategy to a more complex one. The role of instruction is not only to support what students can already do with the simplifying strategy, such as produce narratives of personal experience, but also to lead them into subordinating the simplifying strategy to the more complex one, as in the case of including short personal narratives as examples within a longer expository piece. The simplifying strategy consists of expressing what is on one's mind, and therefore Bereiter and Scardamalia call it "knowledge telling." They describe its workings as both making maximal use of, and being limited by, natural language competence and ordinary social experience. The more complex strategy reprocesses and reshapes what is on one's mind instead of only expressing it, and therefore Bereiter and Scardamalia call it "knowledge transforming." It is a way of independently interacting with one's knowledge, thus doing alone what is usually done socially, that is, with the aid of conversational partners.

In describing knowledge telling, Bereiter and Scardamalia (1987) emphasize its ease and efficiency:

> Knowledge telling provides a natural and efficient solution to the problems immature writers face in generating text content without external support. The solution is efficient enough that, given any reasonable specification of topic and genre, the writer can get started in a matter of seconds and speedily produce an essay that will be on topic and that will conform to the type of text called for. The solution is natural because it makes use of readily available knowledge—thus it is favorable

to report of personal experience—and it relies on already existing discourse-production skills in making use of external cues and cues generated from language production itself. It preserves the straight-ahead form of oral language production and requires no significantly greater amount of planning or goal-setting than does ordinary conversation. (pp. 9–10)

Two writing samples discussed in Chapter 2, Jason's response to the Langston Hughes task and the teacher-authored version of the same task, can now be described as writing produced respectively through the mediation of knowledge-telling and knowledge-transforming processes. Figure 5.1 reproduced these samples.

Knowledge Telling

I have just read a story about a boy who ran into a women knocking her down and braking her purse. The boy fell down from hitting her purse. The women turned around and picked him up buy his shirt. The boy said he didn't mean to hit the women and knock her purse to the ground. "But I think the boy was lieing to the women." The boy had a dirty face and the women said to the boy if I let you go will you run away, and the boy said yes. So the women said I should bring you home and wash your face and give dinner. "I think the women thinks that the boy lives on the street and I agree with the women." The women says that the boy should come live with her.

"I think the rest of the story the boy will live with this women and stay with her for the rest of his life."

Knowledge Transforming

A boy tries to snatch a woman's purse, but fails miserably. He is overcome by the weight of the purse, he falls, and the woman captures him. The boy apologizes, wanting to get away. But the woman wouldn't let him leave her side.

In the rest of the story Mrs. Jones will take him home, wash his face, and feed him. She will try to find out if he has a home. If he doesn't, she'll probably try to care for him or will make sure he's cared for by someone else.

FIGURE 5.1. Writing samples theoretically illustrating two distinct processes.

Jason's response is a double narrative. He tells part of the Langston Hughes story, but he also tells the story of his experience reading the story: "I have just read a story about a boy who ran into a women knocking her down and braking her purse." Jason also tells what he knows of the Hughes story, closely repeating or copying many of the events in the story. He doesn't discriminate between major and minor events or state the gist of the story (as he did, you will recall, in his spoken report of his reading) but instead tells what an observer would have seen. On the other hand, the second response, which was written by an English teacher, transforms her knowledge of events in the Hughes story by summarizing them in her gist-stating opening sentence: "A boy tries to snatch a woman's purse, but fails miserably."

Bereiter and Scardamalia (1987) refer to knowledge telling as a strategy, and it does function as one, but our studies suggest it consists of a collection of strategies. Telling what is known on a topic is certainly one of these strategies, but that one is achieved by three others which seem to be especially characteristic of struggling writers in our research: providing narrative or plot summary where exposition is called for, copying other texts, and visualizing certain aspects of content and form. These four occur so frequently in our observations of struggling writers as to seem to be characteristic of struggling writers in general. My teaching experience and my own experience as a writer, however, make me suspect that a more accurate interpretation of the data may be that narrating, copying, and visualizing are "default" strategies, that is, strategies any of us may turn to more or less automatically when faced with challenging writing tasks. In professional development workshops I sometimes illustrate this notion of default writing strategies by asking teachers to discuss in small groups how they would respond to a seemingly insuperable task, such as writing an insurance policy or a home mortgage contract. When I subsequently invite them to share the processes they identified as ones they would use to attempt to solve the difficult writing problem, teachers invariably describe various combinations of narrating, copying, and visualizing as they tell how they would work toward completion of the task. They report, for example, that they would begin writing an insurance policy by getting one to use as a model.

I am using the label "default strategies" to refer to a group of frequently occurring, developmentally recursive strategies writers may resort to when a writing task becomes sufficiently challenging. I prefer this recursive perspective on writing development to the more popular view in which writers are seen as moving through a series of discrete stages, with earlier stages of writing development giving way to later ones. Ochs (1979) offers a view of language development consistent with the idea that certain strategies are developmentally recursive:

> Becoming more competent in one's language involves increasing one's knowledge of the potential range of structures (e.g. morphosyntactic, discourse) available for use and increasing one's ability to use them. In this view, communicative strategies characteristic of any one stage are not replaced. Rather, they are retained, to be relied upon under certain communicative conditions. (p. 52)

Ochs suggests a key principle for understanding the default strategies struggling writers often use: *Language strategies are not replaced as development proceeds.* We certainly add to our linguistic resources as we go through life, but this does not mean we give up existing strategies as we acquire or learn new ones. Rather, I believe strongly that we retain communicative strategies and go back to them when contexts and topics and other conditions require or when it suits our communicative purposes to do so. The important implication here is that teachers don't have to discourage the use of "old" strategies in order to make room for "new" ones. Indeed, we have found in our research classrooms that the new strategies struggling writers learn most readily are ones that connect meaningfully with their default strategies. Using a web, or a cluster, of lines and circles as a strategy for planning or organizing ideas, for example, works best when it builds on a preexisting strategy for visualizing text components, not only because webs and clusters use visual imagery but also because it is always helpful to approach new learning through familiar pathways. Similarly, instead of simply admonishing students who copy material from sources directly into their own writing, lecturing them about plagiarism and telling them not to copy, teachers might look for opportunities to build on the struggling writer's tendency to copy, to turn it into a deliberate strategy rather than a default one. Such instruction, as I show in the next chapter, helps students take purposeful metacognitive control over default strategies. Indeed, instruction in writing strategies that models a strategy to facilitate its acquisition can be said to be a kind of teaching through "copying" in the sense of duplicating aspects of another person's writing processes and behaviors. In both clustering and modeling, then, strategic writing instruction provides access to "new" strategies by helping students try them on and customize them through the "old," default strategies students are already using to make sense of text. In this chapter I take a closer look at writing development as involving the use of default strategies, and in the next chapter I suggest illustrative ways teachers can use default strategies to promote such development.

Knowledge Telling

As discussed earlier, Bereiter and Scardamalia (1987) call their model of cognitive processes involved in the writing of novice writers "knowledge telling," which they define as a strategy inexperienced writers use to convert writing tasks into problems of telling what they know about a subject. Bereiter and Scardamalia describe writers using the knowledge-telling strategy as producing information on a topic in a form suggested by the writing task, so that the response has both topic appropriateness and genre appropriateness. But the writing falls short of putting together an original response to the task or achieving another intended goal such as explaining an idea or specifying information in one's own words. Instead, the writing may tell what the writer knows by copying text or repeating key words from the assignment or from a text being written about. In addition to Jason's "Hughes" response, we saw other instances of knowledge telling in previous chapters, as in Jeannine's students copying from class discussion and Samuel's test takers replicating their practice essays.

A writer's struggle, in this analysis, does not result from knowledge telling or from the use of default strategies. Writing instead is more or less difficult depending on a complex interaction among writer, task, and sociocultural contexts. A challenging writing task is one that affects the accessibility of plans—mental structures or networks of related concepts and images—that provide the frames for producing text for particular purposes and audiences. The relative inaccessibility of plans, however, doesn't mean the problem is "caused by" default strategies which must be "cured" or "eliminated." Rather, it is more likely the case that the act of writing about a challenging topic within a certain context calls out a tendency to use default strategies to produce writing under difficult conditions because the default strategies are familiar and reliable. Again I am reminded that Jason could talk about the gist of the story but was distracted from stating the gist by the act of writing monologically about the story; when the level of difficulty went up with the switch from talking to writing, he resorted to a tendency to copy material from the original text. Thus, the struggling writer's "problem" is better understood in terms of the interaction between the writer and the task and between the writer and the contextual support (or lack of it) the writer receives. The difficulty the writer encounters with content and contexts makes the struggle seem to be the result of some tendency (or deficiency) within the writer because the writer is attempting to "go it alone," but it is the very process of going it alone that calls out default strategies while grappling with tough pieces of writing. It is as if the challenge inherent in writing about certain contents in certain contexts limits planning to what the writer thinks of at the point of production. Little or no attention is paid to using more appropriate strategies to plan globally or to deliberately frame an argument for an audience because the very act of writing takes so much attention.

Schema theory in reading research suggests one way of understanding the accessibility of plans for writing. Schema theory tells us that we use two types of schemas to select and organize information from texts: text-structure schemas and content schemas (van Dijk & Kintsch, 1983; Ohlhausen & Roller, 1988). Writing about reading is doubly schema-dependent, once to make sense of the reading and again to produce the writing. Writing that discovers and shapes knowledge does so through the mediation of content and text-structure schemas when the writer reads and again when the writer writes. When writing about reading has the character of knowledge telling—telling, narrating, copying, imitating, or summarizing either the content or structure of the reading—then it might be the case that students don't have access to appropriate content and text-structure schemas *on their own* to guide their reading and writing. They resort to knowledge telling to construct an understanding of the writer's text.

In Chapter 2, I said that it is difficult for experienced writers to read the words "business letter" without forming a mental image of one. This is an example of a text-structure schema at work. When I sit down to write a business letter, I can readily summon up a "snapshot" of the structure of the components of the letter: the heading, inside address, salutation, body, closing, and signature. My brain provides the structure not by giving me those names (which I just had to look up in a grammar handbook) but by giving me a mental image of an arrangement of spaces to be filled in with information appropriate to each of the components. This mental picture is a conceptualization of the framework of the letter, an imagined template to guide the construction of the letter if I feel I need such guidance. Similarly, my brain contains other mental representations of text structures for writing articles, chapters, research reports, grant proposals, conference papers, course syllabi, and so on. Such is the mind of a person who writes for a living. For less experienced writers, or even for experienced ones faced with insuperable tasks, such as the English teachers from whom I requested an insurance policy, coming up with a real model and "copying" it takes the place of using a mental image to guide the writing. This is what makes copying a default strategy.

Default Strategies in Composing-Aloud Protocols

Our work with struggling writers in middle and high schools suggests that they have mental representations of text that influence their writing, but their mental representations tend to be generalized across a few basic genres—such as a story, an answer to a test question, an answer to a question at the end of a reading selection—which are undifferentiated by specific structures for writing or by academic subjects, except when an assignment requires differentiation, as in the case of a research paper. The struggling writers in our studies seem often to imagine academic writing in a "minimally acceptable" version of the genre, as "collections" of words and sentences filling a required amount of space on paper, but not as coherent paragraphs or whole texts and certainly not more space than is required. Imagining "collections" of words and sentences probably gives an appearance of laziness or carelessness to their writing, as we saw in the case of Brandon. Perhaps the most frequent representation of text reported in our data is an image of a certain amount of space that must be filled, usually the number of handwritten pages, or partial pages, the teacher assigned. (This may have something to do with why giving an assignment to a classroom full of student writers invariably calls out from at least one of them a question about "how long it has to be.") The default setting on number of pages for the writers in our research, furthermore, seems most often to be *one*. Here are two examples, the first from a 5th-grade writer and the other from a 12-grader, in which the writers seem to be "organizing" their writing by using default strategies of narrating a story and "filling up the required space."

Language arts teacher Sharon Smith and I gave the fifth-grader, Allison, the task of creating a story which ended with the sentence, "When they finally arrived home our young heroes were fast asleep in the back seat," and we asked her to speak her thoughts aloud while writing.[1] Allison worked toward a solution to the writing problem without much hesitation. Using talk to draw from a combination of personal experience and imagination, she produced a 154-word text and 738 spoken words in about 17 minutes.

Allison wrote her story one or two sentences at a time, and she planned each one- or two-sentence segment by first talking it through. Each written sentence is a shortened version of a spoken passage. One of the more extreme examples follows.

---

[1]The composing aloud was done after school, and Allison wrote as she composed aloud by talking with her teacher and me. The session was videotaped, transcribed, coded, and analyzed for evidence of cognitive processing, especially planning and organizing processes.

Allison said:

"It always sort of bored him whenever we got home. He used to lie about why it bored him. He used to say stuff like, 'It makes me sad because my friend, he was moving and his house caught on fire and he was out at his other house, his new house, and his little puppy was at his old house. The house caught on fire and he blew up with the house because he went back in to get his little puppy.' So, I'll write, 'he lies about it a lot about why he is sad when we get back.' "

Then Allison wrote:

"He lies about why he's sad when we get back."

Allison thus writes by thinking of one or two sentences at a time, and the process of talking first and then writing an abbreviated version of the same ideas perhaps contributed to the sense of disconnectedness we find in her first draft:

My Stepbrother

```
He always when we looked at houses. He lies
about why he's sad when we get back. Then we
go look at another house. My father discusses
carpentry.  My  stepbrother  falls  asleep  and
dreams  about  the  day.  He's  driving  to  his
favorite ice cream store. After he get's ice
cream. He thinks my father and his mother are
kidnapped. So he went out to a house that we
had  seen  previously  thinking  they  might  be
there. Of course they weren't! He got worried
and started to wake up, but he started telling
himself that didn't happen. He keeps on driving
and  looking.  He  went  back  to  the  ice  cream
looking for them. He searched all around for
the two, but they were nowhere to be found. He
gets  in  and  drives  home  ready  to  call  the
police. When they finally arrived home our young
heroes  were  fast  asleep  in  the  back  seat.
```

Her imagined narrative supplied Allison with the details of plot: Her increasingly anxious stepbrother makes two trips to the ice cream store, sandwiched around a return trip to a house they had visited. The imagined narrative also allowed Allison to have her stepbrother drive the car and to have the parents sleep and "get lost" in the back seat; these solve important subproblems in the writing task because the target sentence demands that someone drive a car home while others sleep in the back seat.

Throughout her writing Allison didn't do much general planning, though the videotape suggests that toward the end of the story she was carefully rationing her handwritten words so that her draft would fill exactly one page, which it does. The transcript of her composing aloud suggests, further, that she preferred to plan ideas for one sentence at a time rather than for the whole text. She is using a knowledge-telling strategy and moving through the writing one episode at a time first by talking then by writing. Perhaps chronological structure and other formal properties of the narrative genre helped her "solve" the writing problem of getting simultaneously to the last sentence and the bottom of the page without lengthy planning for subproblems of character, setting, plot, paragraphs, and coherence.

While studying the composing-aloud transcript, we noticed a similarity between Allison's planning and reviewing behaviors. Both operate primarily at the sentence and word levels and less at the level of considering paragraphs or the whole text. This emphasis on planning and reviewing at the sentence and word level is characteristic of novice writers, young writers like Allison and inexperienced writers in high school and college. Experienced writers do more planning and reviewing at the paragraph and text level, and considerations of purpose, audience, categories of information, relations between ideas, and overall structure influence the planning and reviewing they do. Still, we must not conclude that Allison is a weak writer just because she is not yet an expert. She is actually quite skilled. She is certainly a quick and fluent writer, at least for narrative tasks. She readily draws on experience and imagination to come up with ideas, and she has no trouble at all expressing her ideas in words. She is comfortable with narrative form and has a good sense of what makes a story interesting. We learned from a postprotocol interview that she is also aware that writing is not a one-shot deal. Allison regularly shares her writing with her parents and edits it accordingly, suggesting that she has some understanding of writing as process. Taken together, the transcript and interview suggest that Allison is ready for new challenges. We might, for example, ask her to reconsider her solution to the problem by requiring her to have children, not parents, fall asleep in the back seat, so that she would have to think about changing her writing globally, at the level of the whole text. Or, we might ask Allison to do some nonnarrative writing. For example, we could ask for a description of a person, because the transcript shows she's able to describe her stepbrother with considerable sensitivity.

In Allison's protocol, the use of a narrative text-structure strategy is entirely appropriate because we assigned a narrative task. What really suggests that narration is a default strategy for Allison is her lack of planning in using the strategy. She tells the story as if the abbreviated written version will automatically represent the specificity and coherence apparent to a greater degree in the spoken version.

In the case of our 12th-grade protocol, which was part of a full case study of a struggling writer compiled by teacher-researcher Lenise Deakin, we see that selecting a narrative text structure is a less appropriate option than it was in Allison's case. This time the narrative default strategy just doesn't get the job done because Lenise had given the 12th-grader, David, a task in which he had to write a persuasive, monological piece to convince a truant student of the importance of attending school regularly. Narration by itself is not the best choice for achieving a persuasive purpose, as David seems to suspect when he asks a couple of questions near the beginning of his composing-aloud protocol:

DAVID: Do I have to give the person a name?

LENISE: You can give the person a name. Sure.

DAVID: Well, I don't know if, I'm thinking like, I don't know if it's like, what kind of a situation, if it's a story telling thing; should I tell a story?
(*Brief pause*)
Like, "I was walking to school one day and I seen this person I know . . . standin' in the corner like smokin' or somethin.' "
(*Brief pause*)
I don't know if it's a story or, it doesn't say anything. (*Reads*

from the assignment) "You are concerned about the student and want to explain the importance of attending school regularly." Should I do it like a story?

Because Lenise was collecting a research protocol, and because it is possible, though difficult, to persuade by narrating, she didn't answer David's question and instead advised him to do what he would do on the state writing test for which he was preparing. The first draft of his essay shows that he selected the narrative strategy:

> The first day of school, I drove into the student parking lot and parked my car. When I got out I glanced over at Primrose Lane, their was John Tree. I figured he was just standing there with a couple of his friends. I knew he was in my first period class because I talked to him on the phone the night before. When I arrived to my first period class he was not there. When it was time for lunch, which is 5th period, I saw John sitting over with a different group of friends, insted of sitting with me. John did this continuously for weeks. Then one day I decided to talk to him about what he has been doing. I said "John why haven't you been in class lately." He replied by saying "cause I don't need to go." This statement shocked me. I said "why is it you don't need school." He said because it is boring and always a drag." I couldn't beleave this was coming out of his mouth. I explained to him the importance of attending school regularly.
>
> I began by saying that you can't get a decent job without a high school Diploma at least, and that if you are successful in high school that will get you into a good college and maybe for free. He finally promised me he would go to class, And I said I would help him.
>
> That was back in 1972, John Tree is now a famous man, who changed his name to billy Pepsi, and ownes a huge corperation.

Lenise reported that David seemed to be confused by the assignment, as evidenced by the fact that he kept reading the directions over and over, both before he wrote and while he was writing. She attributed his confusion to the possibility that the task was, for him, an unusual one, owing to the audience being an imaginary schoolmate and the format a monologue. Lenise added that David apparently felt the need to turn a vague "situation" (his word) into a larger context or framework for the writing, and this framework then became the focal point of the composition. The framework, of course is the story David tells in his first and third paragraphs. The assignment stipulated "a composition of about 200 words" (the state requirement on the test David was preparing for), and he produced 264 words, 209 of which provide the narrative frame for his story. Even his middle paragraph, the one that gives reasons for staying in school, has a narrative structure because it reports what David said rather than saying it directly to his friend. That, and David's question in the protocol—"Should I do it like a story?"—suggest that he is relying on narrative as a default strategy (and his teacher as a default audience) for writing the piece.

It may be that figuring out what to say in a text by telling a story, and even copying parts of it (as David does with "I explained to him the importance of attending school regularly," which was part of the wording of the assignment), is a sufficiently weighty cognitive burden for some students to block or detract from the additional goal of achieving a written representation of a more appropriate response to the task. A linear process of writing to associate ideas with an assigned topic is characteristic of knowledge tellers (Bereiter & Scardamalia, 1987) and can be understood as telling themselves what a writing task requires. This means that writing by knowledge telling consists of planning on paper, in the midst of composing and exploring initial associative thoughts by telling the story of the encounter with a challenging subject. "Knowledge-transforming writing," Bereiter and Scardamalia's (1987) label for writing that epistemically constructs knowledge, doesn't directly tell knowledge associated with a task because the writer transforms the reading first. Experienced writers writing about familiar subjects have sufficient access to the requisite content and discourse plans needed to write epistemically about a passage being read. They produce writing more by forming knowledge than by telling it.

Still, the notions of content and structure plans give us a way of characterizing writing difficulties without hinting at any negative connotations. Labels such as "egocentric writing," "basic writing," and "writer-based prose," all of which are used to describe the writing of struggling writers, are not entirely free of negative associations because they suggest something unusual, childlike, incorrect, or otherwise inappropriate or abnormal is happening when writers have trouble shaping meaning. Admitting that difficulty arises as a result of the relative inaccessibility of appropriate content and text-structure plans within a complex writer–task–context framework helps to erase the deficit labels usually applied to struggling writers.

Even Good Writers Use Default Strategies

Even experienced and fluent writers, when faced with writing about challenging new ideas, can produce writing without the mediation of text-transforming plans. When that happens, early drafts of the writing will most likely have a lot in common with writing produced by struggling writers. This happens, I believe, because writing development is recursive. Even skilled, published writers can find themselves using default strategies when conditions warrant.

I illustrate that idea with an example from my own writing experience. The example records a struggle I had composing an invited chapter for a book on literacy development. Like much of the writing of writers who struggle in secondary schools, my chapter called for writing about reading. Writing about reading presents writers with three major problems: generating content for writing by determining what the author(s) of another text(s) is saying, organizing ideas for writing by recasting the ideas from other texts into a planning framework appropriate to responding to the assignment, and making sure the writing is structurally and mechanically well formed.

The first step of a writer's task in writing about reading consists of following the author's words to apprehend the meaning of the text and restructuring the author's remarks in accordance with the writer's own schema. If the writer has access to cognitive schema intersubjectively shared by members of a social group, such as the teacher and students in a classroom, the content and form necessary for writing are relatively more available and the writing is relatively less challenging. If shared cognitive models are not readily available, the writer may resort to copying or paraphrasing the author's words, thus allowing knowledge telling to supply a model of form and content.

Writing is more or less difficult, in other words, depending on the accessibility of appropriate plans, frames, and images for producing text. Here again, in place of a two-component system for analyzing the writing process—a writer and a writing task—I am advocating a three-component system: a writer, a task, and the sociocognitive activity of sharing the writing. This three-component system has the advantage of getting the teacher or collaborator in on the process as an integral participant rather than as an outsider or intervenor. Using my own experience to illustrate the meaning of this three-component system gives me access to information usually hidden in the analysis of cognition through protocol analysis or other methods.

In my example, the role of collaborator is filled by an editor, rather than a teacher, because the writing under discussion was part of an early draft of a chapter I wrote on the development of writing abilities during the school years. The chapter was subsequently published (Collins, 1984) and even reprinted (Collins, 1993), but as the following excerpt from the first draft suggests, the writing did not come easily. The excerpt, necessarily rather lengthy, discusses *Language Development: Kindergarten through Grade Twelve* (Loban, 1976), a book reporting a longitudinal study of writing development. Here is the excerpt:

Loban collected data on 211 urban students throughout their 13	1
years of schooling. These data consisted primarily of typed	2
transcripts of oral interviews and compositions written in	3
connection with school work; a variety of test, questionnaire and	4
teacher-supplied data was also included. The investigation	5
concentrated on three groups of subjects (each N = 35), which were	6
established to represent high, low, and random ability levels,	7
according to averages of teacher ratings for the 13 years. Other	8
variables in the study were socioeconomic status (*Minnesota Scale*	9
for Paternal Occupations), race, sex, and IQ scores	10
(Kuhlman-Anderson). Loban found a consistently powerful	11
relationship between ability and socioeconomic status throughout	12

the developmental span he studied, and that finding looms large in   13
his conclusions.   15
    Specific measures were derived from these methods of   14
analysis: Segmentation of language samples into communication   16
units (similar to the T-unit frequently used in writing research but   17
including the abrupt utterances possible in oral language; an   18
independent clause with its modifiers); Mazes (unattached   19
fragments, tangles, repetitions, false starts which interrupt the   20
flow of communication units); Elaboration of language by   21
expanding subject or predicate portions of communication units;   22
Verb density and diversity.   23
    Loban reports his findings by describing achieved levels of   24
proficiency in oral and written language for the high, low, and   25
random groups. The following is a summary of the findings   26
relevant to writing development.   27
    In average number of words per communication unit, there was   28
no smooth pattern of increase with grade; upward trends are usually   29
followed by plateaus and downward shifts in all groups. Loban reports   30
that his high group had scores similar to those presented in Hunt   31
(1965) O'Donnell, Griffin, and Norris (1967) and that the   32
high group duplicated the superiority in written language over the   33
low group that had been shown in oral language, with the random   34
group falling consistently in the middle at each grade. Oral   35
average number of words per communication unit is slightly   36
higher than the written average in grades one through seven; these   37
tend toward balance in grades seven through nine, and in grades   38
ten through twelve the written average becomes higher.   39
    In average number of dependent clauses per communication   40
unit in written language, the high group is superior to the low and   41
random groups through grade eight. This pattern reverses in   42
grades nine through eleven. Loban attributes this reversal to the   43
high group's increased use of alternative methods of subordinating   44
thought, such as appositives, gerunds, participles, and   45
infinitives. This argument is supported by the data he presents on   46
proportion and development of clause types, on elaboration of   47
written language, and the special transformational analysis of the   48
language of six subjects in the study.   49
    Loban made a special study of verb density per words in   50
communication units and of nonfinite verbs per total verbs. He   51
found that verb density did not distinguish among the groups, and   52
that nonfinite verbs did in written language. Here the high group   53
showed a superiority to the low group and the data moved in   54
opposite directions. The high group used more nonfinite verbs in   55
written than in oral language; the reverse is true of the low   56
group.   57

I want to begin my discussion of this passage by admitting that it was typical of the whole manuscript. The early draft of my chapter closely resembled the notes I took on my reading. The passage was excessively wordy and insufficiently communicative, and it flips back and forth between present and past tenses and between active and passive voices. These difficulties and other, more important ones I come to shortly probably reflect the fact that at the time of the writing I was grappling more with understanding Loban and the other authors I read for the chapter than with restructuring their ideas for communication to my audience. This is knowledge telling instead of knowledge transforming. A first step in writing about reading can be to describe the experience of the reading, and that's what I was doing. The initial draft of my writing was less a synthesis of newly acquired ideas than a record of the process of idea acquisition.

In my passage the main evidence that ideas were still under construction was that the draft provides a summary of Loban's major points. I condensed Loban's ideas and recast them in my words, but I didn't relate the ideas to other content or to a conceptual framework. The narrative form of the passage was another result of idea formation in progress. I subordinated an arrangement or schemas for organizing research reports—problem, method, measures, findings, conclusions—to a chronological arrangement, one listing Loban's ideas in the order in which he presented them, but also one telling the story of the research as if I had observed it. Of course, I hadn't; the narrative here instead reflected my experience encountering Loban's research for the first time, as well as the experience of writing about my reading. This is both narrating and knowledge telling, because I was reconstructing the story of Loban's research and telling what I knew about his ideas. The chronological arrangement of narrative is especially visible at the beginning of several paragraphs:

Loban collected data (line 1)
Loban reports his findings (line 24)
Loban made a special study (line 50)

Because I used narrative form to begin three of the six paragraphs, I was also using it to connect important ideas in my thinking about my reading of Loban. I also used the narrative form in two other places, lines 11 and 42, and there, too, the form marked what for me were main ideas in Loban's book. Indeed, the sentence in lines 11–14—"Loban found a consistently powerful relationship between ability and socioeconomic status throughout the developmental span he studied, and that finding looms large in his conclusions"—was a tentative formulation of the most important of Loban's ideas discussed in the whole passage, as I show in a moment.

My editor's response to the draft of my chapter asked in two places for clarification of meaning; in one, "that had been shown in oral language" (line 34), I was guilty of elliptical reasoning, and in the other, "tend toward balance" (line 38), I was using an inappropriate image. The editor also pointed out several more minor slips on my part and this major one: He wrote, "Is this surprising? So what?" in reference to my sentence about a powerful relation between socioeconomic status and language abilities (lines 11–14 again). Now, in Loban's last chapter he makes it clear that he attaches considerable importance to the connection between socioeconomic status and language, and what my editor's response told me was that I had failed to communicate the value of this connection in my chapter. Prompted by this oversight, and by my editor's pointing it out to me, I revised the Loban passage in the published version of the chapter to say this:

> We have suspected for some time that writing development is connected to societal contexts: socioeconomic status affects language development (Loban, 1976) and language performance (Bernstein, 1975; Hawkins, 1977); adult basic writers hold membership in residually oral subcultures (Farrell, 1977); writing ability is unevenly distributed along class lines (Hendrix, 1981).

The Loban passage in the published version of the chapter thus became part of a single sentence, and in doing so it shrunk from 515 words to 5, a 97% reduction. For me, though, and for others who have read Loban, the reduced version still carried the full import of the initial draft; the 97% reduction in words has abbreviated my meaning but not deleted it. In fact, the reduced version can be said to carry more meaning than the original. The reduced version emphatically states Loban's conclusion about a causal connection between socioeconomic status and language development, whereas the original only alluded indirectly to that conclusion.

During the process of writing the chapter, my reading of Loban developed from summarizing the "plot" or gist of his book to achieving a thematic statement, one that stated his main conclusion and established a connection between his conclusion and those of other researchers. The change from narrative, knowledge-telling-based "plot summary" to thematic statement is indicative of the sociocognitive dimension of writing, as is revealed through a closer look at the process of revising the chapter as recorded in initial and published drafts, my notes, my editor's instructions and his response recorded on the first draft, and the letter from my editor including his reaction and comments on the chapter from another reviewer.

My stated purpose in the first draft was "to review research studies concerned with the development of writing abilities during the school years," and reviewing studies, in the sense of summarizing them, is exactly what the draft does, as the Loban excerpt illustrates. My stated purpose in the published draft is quite a bit more ambitious than the earlier one was:

> My purpose here is to modify a rather conventional approach to understanding the development of writing abilities. This approach describes writing development in terms of a linear or hierarchical model, as a continuum consisting of identifiable, sequentially ordered stages. I argue that this conception is problematic on two related counts: it appropriately describes only one dimension of writing development, and it neglects societal and instructional influences on writing abilities. It emphasizes cognitive processes and tends to exclude social ones. In place of this conventional approach, I argue for one that includes a functional perspective on writing development during the school years. (Collins, 1984, p. 201)

During the revision process my purpose changed from reviewing studies to determining what they collectively mean. I moved beyond narrating a review of studies and telling knowledge to looking for patterns of relatedness across studies, categorizing them, and presenting a thesis statement.

The thesis statement eventually became this: Writing development varies with the functions of writing because writing development is social as well as cognitive. The record shows that 13 months passed between initial assignment of the chapter and mailing of the final draft, and it also shows that in the 10th month a letter from my editor provided the idea for the final classification of studies in the chapter. This classification helped me establish the form of my revised chapter and discover my thesis, which events happened in exactly that order.

In the revision the chapter remained 20 double-spaced pages long, but the content became fuller; the list of references, for example, grew from 43 items in the first draft to 72 items in the published draft. The organization changed from a simple division into longitudinal and cross-sectional studies in the first draft to a categorization of studies by their degree of contextualization, from psychological through institutional to social and cultural, in the published version.

The most important change, though, was at the level of a deep-structure image. Throughout the writing of the first draft I held in mind an image of the relation between writing development and schooling as two intersecting lines. One line represented cognitive development, conceived of as a process of organic growth programmed into the human brain; development as represented by this line is wholly a psychological construct and consists of the working out of a genetic pattern of growth. The other line represented writing and schooling and other social influences on development. The problem arising from this "double linear" image of development is deciding how or where the lines intersect, for intersect they must if writing and schooling are to be related. I solved the problem, temporarily at least, in the first draft by referring to Kroll's (1980) distinction between two types of learning: maturationism and interventionism. Maturationism is an individual's learning by fulfilling an innate capacity for growth, and interventionism is learning through the transmittal of skills and knowledge from teacher to student. I saw in Kroll's labels a correspondence with the lines in my image, and, like Kroll, I saw a third position, the interactionist perspective, as indicative of the way writing development and schooling come together. They interact with each other.

What could be simpler than that? No matter how or where they interact. We need only know, I told myself, that they do, indeed, interact.

And so I wrote and mailed the first draft, but still the troublesome image persisted. I simply couldn't decide how to reconcile the fact that writing abilities develop along a cognitive dimension with the fact that learning to write is at every turn a social process. Writing development doesn't take place in a noninterfering environment: how to bring together development and environmental influence? Finally, an alternative image came, contained in the letter from my editor accompanying the return of my manuscript. The letter suggested a new schema, a reorganization of the chapter according to widening contexts of influence on writing development: studies divorced from context, studies in a rhetorical context, studies in an institutional context, studies in a social or cultural context. The letter also reported several comments from an outside reviewer urging me to think of writing as a hybrid between development in the sense of genetic maturity and learning in the sense of instruction and socialization. Thus, my new image of writing development and schooling was conceived socially, through long-distance "dialogue" between the reviewer and me. The word "hybrid," and its mental representation as a single kernel of corn, supplanted the image of intersecting lines. I solved the problem of how the lines intersect, how the social influences the cognitive, by abandoning the linear image and by determining that in the case of writing, cognitive and social aspects are always present and always unified because writing is a hybrid, the product of cross-breeding cognitive processes with a social code and cultural knowledge. Once I formulated this theory, the fact that I, a writer, learned it by means of a letter from an editor seemed to confirm the theory on the spot. In the second paragraph of the published version of my chapter, I put the matter this way:

> Writing development is a hybrid; it combines development in
> the sense of genetic maturity with development in the sense
> of learning from instruction and socialization.[2] In the first

---

[2] The reader may recognize this sentence from its "copied" version in Chapter 2.

sense, writing development resembles the learning of oral language or of a second language; the pattern of development shows emphasis on phonology and lexicon at early stages and on syntax and discourse at later ones (Shuy, 1981). In the second sense, writing development is less concerned with form and more with function. Here writers learn to write (or not to write) for socially and educationally determined purposes; the pattern of development becomes dominated particularly by school-sponsored functions of writing. As Bereiter puts the matter, "writing development, in a highly schooled society, is whatever the schools make it to be" (1980, p. 88). (Collins, 1994, p. 201)

So, writing development, as represented by my new image of a kernel of corn, combined the cognitive and the social. In contradistinction to the traditional view of the writer working alone, the sociocognitive view is based on an interaction between cognition and social contexts. This second model supports the argument that struggling writers, and *every* writer faced with seemingly insuperable difficulties while writing, can benefit from interaction with a person having the cultural capital to help complete the task. In this manner, writers transform default writing strategies into new ones at the same time they use writing to transform their knowledge.

The traditional image of the writer at work is that of a solitary figure, trusting herself and her own ideas, looking inward through a computer screen or writing tablet to discover new meanings. Writing instruction often takes this view of writing as a solitary act of discovery, even in process- and conference-based approaches, which often are seen as facilitating the writer's "natural" development, as I argued in Chapter 1. Writing is often described as *making meaning for oneself,* and teaching as *intervening in writers' work* while preserving the *writer's ownership of ideas* in the writing. Each of the italicized phrases reflects an individualistic image of the writer, the solitary scribe who somehow manages to work alone, ironically, even when under the influence of instruction.

Contrary to this image of the solitary writer, our studies indicate that development is recursive and social. To put the matter simply: Struggle is individual; development is social. What leads writing development beyond the default options we've been considering in this chapter is interaction with others, both other writers and other texts, which transforms the default options into new writing strategies as writing is used to transform knowledge. The metaphor of the zone of proximal development (Vygotsky, 1978; Cole, 1985) is an apt description of the difference between independent problem solving and a higher level of "problem solving under adult guidance or in collaboration with more capable peers" (Vygotsky, 1978, p. 78). This concept of shared or joint activity with more expert partners is central to a sociocognitive theory of writing development. From the perspective of a cultural view of cognition, the sharing of ideas, frames, schemas, images and words is the real impetus behind writing development. Successful academic writing is writing attuned to the culture of school, and a writer's ability to achieve such writing varies with communicative interaction and participation in the culture.

They're Not So Different

Struggling writers have the same difficulties as the rest of us when we're faced with challenging writing tasks; the only major differences are that they encounter difficulties more often and have fewer options for overcoming them. When the going gets tough, the first step in writing about reading for novices and experts alike may be to describe the experience of the reading. The initial draft of the writing in that case is less a synthesis of newly acquired ideas than a record of the process of idea acquisition. The original author's ideas may be repeated, even copied, in the writing without being shaped or related or otherwise transformed epistemically by the act of writing. The real differences between struggling writers and us is not simply in the use of a knowledge-telling strategy rather than a knowledge-transforming one. We all do that when we resort to default strategies to make sense of challenging new ideas. Struggling writers, however, have the additional difficulty of not knowing where to go from there. Formulating the content and structure of the writing according to default patterns such as narrating, copying, and visualizing stops short of two crucial next steps: (1) reformulating content and structure to construct one's own understanding and (2) managing the demands of producing written language appropriate to the subject and audience. Little attention is left for matters of revision, style, and correctness when default patterns of arriving at content and form take up so much of the writer's attention. These patterns give us the main characteristics of the writing of struggling writers, characteristics we noticed as early as the "pep rallies" essay in Chapter 1: a chronological arrangement of content where a logical arrangement is called for, associative details copied from memory or observation, sound-based misspellings, and so on.

I don't believe something unusual, childlike, incorrect, or otherwise inappropriate is happening when writers resort to personal levels of meaning, to experience and imagination and records of initial encounters with texts, to make sense of their subjects. Nor is it unusual to overquote or copy from references; this is what happens when writers don't have schemas to make sense of their reading. Resorting to expressive, narrative, and associative elements in writing is normal in challenging situations. This is when personally meaningful frames and images, or even the raw data of experience including the experience of reading, show up in the writing without being shaped by the writer for explicit communication to a reader.

If even strong writers can get stuck and resort to expressive, chronological, presentational structures in writing, we should stop expecting struggling writers not to have such difficulties. They need default writing strategies just as we all do. When faced with writing about challenging new ideas, the mind takes its approach through familiar ideas, those leaning on experience and perception and personal insights into the subject. If we know exactly what we're writing about, if we have readily available content schemas, we have less trouble generating appropriate elements of content for the writing. And if we are familiar with the typical arrangement of ideas in the type of writing we're doing, if we have access to structure schemas, we have less trouble relating ideas. If we don't know much about the subject of the writing, or don't have ready access to an appropriate pattern for relating ideas, however, we must search experience or imagination to build schemata from the ground up. Helping with this search is where default strategies come into play.

I once asked 17 advanced English majors in a methods

course—seniors and graduate students getting ready to teach—to read Sylvia Plath's "Blackberrying" in preparation for writing about the poem. I also had them take careful notes on their processes of reading the poem. They kept response logs to record their thoughts while reading, and I used the response logs to study the reading processes of the participants. What I learned from this informal inquiry was that the participants worked very hard to construct their understanding of the poem. The English majors used multiple readings of the poem; some, for example, read it four times, others as many as eight. All reported reading certain lines over and over. They used dictionaries, prior notes, and other writings of their own, and they wrote short notes in the margins and between lines of the poem and longer notes in their notebooks. They discussed the poem with friends. Participants paid careful attention in their response logs to images and words, and they grouped these into categories, usually by similarity. They started their analyses somewhere in the middle of the poem, and they jumped here and there as they traced emerging patterns of meaning. No one wrote by starting at the beginning and working through the poem line by line.

When I repeated the experiment with two ninth-grade classes composed mainly of struggling writers, the ninth-graders behaved similarly to the English majors in every respect except two. The ninth-graders used multiple readings of the poem and of certain lines; they used dictionaries and prior notes; and they made notes in the margins and response logs, discussed the poem with friends, and paid particular attention to certain words and images. The ninth-graders were different from the English majors in that they didn't group their observations into categories, and they insisted on trying to write about the poem from beginning to end, line by line. In short, they were using knowledge telling and reporting their encounters with the poem, top to bottom, as I did in my first draft of the Loban piece.

The English majors, by virtue of their experience, had plans or patterns or schemas for organizing writing about poetry, and they were highly familiar with codes for academic written language, so they could focus most of their attention on the problem of generating content. The overall shape of the writing and the construction of paragraphs and sentences required so little attention from them that these aspects of writing seemed almost to take care of themselves. They were like experienced drivers on a familiar road, free to think about other things rather than the route being traveled or the rules of the road. Even content generation was relatively automatic for the English majors, especially those who had prior familiarity with the works of Sylvia Plath. Attention to content became mostly a matter of noticing and classifying data. For them, this writing was a matter of filing information from their reading and their response to the reading in accordance with a mental plan. The ninth-graders were relatively less familiar with the tasks of generating content and organizing ideas for writing about poetry, and this probably contributed to their trying to understand the poem line by line, repeating parts of it, making sense of their encounter with it, writing about the encounter by narrating their developing understanding, all the while telling what they know.

What can we do to help the ninth-graders develop as writers? The short answer to that question is *combine process and strategies*. The long answer will take me the next two chapters to spell out. Process-based approaches recommend taking component tasks one at a time, prewriting through final draft, and strategies-based instruction recommends using writing strategies with each component task. Prewriting strategies such as listing, brainstorming, or freewriting could focus the writer's attention on generating content, and then strategies for organizing the writing such as clustering, branching, or outlining could focus on shaping content. The writing and revising stages then might continue to focus on content and organization, generally by adding to, expanding, and rearranging what was already written. Surely these are useful strategies, and I describe them and others in greater detail in Chapters 6 and 7. By now it should be clear, however, that I am not just recommending a list of validated writing strategies for teachers to choose among and pass along in their work with struggling writers. If writing development is a recursive process which includes cycling back and forth between knowledge telling and knowledge transforming, if it is a continuum consisting not only of stages but of problems matched with solutions, a process of negotiating one's way out of difficulty rather than simply prewriting, writing, and revising, we should look for writers' problematic moments and help them to construct solutions.

The recursive view of development holds that writing abilities develop when writing tasks and contexts are sufficiently challenging to cause difficulty and sufficiently manageable to overcome it. Strategic writing instruction, especially in its emphasis on co-constructing writing strategies with writers, is an approach that looks for writers' moments of difficulty and combines strategies students bring to the classroom with strategies for transforming their writing to assist them in overcoming their difficulties. The long answer to the question of how to help struggling writers thus focuses on bringing together students' own strategies, the default strategies discussed in this chapter and the next, with new strategies to get them past their difficulties.

Chapter Six

Bringing Together Old and New Writing Strategies

The distinction between knowledge telling and knowledge transforming suggests a qualitative change in writing abilities that comes with the mastery of increasingly complex writing tasks and communicative purposes. I argued in the last chapter, however, that the change is socially constructed and is negotiated each time writers encounter new and greater challenges. Writing development is a journey, to be sure, but it is not so much a direct flight leading only to one prearranged destination as a combination of familiar routes we traverse again and again as we look for exploratory paths to get to new places. The writing-process approach to the teaching of writing, by itself, seems better suited to the direct flight/one destination theory of development and might contribute to holding struggling writers in one developmental place by insisting that we all traverse the same route to writing development. The hallmarks of process teaching—responding mostly to encourage the expansion of ideas through successive drafts, letting students choose their own topics and genres, presenting generic minilessons, postponing attention to spelling and other conventions—certainly provide practice at current levels of achievement, but for struggling writers these provide little incentive or assistance to attain new levels. Recall Greg in Chapter 1, for example, who, in a process-based workshop, usually wrote about what he knew well, such as sports, in forms he was already familiar with, such as personal narrative. Writing about familiar topics in familiar forms and receiving little help with mastering conventions of written language were not helping Greg with his writing difficulties and with achieving self-regulation of his own learning. At best, the workshop exercised "old" writing strategies Greg was already accustomed to using.

Using the metaphor of default strategies from Chapter 5, I want to say more about writing development in terms of adding new strategies to already existing ones. By themselves, default writing strategies are not signs of weak writing abilities as much as they are basic or prototypical means of solving difficult problems. Default strategies are the fundamental plans we use for problem solving: copying from models or prior experience; visualizing or imagining structures and relations among entities; narrating lived and observed events. We use default writing strategies *precisely because we can do so without thinking much about them*; this frees the mind for thinking about problems and challenges encountered while writing. These problems and challenges are of three general types: generating content, structuring texts, and using conventions of the written language system. The problems and challenges, furthermore, are overlapping. It is unwise, for example, to focus all of our cognitive energy on just brainstorming the content for a piece of writing because "background planning"—for example, visualizing text structures such as steps in an argument, elements in a narrative, or even parts of paragraphs and sentences—can help tell us what content to look for and how to shape it for expression. Struggling writers, however, do attempt to solve the tripartite challenge of content, structure, and conventions by taking them on one at a time, beginning with content generation. This is a result in part of the fact that content generation, as we have seen, is such a dominant problem for struggling writers. Generating content, even in its basic forms of telling what is known on a topic or deciding what to say next in the writing, can use up much of the struggling writer's cognitive resources.

Another reason why struggling writers take up content,

structure, and conventions one at a time, however, is that teachers often require exactly that by asking writers to follow a fixed list of steps in the writing process:

1. Brainstorm ideas.
2. Rearrange ideas in columns, circles, webs or other loosely associated groups.
3. Write.
4. Revise.
5. Edit.

This "separate steps" view of the writing process occurs frequently in our data, so frequently in fact that for a while we wondered whether the steps, especially brainstorming to make lists of ideas and arranging ideas in groups, might reflect one or more additional default strategies writers use to solve writing problems. After studying the correlation between instructional practices of teachers and writing processes of students, however, we decided that brainstorming and rearranging were more likely the result of teacher influence than student default preferences. It is possible that there is an instructional irony involved. Teaching the writing process as separate steps can reinforce the mistaken notion that writing involves the separation of content from structure and conventions and thus contributes to the misguided tendency to solve the tripartite challenge of content, structure, and conventions by taking them on one at a time. The opposite is more nearly true: content, structure, and conventions permeate and construct each other.

How can we teach writers that writing is a process of integrating content, structure, and conventions instead of separating them? Surely asking struggling writers to grapple with all three simultaneously would tend to overwhelm them. A better answer is to let them focus on one of the tripartite challenges while we assist them with the other two. We can let them work on content generation, for example, while we assist them in procuring a framework for arranging and expressing the content according to an appropriate plan for a given piece of writing. This is exactly what happened, for example, as students completed the study pages I described from Garland Godinho's classroom in Chapter 4. Frequently occurring academic text plans are recognizable in the observations that discourse generally "runs in a line" with thesis sentences and topic sentences followed by clarifying information, and that texts or stand-alone paragraphs generally show a three-part structure (beginning, middle, end for narrative; introduction, body, conclusion for nonnarratives). These are some of the plans experienced writers use to structure their writing.

Teaching the plans experienced writers use can be thought of as connecting "new" writing strategies to "old" ones. The old strategies are the default ones. Default strategies are like default settings in a word processing program, settings that operate independent of user control. Unless I tell Microsoft Word otherwise, it will automatically record my words as I type them in 14-point characters and double-spaced lines with an inch margin at the top and bottom of the page and an inch and a half at each side, and so on. Similarly, when struggling writers are not assisted in doing otherwise, they tend to use familiar or preferred strategies to produce writing, especially when topics or communicative contexts prove challenging. These familiar or preferred strategies are the ones I'm calling defaults, and the most frequently used examples of such strategies in the writing processes of students in our studies of struggling writers are the three major strategies I identified in the last chapter—copying, visualizing, and narrating—and several other, more minor ones: spelling by sound, asking for a correct spelling,[1] estimating page length, counting words, filling up a single handwritten page, and settling for the shortest possible text. In our data many other strategies also have the appearance of possibly being default settings, but they don't occur as regularly as the ones just listed.

All the default strategies we identified in our data seem to be used primarily for generating text rather than monitoring its production. This is consistent with Bereiter and Scardamalia's

---

[1]That students regularly asked for help with spelling but not with other difficulties (until we invited and encouraged them to do that) seemed curious at first, but interviews with students and teachers suggested that students are simply looking for the least obtrusive way to spell a word they need to use so that they can get on with the writing task. A teacher's or peer's assistance is certainly less obtrusive in the writing process than looking the word up, and probably sometimes less obtrusive even than using an electronic spell checker.

(1987) description of the knowledge-telling model and suggests that what is really on the mind of struggling writers is the problem of generating content and writing it down. Recall how Allison, in one of the composing-aloud protocols in Chapter 5, was more fluent and articulate when talking about her subject than when writing about it, and how David resorted to narrative to write about his topic even though he questioned the suitability of telling a story for accomplishing his purpose. Generating content and writing it down in an appropriate form, thus, appear to be the broad categories of difficulty behind the use of default strategies, especially copying, visualizing, and narrating. The result of concentrating on content is a kind of planning at the point of production by letting default settings such as copying, visualizing, and narrating supply the structure and some degree of conformity to conventions.

From the theory of writing development I outlined in Chapter 5, it should be clear that helping struggling writers to plan while writing is not simply a matter of displacing default strategies and replacing them with more advanced strategies typical of expert writers. Rather, instruction should aim for a gradual transformation of default strategies by building on them. I want to illustrate how this may work for each of the primary default strategies, and I do so by discussing copying, visualizing, and narrating in turn.

Copying

Copying, of course, seems endemic among struggling writers, and every teacher has encountered occasional students who try to pass off the work of others as their own. For that reason, copying has a bad reputation. In a *Doonesbury* comic strip (Trudeau, 1996), for example, a student who appears to be in middle school consults an encyclopedia before writing his history paper. He reads silently from the encyclopedia:

> Lousiana Purchase (1803): The purchase of the vast Lousiana Territory from France, initiated by Thomas Jefferson. The purchased area, which extended from the Mississippi to the Rocky Mountains, doubled the size of the United States.

After reading this report, the young man writes:

```
The Lousiana Purchase in 1803 was the purchase
of the vast Lousiana Territory from France at
the initiation of Thomas Jefferson. The area
that was purchased extended from the Mississippi
to the Rockies and doubled the size of the
United States.
```

In the final panel, the boy's mother is reading his report, and she says, "My . . . what a dramatic improvement in your writing." He replies, "Thanks." The comic strip illustrates two facts about copying in secondary schools: Students do it, and adults think it's cheating.

Contrary to its bad reputation, I want to make a case for seeing copying as a learning strategy and a planning strategy useful for promoting writing development. With writing that consists primarily of making sense of reading (probably the most typical school-sponsored writing task), knowledge telling may take the form of taking notes from the reading and even copying from the text or from the teacher's remarks or class discussion about the text. We saw such instances of copying in the writing of Jason in Chapters 1 and 2 and in the essays of students writing about censorship in *The Catcher in the Rye* in Chapter 5. Such examples suggest that a passage copied from a text being studied or a reference text may not necessarily carry the intent of plagiarism. Copying could simply be evidence that the writer's understanding of the passage being read and written about is still under construction and dependent on the original author's words rather than on the writer's own formulation of a response to the reading. The tripartite elements of the writing process—content, structure, convention—have their parallel, in reverse order, in the tripartite elements of the reading process—decoding, comprehending, and interpreting. Material that is copied inappropriately but without intentional deception from reading can be understood as awkwardly suspended between decoding and comprehending. Students in that case have not achieved an independent interpretation in which they explore the meaning of a passage in their own terms. Instead, their sense of the meaning of the passage leans on the original author's words. The words being written take Bakhtin's (1975/1981) observation about language learning quite literally: They are half someone else's. Struggling students in our studies generally reported and demonstrated such a tendency to use copying to formulate an initial understanding of their reading. This apparent basic tendency or need—to copy to understand a passage—is probably why students are often surprised when teachers get upset about their copying from source materials.

I want to argue as effectively as I can against the prevalent view that copying is universally bad for writers. Writing about reading usually asks students to communicate an original understanding of another author's ideas, and this can lead quite naturally to using the other author's words, especially when that author's ideas are difficult to comprehend. Writing about reading is never an easy task for struggling writers, at least not as easy as it is for those of us who went to college and majored in English and spent many years writing about ideas encountered in reading (which, I am certain, is one of the ways I became the "text-oriented person" I described myself as in Chapter 2). Ask a college English major to write about black and white imagery in *Othello,* for example, and chances are you'll rather quickly receive an original, polished essay. Ask a struggling high school writer for the same essay, or any essay on Shakespeare, and you risk getting material copied from an encyclopedia or from another reference book. (Ask for manifestations of other skills, such as changing a spark plug or baking a soufflé, and the college English major may also look for someone to copy; in the latter case, however, copying is likely to be seen as modeling, that is, as an intelligent learning strategy, rather than as stealing ideas from another person.)

Our studies suggest that the knowledge-telling strategy and the component strategy of copying from sources are default strategies writers use when gaining access to independently construed plans for content or structure, or both, during writing processes. As we observed frequently in previous chapters, the first step a struggling writer may take when responding to an assigned task, especially in writing about reading, often consists of following an author's words to apprehend the meaning of the topic or text. Copying or paraphrasing the author's words can take the place of independent content generation, and summarizing the plot or repeating the author's order of ideas can take the place of independently structuring one's own writing. As in the example from my own writing in the last chapter, writers may also use the narrative default strategy to make a first pass at constructing meaning from reading by telling the story of their encounter with the ideas they are reading about.

There is nothing wrong with the copying strategy when it is used to conceive but not to deceive. Copying, in short, is a learning strategy. My wife and I have a photograph of our daughter lying on her stomach on the floor with a wide-open newspaper in front of her. She is obviously enjoying her perusal of the paper, and you'd swear she was reading—until you notice that the newspaper is upside down. Kathleen is only a year and a half old in the picture, but she is already imitating some of her parents' reading behaviors. I tell this story both to indicate the broad range of literacy behaviors I am including in the category of "Copying Strategies" and to suggest how commonplace these strategies are. You don't have to look very far to gather evidence that writers learn and accomplish much by copying. In fact, if you're like me you don't have to look beyond your own desk. Right now, I have a stack of 19 books in one corner of my desk and three others open closer to where I'm typing. And while I'm typing in this file, I have two other files waiting in the electronic background, holding information I know I'm going to copy and paste into a later section of this chapter as I just did with the "Doonesbury" reference. Immediately to my left I have a folder of materials, one of which is an interview with Hunter S. Thompson from *Rolling Stone* (O'Rourke, 1996).[2] Because it suits my purpose to do so, I now copy a small portion of the interview right here:

> [INTERVIEWER:] So what do you tell people who say they want to become writers?
> [THOMPSON:] Ye gods, that's a tough one. I think that one of the things I stumbled on early, as really a self-defense mechanism of some kind, was typing other writers. Typing a page of Hemingway or a page of Faulkner. Three pages. I learned a tremendous amount about

---

[2]I am grateful to English teacher Paul Lasch for bringing this interview to my attention.

rhythm in that way. I see writing really as music. That's why I like to hear it read out loud by other people. I like to hear what they're getting out of it. It tells me what you see. I like to have women read it. If it fits musically, it will go to almost any ear. It could be that's why children relate to it. (O'Rourke, 1996, p. 68)

What Hunter Thompson calls "typing other writers" is surely a form of copying or modeling, and he claims to have learned much that way, especially about the regularities and rhythms of written language. It is obvious that when we copy from our own writing and from others, we temporarily borrow ideas. Thompson reminds us that when we copy a page or so of writing we are also borrowing patterns of language in use. In our research we discovered that this second type of borrowing makes an excellent learning strategy; in fact, we think it is closely akin to many ways we all learn the regularities and rhythms of written language, such as the tacit acquisition of familiarity with the forms and lexicon typical of academic written language that happens when readers read schoolbooks.

Copying can assist with each of the tripartite elements of the writing process. Copying can help writers generate content, plan structure, and conform to writing conventions. The last of the three is the most obvious example: Copying is exactly what we do when we consult a dictionary or handbook or style sheet for assistance with matters of usage or mechanics or spelling. What is perhaps not so obvious are the legitimate ways writers can, and do, copy content and structure. Special education teachers, for example, often ease some of the cognitive burden involved in writing by writing down ideas as students speak them. In our research we turned this into a copying strategy we call "double dictation." This strategy consists of having students dictate a story or essay while a teacher or peer writes it down. The teacher or peer then dictates the story back while the student writes it down. Finally the two written versions are compared for work on conventions. At first glance, this process of double dictation seems to separate content from structure and conventions, but that is not really the case. Content generation and scribal activity are happening at once; they are simply being performed by different people. Nothing is left out, all aspects of writing happen at once, but through the implementation of a controlled double copying strategy the writer benefits by focusing on content, writing, and editing one at a time while another person assists with the other two.

In our work with struggling writers we developed another strategy which builds on learning by copying and manipulating written language. We refer to the strategy in our conversations with students as "I Wish I Could Write Like That" because the strategy consists of having them write in emulation of short excerpts from the literature they are studying. Putting literature in the service of improving writing skills is a natural for English classes because English teachers are responsible for both literature and composition, and the deliberate imitation of the structure of literary models which is at the heart of "I Wish I Could Write Like That" teaches sentence craft and sentence structure as well as paragraph and text conventions. The imitation of literary models, however, is not the only way of using the emulation strategy to practice the rhythms and conventions of written language. We found that *Time* and *Newsweek,* for example, also do an excellent job of modeling the conventions of educated writing for secondary students, and they have the additional advantage of modeling expository prose.

"I Wish I Could Write Like That" is both a strategy for learning rhythms of writing and an exercise in writing to study conventions of written language at levels of text, paragraph, sentences, words, and mechanics. We first introduce the strategy with teachers, who, in turn, construct it with students. In the following example, English teacher Lenise Deakin wrote in imitation of a paragraph from Annie Dillard (1974). Here is Dillard's original text:

> As I walked along the grassy edge of the island, I got better and better at seeing frogs both in and out of the water. I learned to recognize, slowing down, the difference in texture of the light reflected from mudbank, water, grass, or frog. Frogs were flying all around me. At the end of the island, I noticed a small green frog. He was exactly half in and half out of the water, looking like a schematic diagram of an amphibian, and he didn't jump.
>
> He didn't jump; I crept closer. At last I knelt on the island's winterkilled grass, lost, dumbstruck, staring at the

frog in the creek just four feet away. He was a very small frog with wide, dull eyes. And just as I looked at him, he slowly crumpled and began to sag. The spirit vanished from his eyes as if snuffed. His skin emptied and drooped; his very skull seemed to collapse and settle like a kicked tent. He was shrinking before my eyes like a deflating football. . . . I gaped bewildered, appalled. An oval shadow hung in the water behind the drained frog; then the shadow glided away.

I had read about the giant water bug, but never seen one. . . . The frog I saw was being sucked by a giant water bug. I had been kneeling on the island grass; when the unrecognizable flap of frog skin settled on the creek bottom, swaying, I stood up and brushed the knees of my pants. I couldn't catch my breath. (pp. 5–6)

And here is Lenise's imitation of Dillard's text:

As I approach the entrance, the mall looks different than I remember. For the first time I am able to take a wider view of this remarkable structure. The smooth white concrete walls meet to form angles which contrast against the flat, blue sky. I do not understand even what I can easily see. Let those who dare worry about shoddy roof construction and the growing number of failing retail shops. I must start somewhere, so I try to deal with the two-for-one bra sale at Victoria's Secret and the skirt I need to return to Ann Taylor.

Just outside of the doorway, I come upon a group of Canadian bargain hunters, most of them senior citizens. Canadians shop together in vast hordes and droves, migrating south of the border to avoid the G.S.T. They have their favorite spending sites, which they return to week after week, the Galleria foremost among these. I surmise that they are waiting for the chartered bus which will transport them back to their native region. At the edge of the curb, I notice a short, elderly woman in a pink pantsuit. She is barely visible, hidden by a mound of bags and packages which surround her. I creep closer and am just able to make out the label affixed to her breast pocket. "HELLO, my name is . . . Mildred," it reads. She is a pale old lady with red drooping eyes. And just as I look at her, she slowly crumples and begins to sag. She is shrinking before my eyes like a deflating balloon at T.G.I. Friday's. I stand, open mouthed, as she slumps over onto a J.C. Penney shopping bag. I have read about people who "shopped till they dropped," but never seen it. Unable to catch my breath, I stagger toward the heavy glass doors hungry for the solace which lays beyond.

As the previous example suggests, "I Wish I Could Write Like That" consists of asking students to put their own words in a professional writer's text structure as they write in emulation of that writer. This is a kind of English-class equivalent to a musician's composing a song to the tune of an already existing song. In a class of eighth-graders taught by Cathy Fairbend we examined the possibility of stretching student writing abilities by having them imitate, as precisely as possible, the structure in selected brief pieces by published writers. We brought two basic assumptions to our trials of the approach: (1) that language learners acquire many aspects of language through imitation of what others do, and (2) that writing is partly learned, both intuitively and deliberately, through exposure to written texts, especially while reading. We wanted to build on these tendencies to acquire language forms through imitation and intuition by asking students to consciously imitate literary models. The objective of "I Wish I Could Write Like That" in Cathy's classes was to have students acquire control over the use of structural patterns in written language by plugging their own words and sentences into a published writer's text. She gave students brief excerpts from exemplary texts, and she told them to read and rewrite the texts by keeping the form and sentence structure but using their own words. The basic rule was "Keep the form, but change the words and the meaning." We wanted to see whether students could do the kinds of imitation we were asking them to do, and we wanted to see whether repeated practice (once a week for half an academic year) with the method would improve the quality of their writing and expand the variety and control their writing shows in matters of syntax and paragraph structure. The answer was yes to both questions.

Cathy had two classes write short paragraphs once a week, on Fridays. Each week she gave them a short excerpt from a literary text, and she tried various ways of modeling and assisting her students in rewriting the text by putting their own words into the spaces occupied by the author's words. The texts were short, only two or three sentences, and they came right out of the literary selections the kids were studying. Here are some early examples from the project:

Sample 1:

In another corner of the room behind a screen was a gas plate and an icebox. Mrs. Jones got up and went behind the screen. The woman did not watch the boy to see if he was going to run now, nor did she watch her purse which she left behind her on the day bed. (Hughes, 1994, p. 181)

Student versions:

1. The other end of the Building on the cabnit was a Hockey puck and a stick. Mrs. Johnson stood up and walked across the Floor. The Man went to observe the water to see if it was driping on the floor, litle did he know his walet that he left back lay on the reclining chair.

2. The other side of the fence under a tarp was a bike and a boot. Mr. Thomas stood up and went under the tarp. The man did not watch the girl to check if she was going to leave now, or he didn't watch his wallet wich he left sitting on the small black table.

3. In the back of my closet next to a bunch of clothes sat a white dress. I got up and went to the closet. I picked up the dress and headed over to see if it was going to fit me, But as all things happen, my favorite dress did not fit me.

Many students made several successive attempts at the first sentence, as in this example:

Across the hall in the corner was a picnic table and a poster.

Across the hall in the right corner behind the picnic table was a garbage can and a poster.

Across the hall in the corner behind a window was a picnic table and a tree.

Notice that in this early example from our data in the "I Wish I Could Write Like That" study students are "matching" their words with a professional writer's structure quite successfully with one exception, the "woman did not, . . . nor did she" pattern in Hughes's original sentence, "The woman did not watch the boy to see if he was going to run now, nor did she watch her purse which she left behind her on the day bed." Apparently Cathy's students were not "seeing" that pattern in the original, not picking it up by acquisition alone. Later in the project, after considerable direct modeling and instruction from Cathy, they became much more successful at noticing and replicating patterns in the original texts:

Sample 2:

He was a blind beggar, carrying the traditional battered cane, and thumping his way before him with the cautious, half-furtive effort of the sightless. He was a shaggy, thicked-necked fellow; his coat was greasy about the lapel and pockets, and his hand splayed over the cane's crook with a futile sort of clinging. He wore a black pouch slung over his shoulder. Apparently he had something to sell. (Kantor, 1993, p. 149)

Student version:

Joe was crooked theif, wearing the usual dark cloak, and walking his way towards her with the slick, slight cautious movement of the talented. He was a short, rough-necked person; his wardrobe was muddy about the boots and leather pants, and his hand layed over the pockets opening with a sort of clinging cautious kind of slickness. He wore a black glove carefully put on his hand. Apparently there was something to steal.

Copying, of course, can also help with the generation of content for writing, and again we don't have to look far to find professional writers who exemplify this strategy. Certainly the book you're looking at right now is one example, as is all scholarship that includes library research. Creative writing, too, provides many examples of borrowing from others. Jane Yolen calls herself an "empress of thieves":

> It is no secret to those who know my books that I am an empress of thieves. I have sneaked into the story rooms of a hundred cultures and taken characters like selchies from Scotland (*Greyling*) or mermen from the cold Northern seas ("The Lady and the Merman"). I have stolen magical implements like swords in stones (*Merlin's Booke*) and mythical beasts like dragons (*Dragon's Blood*). I have lifted plots from ballads like "Kemp Owain" (*Dove Isabeau*) and borrowed landscapes from the Blackfeet people (*Sky Dogs*) and the Scottish borders (*Tam Lin*). I have filched rooms from Indian orphanages (*Children of the Wolf*), Chinese palaces (*The Seeing Stick*), and a friend's memory of life in a concentration camp (*The Devil's Arithmetic*). I have pulled threads from magic tapestries already woven and used them to weave my own cloth. (Yolen, 1991, p. 144)

Kids, too, can borrow from the "magic tapestries already woven" by other writers. My writing development had its J. D. Salinger phase and its Ernest Hemingway. For a while in college I was fascinated by the poetry of Alexander Pope and wrote dozens of couplets like his for the fun of it ("His face proves that humans once depended/On the same tree from which apes descended"). Also in college I fine-tuned my control over the discourse of English studies by borrowing stylistic tricks from Russell Murphy, then my roommate and now a published novelist.

My best example of copying as a mode of writing development involves teacher-researcher Jody Rabinowitz, a seventh-grader I'll call Randall, novelist Dean Koontz (1984), and me. The four of us are connected in a chain of language styles and words taken from other people and their contexts and intentions that would make Bakhtin (1975/1981) proud. Jody explains that at the end of each term students must turn in writing portfolios with their two best pieces and a reflective letter on top. The reflective letter is based on choices they make from a list of questions she provides. One of the questions they can answer is, "In what ways are your reading and writing connected?" Few students choose to answer this question, but Randall decided to. He wrote that he is getting ideas for writing from reading he's doing outside of class:

```
    I feel my best piece of writing is "Microproc-
    essor Murder." I chose this because it is my
    longest piece, it is the most exciting and I
    enjoyed writing it. Several things inspired me
    as I wrote this story. I began reading Darkfall
    by Dean Koonz. I really enjoyed the book. It
    is a horror mystery book. I also found an
    article in the newspaper which gave me ideas.
    I thought it would be fun to try and write a
    short horror story myself.
        My biggest problem that I encountered was
    not knowing what to write about. I thought about
    a lot of things and several times I tried
    writing different stories but I didn't like what
    I wrote. These stories seemed to be going
    nowhere. I found the solution to the problem
    when I started reading Darkfall. I enjoyed it
    so much that I decided to try writing a horror
    story myself.
```

When Jody read Randall's "Microprocessor Murder" piece she discovered that it was "so far above the seventh-grade level" that she wondered whether he had plagiarized all or part of it. She checked it against *Darkfall* and then reported this reaction to me:

"I was thrilled to find that Randall's story did not follow the plot line of *Darkfall,* but rather the writing style. The structure of his sentences, his word choice, and his use of dialogue provided the evidence that Randall was emulating Dean Koontz' writing style. Randall was writing strategically; he altered his writing style in an effort to emulate professional writing. . . . Randall's ability to apply the writing conventions he observed in a published novel indicates his metacognitive awareness of both his reading and writing processes. In Randall's case, reading acts as a catalyst for his development as a self-regulated writer."[3]

Copying, in short, can be a form of emergent self-regulation.

[3]Jody shared this reflection by means of personal communication (January 30, 1997).

Not All Copying, of Course, Is Good Copying

In an article I wrote with Kathleen Collins (Collins & Collins, 1996) we describe the case of a ninth-grader we called Margarita who was overly dependent on copying. Our report[4] began at the point at which Margarita's class read and discussed newspaper articles, and their teacher asked them to write about one of the articles, summarizing and evaluating what it said. Margarita wrote her response quickly and she seemed to have no serious difficulty with the task. When she finished, however, her writing contained many ideas copied directly from the article, as indicated here by italics:

> My essay is on article entitled "Just take away their guns." It talks about tougher gun-control legislation and if it works or not.
>
> *The President thinks tougher gun control will work. But the public supports it but thinks it won't work.* Who is right? The public is right.
>
> *Only about 2% of 65 million or so privately owned handguns are employed to commit crimes, and about one-sixth of those are purchased from a pawn or gun shop. Most handguns used by criminals are stolen, borrowed, or bought privately.* If they *shrink the stock of legally purchased guns or ammunition, it would reduce the capacity of law abiding people to defend themselves.*
>
> *According to the Bureau of Justice Statistics, people who defend themselves with a weapon are less likely to lose some property in a robbery or* [be] *injured in an assault than those people who don't defend themselves.* Most people say that *owners are more likely to shoot themselves or hurt their loved ones than to stop a criminal.* Is that true? *No, half of the firearm accidents known involve rifles and shotguns, not handguns.*

[4]This section is only slightly revised from its original published form coauthored by Kathleen M. Collins (Collins & Collins, 1996). It is used here with Kathleen's permission and the permission of the National Council of Teachers of English.

> The article also stated that *the National
> Rifle Association urge the government to punish
> more severely people who use guns to do crimes.
> Modern science can help,* too. *Metal detectors
> at airport have reduced skyjackings and bombings
> to* just about none. But *the police need
> something that will work from a distance of ten
> to 15 feet* that would [let] them know if someone
> were carrying a gun. Hopefully the *engineers and
> scientists will be able to design a better gun
> detector.*

Margarita's main writing strategy apparently was to copy key ideas nearly verbatim from her reading. She told us that she knew she needed facts to support her position, and she found the facts in the news article. Here, again, many teachers might see this as plagiarism, and perhaps it is, but we didn't think Margarita was being deceptive or dishonest. Instead, her copying directly from material she was writing about seems to be part of the tendency I've described as resorting to copying as a default strategy for solving one of schooling's toughest and most frequently encountered intellectual problems, the critical reformulation of ideas from another writer. From this perspective, Margarita's quick and facile writing process belies a struggle she has with thinking through the meaning of a passage for herself. Margarita fits the description I provided earlier of readers who are awkwardly suspended between decoding and comprehending, students who have not reached the level of interpretive inference making where they state the meaning of a passage in their own terms.

Kathleen Collins worked with Margarita by using the four-step process at the heart of strategic writing instruction: identifying a strategy worth teaching, introducing the strategy by modeling it, helping students to try the strategy out with workshop-style teacher guidance, and then helping students work toward independent mastery of the strategy through repeated practice and reinforcement. She prepared for the first step, identifying a strategy worth teaching, by asking Margarita's class to bring newspaper or magazine articles they were interested in to class. She led discussions of the content and organizational patterns of many of the articles they brought in, including, for example, such matters as how the author of an editorial organized her writing differently from the author of a front-page news story. Kathleen then asked her students to respond to their articles by writing an essay, and in addition she asked them to fill out a brief questionnaire regarding how they had completed the assignment. She had two other teachers rate the compositions for overall quality, and Kathleen then observed a correspondence between the holistic quality of the writing and the responses writers made to the questions, as in these excerpts:

Question 1: How did you begin writing?
These responses are from writers of pieces rated highest in overall quality:
"I began with an opening sentence that explained what I was writing about."
"I began writing by stating the main idea of the article."
"I tried to start off with a good sentence to let you know what I was going to be writing an essay on."
"I began writing by trying to start off with the main points of the article."
"I began writing by rearranging the first sentence of the article."
"I followed how the author of the article started the article and used my own words."
"Before I started writing, I brainstormed and . . . I read another article on the same topic . . . that helped a lot."
These responses are from writers of pieces rated lowest in overall quality:
"I began writing messy."
"Well, I asked my sister how would I start off and she couldn't tell me so I guessed."

Question 2: How did you organize this piece of writing?
These responses are from writers of pieces rated highest in overall quality:
"I followed the way the author of the article organized his."

"I wrote like the article."

"I went in the order of the action that took place."

"I organized my writing in order. For example, what happened first, second, third, and so on."

"I started with an introductory paragraph, put supporting paragraphs in the middle, and gave a closing paragraph in the end. My supporting paragraphs are what explained my topic in detail."

These responses are from writers of pieces rated lowest in overall quality:

"I did it in cursive and wrote in paragraphs."

"I organized it by just thinking of a first sentence and then going from there."

"I didn't"

"I really didn't. I just started writing."

A comparison of the strategies correlated with higher- and lower-quality ratings led Kathleen to the conclusion that the strategies associated with the higher-quality writing are self-regulatory in that they provide ways of thinking about writing which help students control their writing processes by setting goals and monitoring progress toward achieving them. The writer who wrote, "I began with an opening sentence that explained what I was writing about," in other words, probably used that strategy to accomplish the rhetorical objectives of getting started and planning or organizing the writing, and the writer probably also used that strategy to signal for herself when those objectives were met. Not only did the writer possess a strategy for getting the writing going by framing her response, but she monitored her own use of the strategy. According to their questionnaire responses, writers of the pieces rated lower in overall quality seemed to get started by just beginning to write, at best a default strategy that offers little in the way of planning the whole piece and monitoring its production.

In the class of ninth-graders, Kathleen determined that writers of the pieces rated highest in overall quality were basing their thinking on close readings of the articles they were writing about. They used multiple readings of the news articles, and they relied on the articles as models of organization and as sources of content. They didn't copy directly from the articles but instead reworded and summarized and evaluated what the article said. Kathleen's way of explicitly describing the thinking behind the strategy the student reported as, "I began with an opening sentence that explained what I was writing about," is to say that the student read the article closely, decided what it was saying, and then wrote a sentence summarizing and interpreting its content. We called this strategy "Read–Think–Summarize–Interpret."

Step two in the strategic instruction process is to introduce the strategy by modeling it. Kathleen selected double-entry note taking as an external framework to support the "Read–Think–Summarize–Interpret" strategy. In double-entry note taking for this purpose, students divide a sheet of paper in half vertically, and on the left side of the page they record notes on their reading or copy excerpts from it. On the right side of the page they write reactions to and interpretations of their reading (David, 1992). The note taking thus provides constructive and repetitive practice with reading, thinking about, summarizing, and interpreting text. Its purpose is to get students beyond decoding and comprehending and into inference making as they read and write.

Margarita was one of the students who benefited from the "Read–Think–Summarize–Interpret" strategy. She was a good candidate for needing to learn the strategy because her writing, as we indicated earlier, showed many portions copied verbatim from the news article about which she was writing. Margarita knew that she needed facts to support her position, but she apparently lacked the strategy of reformulating and restating ideas in her own words rather than reproducing them in the original author's words.

Kathleen helped Margarita overcome her overreliance on copying by teaching double-entry note taking to the whole class to model summarizing and interpreting the main ideas and facts from a text and expressing them in one's own words. Kathleen selected three articles from *The Washington Post* that all dealt with the same incident, a recent fatal automobile accident in a nearby town that involved teens and alcohol. Two of the articles were editorials (of opposing viewpoints) and the third was a factual report of what had happened. She began with the factual article and started taking notes on an overhead, recording and discussing comments from students in Margarita's class, as in this excerpt:

Summary of reading	Responses and interpretations
(Important facts, quotations, main ideas, statistics *"from the text"*)	(Thoughts repeating and reacting to what the text says *"from your head"*)
She started out with a personal experience [her son]	I like the way she started it!
Traffic accidents are the number one killer of teenagers	Why did the NHTSA wait to have so many tragedies before doing anything? They shouldn't have waited so long.
Fatality rate for teen drivers is about 5x's that of any other age group, 40% of those involve alcohol	
The National Highway Traffic Safety Administration is pushing for the provisional licensing program in all states. 13 states, inc. Maryland and West Virginia, have started it.	I think that is a little too strict for the young teenagers. I also think it is a good way to reduce such crashes and violations. . . . it's going to have some problems. Teens haven't gotten the point yet.

The students in the class then wrote their own double-entry responses to the second article. This is the third step in strategic writing instruction, helping students as they use the strategy to work on their writing. Here is an excerpt from Margarita's notes, followed by the essay she subsequently wrote in writing workshop:

Summary of reading	Responses and interpretations
Walt Whitman High School lost 2 classmate and almost lost 2 others 16 yr. old's license was 3 weeks old Most parents can't wait until their kids are driving, but that means they can get to parties easier	This is a very sad story
	Why was she driving?
	Teenagers aren't dumb, they just do dumb things. It is true that most teenage parties have no adult supervision. I think if parents knew they wouldn't want their kids driving.

Teens and drunk driving is very common these days. You are probably asking, "But how do they get the alcohol?" But it's very simple. They get it from parties, friends, and even family members. Family? Yes, most households have alcohol in them. What I mean is, most adults drink, don't they? Yes, most adult drink most of the time. Most teens just go and get the alcohol from the refrigerator, cabinets, or any hiding place a family member thinks no one knows about but that's how it is.

To stop this drinking and driving among teens we should enforce the provisional licensing program. The provisional licensing program is a program that the NHTSA is trying to enforce in all states. So far only 13 states have this program that requires a teen to have an adult (21 years or older) with a license in the car to be able to drive between the hours of midnight and 5 A.M. And if you get caught drinking and driving or driving recklessly, your license will be taken away on the spot.

Another way we can prevent drunk driving to organize a club or activities for teens. That [way] kids have a place to go on the weekends instead of going to alcoholic parties. Also, have parties that are chaperoned by responsible adults. But pretty much don't say nothing, just watch that there aren't any fights, alcohol, or smoking of any kind.

The final way is if teens get caught drinking and driving, take their license away on the spot until they show some responsibility. For example, make them have to do community work until get there license back.

These days drunk driving is very common among teens. We could do a lot of things to change that. For example, we could have provisional licensing, clubs and activities to keep kids busy on weekends, and finally, if they are caught driving drunk, their license should be taken away until they show some responsibility by doing community work.

This second essay is longer than Margarita's first one. It is also much more specific. More important, Margarita composed the essay herself rather than copying most of it from the text she wrote about. When asked what academic activity she felt benefited her most in ninth-grade English, Margarita wrote, "The DEN's [double-entry notes] helped me because I usually have a hard time writing essays.... DEN helped me because it helped me write down what I'm thinking about while I'm reading." Step four in strategic instruction is helping students work toward independent mastery of the strategy through re-peated practice. Margarita will need such practice before she has mastered the "Read–Think–Summarize–Interpret" strategy, but we think she is well on her way toward being able to use the strategy to help control her writing.

Visualizing

Visualizing is the second "old" strategy I want to discuss in terms of its capacity for providing a foundation for learning "new" writing strategies. Elementary school teachers are well aware of the close developmental connection between drawing and writ-ing, as are parents of young children and authors and illustrators of children's books. Writing by young children often occurs in connection with drawing (Graves, 1975; Dyson, 1983), as in this example:

```
I was wawking thrue the wds,
Wan I saw a pritty brd. It
was bringing the babby brds
a wrm to eat. It was a
butifl day. The sky was
blue and clear. I was waring
my red shrt with the blue trimming
and my blue geandges.
```

This paragraph was spontaneously written by a first-grade girl on the back of a piece of paper. On the front side she first drew the scene described in the writing.[5] The drawing obviously suggested the content of the writing and probably its descriptive

---

[5]This might be a case in which all three of the default strategies I am discussing are operating, because the descriptive content of the writing was copied from a visual form and expressed within a narrative frame.

purpose as well. Perhaps it is natural to expect that this child's use of visualizing a walk in the woods to get ideas for the content and scope of her writing will later disappear along with her sound-based invented spellings, but I want to argue against that expectation. It is more likely that visualizing ideas and relations will "go underground" so that actual drawing developmentally turns into mental imaging, in a manner similar to what Vygotsky (1934/1986) says happens to the child's tendency to think aloud, which he claims turns into verbal thought or inner speech. If that is the case, visualization becomes an inner capacity that acts as a foundation for highly specialized cognitive strategies available to writers and readers. Our data support that interpretation by suggesting that writers continue to rely on visualization in secondary school (and beyond) to solve problems in their writing, especially problems related to planning globally or envisioning the whole structure of the writing, as we saw in the cases of Jason and Brandon and my own writing in earlier chapters.

Eisner (1993) attributes the structuring capacity of imagery to its simplifying function. Mental images can render complex information, for example, as graphic representations such as pie charts, histograms, scattergrams, spreadsheets, and models. These spatial analogues simplify by "displaying the structural features of the phenomena people wish to understand" (p. 3). The capacity to *display the structural features people wish to understand* is doubly useful in writing: once to show us the structure of the topic or content of the writing and again to show us the structure of the writing itself. Images can help with this double structuring involved in the task of constructing meaning in language precisely because they present whole structures "at once" rather than "in a line," as language does. Images are synchronic, giving the whole picture at once, while language is diachronic, giving us meaning over time. Images therefore can help us see, quite literally, where our understanding of both topic and words is going. Picturing the structure of content relevant to a topic tells us much about constructing our understanding of it, and picturing the shape of a whole text shows us the route our sentences and paragraphs need to take to get the writing where we want it to go to express our understanding. For example, in the middle of the last paragraph, I suddenly hit the return key a couple of times and typed three words in a column:

Eisner
Wilhelm
Examples

This list of words is an attempt to capture a "planning image" that just came to mind. The full image, the one in my mind as I typed that paragraph and this one, tells me where I am heading in this section by outlining the next several topics I want to cover, and it also suggests approximately how much space each topic will occupy. The order in which I will get to them is flexible, however, because I plan to use examples in the Eisner and Wilhelm sections and not just at the end. The three words thus represent a planning image by recording it in abbreviated form on my monitor as a simple list. Writing the list down as I type is my way of structuring this section by displaying my plan for myself and by using my computer's memory to supplement my own. If need be, I can go back to where I typed the abbreviated image to help myself retrieve the full planning image in case my memory of it begins to fade. My experience tells me, though, that typing the words in my list has fixed both the structure of the image and its informational content in my memory. I'm always making short planning lists which I don't need because writing the list down fixes the plan imagistically in memory. It's a little like writing down ideas that come to you during the night. A couple of nights ago while falling asleep I had another one of those flashes of insight which deliver a good idea related to my writing, an idea establishing an important and hitherto unrecognized relation. I didn't get up to write it down, as I learned to do by losing a thousand other good ideas. Of course, by morning the idea was gone. I remembered that I had the idea, that the idea was relevant to a central problem in the writing I was doing yesterday, and that the idea established an important relation. But the information contained in the image, the content or words or text associated with the message, was gone. My interpretation of this phenomenon is that the mind remembers the experience and framework of an idea but forgets its content because images are more concrete and complete than words. Perhaps the frame and content, imagistic structure and verbal meaning, come from different parts of the brain, and the imagining part is more amenable to storing and retrieving than the other, but that "neuroanatomical" explanation only enhances the previous one. The obvious insight here is that the frameworks and images on which we hang our ideas and words are basic to constructing meaning. We see mental pictures as friends to be trusted when we are working on understanding complex phenomena. And the fact that I even need to make that point in a book for teachers tells me something is amiss in an educational system that has always taken pictures less seriously than words and given us little practice translating between images and text; little wonder we can sometimes recall an image but not its symbolic import. An astonishing account of the variety and value of mental imagery is available in *Thinking in Pictures* (Grandin, 1995). The book tells the story of an autistic child who became a professor of animal science. She describes her mind as a videotape library. For example, she can translate written words into color movies or store a written page to be read later as a photocopy of the page in her imagination. My belief is that these are abilities we all possess to some degree, abilities we can learn to use by associating words and images.

Eisner (1993) would agree with that last analysis. He makes an argument for using visual forms extensively throughout education, and part of his argument is powerfully relevant to helping students who struggle with literacy:

> We would develop and use these resources because of our understanding that human intellectual capacity is extraordinarily diverse, that the varieties of meaning are many, and that the comprehension of a subject profits from more than one perspective and form of representation. . . . Finally, the use of such resources in our classrooms would contribute to greater educational equity for our students. The singleminded narrowness inherent in the dominance of text in teaching impedes the life chances of students whose aptitudes are more attuned to nontext forms. (p. 6)

In Chapter 2, I suggested that Jason might be more attuned to visual and spatial understandings than textual ones. This might frequently be the case with struggling writers. English teacher Jody Rabinowitz, for example, recently told me about a visit she made to a third-grade classroom. Students there were supposed to be writing about a topic of their choice, and most were, but Jody noticed a boy who hadn't written one word on his paper. She sat down next to him and asked if he was having trouble finding something to write about. Of course, he said, "Yes." Jody also noticed that his notebook was covered with detailed drawings of people and machines. She asked the teacher if he could draw one of his inventions and then write about it. The teacher approved, but when Jody relayed the message to the boy, he was in disbelief. "You mean I can really draw in my journal?" he asked.

"Yes, your teacher said it was okay. I promise you won't get in trouble."

Once Jody made that promise the boy's pencil began to move and within minutes he had a detailed drawing. Jody reports that the student needed a topic, a little motivation, and a real purpose for engaging in the writing task. She gave him a little help with the topic, and the drawing activity increased his motivation while also tapping into his visual/spatial intelligence. The fact that he could write about something real and meaningful to him, his drawing, gave the activity some purpose.

Wilhelm (1995) tells a similar story of students failing to recognize their ability to use the power of visualization for literacy learning. The story reports on his work teaching reading to Tommy and Walter, two learning-disabled (LD) seventh-graders. Both were reluctant and resistant readers, locked into "can't do" identities when it came to reading. Both students, Wilhelm discovered, were also highly visual learners. At one point while discussing a story, Tommy explodes: "I can't think about it, talk bout it, do anything about it, if I can't see it!" (Wilhelm, 1995, p. 476). Similarly, Walter was reluctant to talk about a story but once released from the discussion, he hurried back to his desk and immediately began chuckling to himself over *Calvin and Hobbes*. Wilhelm took further note of the artistic skills of Tommy and Walter and asked them if they had ever used these skills in the classroom. "Usually we get in trouble for it," Walter said (p. 477)—a response, I remember, that made me think that visualizing meaning has the same status in schools that I attributed to copying earlier in this chapter. Wilhelm put together and launched a project in his two LD mainstreamed classes to convince reluctant readers that reading involves seeing. He included student drawings and visual protocols, illustrated books, collages, and picture maps based on readings. For example, Tommy and Walter each eagerly drew several pictures—Walter: "I've gotta stop here" [to draw]; Tommy: "Wait, I need to draw now" (p. 488)—to construct and begin to communicate their understanding of "The Sniper." Wilhelm (1995) provides a concise analysis of his findings: "Artistic response activities help less proficient and less engaged readers to respond on various dimensions to enter, evoke, comprehend, remember, elaborate, and reflect upon the experience of reading" (p. 495). Wilhelm also makes note of the fact that Tommy and Walter became active members of a learning community, reminding us again of our sociocognitive theme. It is not the visualization strategy in isolation but, rather, in communities and especially in partnerships between students and teachers that facilitates literacy learning.

Getting the Big Picture

One of the main insights I gained from our studies of writing strategies with struggling writers is that many, perhaps most, of the strategies reported in the literature on strategies and literacy instruction make an appeal to visual learning. Throughout the strategies research, visualization of the whole is the favorite way to teach "getting the big picture," the reader's sense of a whole text or the writer's plan for a whole piece of writing. Semantic mapping and notesheets to enhance reading comprehension, for example, help readers to see patterns of meaning in their reading. Even seemingly mnemonic-based strategies are often presented as visual information, as in Willoughby and Wood's (1995) taxonomy of hierarchical relations among plant groups and Harris and Graham's (1992, 1996, p. 49) story grammar strategy, which is remembered most easily by its appearance:

W-W-W
What = 2
How = 2

Once called to mind, the strategy in turn gives access to key questions to guide the writing of a story:

Who is the main character; who else is in the story?
When does the story take place?
Where does the story take place?

What does the main character do or want to do; what do other characters do?

What happens when the main character does or tries to do it? What happens with the other characters?

How does the story end?

How does the main character feel; how do the other characters feel? (Harris & Graham, 1996, p. 49)

In an ongoing series of studies, to give one more example, Carol Sue Englert and her colleagues studied the effectiveness of teaching literacy strategies in a sociocultural framework in elementary and special education classrooms, and many of their

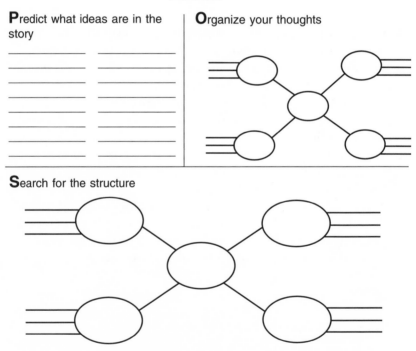

POSSE

Predict what ideas are in the story

Organize your thoughts

Search for the structure

Summarize. Summarize the Main Idea in your own words.
Evaluate. Ask a question about the Main Idea. Compare. Clarify. Predict.

FIGURE 6.1. Graphic for using the POSSE reading comprehension strategy. From Englert and Mariage (1990). Copyright 1990 by PRO-ED, Inc. Used with permission.

strategies use graphic representations of planning, as in the case of POSSE, a strategy for focusing on and enhancing reading comprehension (Englert & Mariage, 1990), in Figure 6.1.

In other studies Englert and her colleagues use graphic strategies for teaching structures of writing, such as the narrative story frame, explanation and comparison/contrast organization forms (Englert & Mariage, 1991; Englert, 1995), and planning think sheets (Englert et al., 1992; Englert, 1995). Each of these strategies uses lines and boxes to help writers plan the overall structure of pieces of writing. In our studies we used similar graphics employing lines, spaces, and arrows to represent parts of texts, as in the cases of Jason and Brandon, and we also used sample texts to picture the same patterns of organization, as in Figure 6.2. This figure presents a strategy sheet we used to work with sixth-graders on paragraph structure and connecting paragraphs. The strategy combines copying and visualizing to show students how we achieved well-formed paragraphs and cohesiveness across them in a model essay we called "Washing the Car." One caveat: Strategy sheets such as this one should not just be given to students without the steps in strategic writing instruction; remember, strategies must be co-constructed by teachers and students actively engaged in writing. Handouts cannot be just "handed out."

In a variation of the theme of using visualizations of three-part structure to teach planning and control of writing, we sometimes give students one or more parts of an essay and ask them to supply the other parts. Figure 6.3 illustrates an example from another one of the tasks we used with sixth-graders. In this case, they had already themselves completed the task Aquell is doing, the task shown inside the rectangular box.

In another one of our studies, teacher-researcher Jennifer Calzi reported that an 11th-grade writer I'll call Kelly benefited from strategy instruction focused on "boxes" or rough outlines of the borders of paragraphs similar to the ones we used with Jason (see Chapter 2), as in Figure 6.4. Jennifer described Kelly as not having a mental representation of what a finished academic essay should look like, and she added that Kelly did not plan her writing at all. As Jennifer put it, "You could say that Kelly was writing blindly." After instruction in the boxing strategy, however, Kelly became able to have a picture in her head

Structure in the "Washing the Car" Essay

This sentence ties the essay to the text question

I have many responsibilities, but the one I (enjoy) most is washing the car. Washing the car is a little complicated, but if I do it right, it's not that bad. ⟨First I⟩ get the soapy water ready, ⟨then I⟩ wash each section of the car and rinse it off.

Getting the soapy water ready is easy. I pour two capfuls of the liquid car soap into a two gallon bucket. Then I add warm water to almost the top of the bucket. Then I get a sponge and the hose and I'm ready.

I begin washing the car by putting soapy water on the roof. I rub gently in a circular motion until the whole roof is sudsy. Then I rinse it off. Starting with the highest part of the car is important to keep from rinsing dirty water over clean parts of the car. After the roof is done, I do the hood and the trunk. Then I do the sides of the car and wheels, one side at a time.

I like washing the car because it only takes about a half hour. Also, I don't have to do it every day, only when it's dirty and the weather's nice.

Introduction

Middle Paragraphs

Conclusion

The first sentence of each paragraph is the focus of the paragraph.

FIGURE 6.2. Strategy think sheet combining text and graphics.

for what writing should look like; in Kelly's own words, "the boxes work."

Using visual means to assist writing is something even accomplished writers do, not just struggling ones. Consider this testimony from writer Joan Didion:

> To shift the structure of a sentence alters the meaning of that sentence, as definitely and inflexibly as the position of a camera alters the meaning of the object photographed. Many people know about camera angles now, but not so many know about sentences. The arrangement of the words matters, and the arrangement you want can be found in the picture in your

Directions: Aquell has written the middle paragraph of his treasure map story about what happened to him and his friend James. Help Aquell by writing a beginning paragraph and an ending paragraph to complete his story. Here's the assignment Aquell was following:

> Pretend that you and a friend found a map that showed where a treasure was buried.
> Write a story of about 150 words telling about the adventure you and your friend had trying to find the treasure.*

_____
_____
_____
_____
_____
_____
_____
_____

We followed the map and walked for about three hours through the city down to the river. At the end of Ontario street we asked a friendly old man with a boat to take us to Strawberry Island because that's where the map said to go. He took us there and we followed the map to get to a huge old oak tree. The map said the treasure was buried under the rock next to the tree. We found a long branch that had fallen off the oak tree to move the rock. We forgot to bring shovels, so we used sticks to dig in the sand under the rock. After digging about three feet, we struck something hard. It was a small treasure chest about the size of a football. When we opened the chest, we found it was full of diamonds.

_____
_____
_____
_____
_____
_____
_____
_____

FIGURE 6.3. Three-part structure visualization task.* This topic was originally part of a fifth-grade competency test in writing.

FIGUR 6.4. Graphic representation of paragraph structure for a five-paragraph essay.

mind. The picture dictates the arrangement. The picture dictates whether this will be a sentence with or without clauses, a sentence that ends hard or a dying-fall sentence, long or short, active or passive. The picture tells you how to arrange the words, and the arrangement of the words tells you, or tells me, what's going on in the picture. *Nota bene*:

It tells you.

You don't tell it. (Didion, 1984, p. 7)

By "picture" Didion appears to mean a mental image of the scene or character she is describing and also a picture of the actual sentence she is writing. These two, topic and sentence, are inseparable. The imagined graphic representation of both the topic and the sentence gives the visible, expressed grammar of the sentence. Grammar in this interpretation results from a visual strategy and a strategic mind-set, not from an application of rules. The conventions of language are learned when needed, as language is made to fit the mind's image of the topic and the text. When the fit is most comfortable, language becomes one with the image and we know the fit is right.[6]

This lends credibility to the idea that controlling the writing process is, partly at least, a matter of paying attention to real or imagined graphic patterns. As Kelly reported in the previous example, "the boxing works." It is helpful when preparing a tightly organized arrangement of words that will become a diachronic text, to picture the arrangement as a synchronic image. A picture of a sentence or text is a functional planning device, and like the copying strategy already discussed and narrating strategy I come to next, visualizing can assist writers with content generation and organization.

Narrating

Of the three default strategies I am focusing on in this chapter, narrating is by far the most popular with teachers. In fact, our studies suggest that although copying and visualizing are frequently underused in writing instruction, narrating is sometimes overused. A dominant belief in process-based writing instruction seems to be that if students have trouble with expository writing, we should have them write narratives, especially narratives of personal experience, because narration is developmentally prior to "more advanced" modes of composition such as exposition and persuasion. The trouble with that assumption is that it contributes to a two-tiered system of writing instruction, with the "developmentally advanced" modes of composition reserved for some writers and personal narrative writing for others. Freedman (1987), for example, suggests that students in U.S. schools

---

[6]In our current research we are investigating the learning of grammar and usage in the form of strategic thinking in addition to rules.

receive differential writing instruction because non-college-bound students and inner-city students are not taught academic forms of analysis or exposition, as are their college-bound counterparts, but instead receive instruction focused on personal-experience narratives.

One irony in such two-tiered writing instruction is that it underestimates the value of personal narrative; indeed, it treats narrative writing with disdain (DiPardo, 1990). When narrative writing, especially in the form of telling stories of personal experience, is viewed as the primary form of writing struggling writers are capable of and as the only place to begin the teaching of other, so-called higher-order modes of thinking and writing, then narrative writing is being associated with weakness and inexperience. Such an association, furthermore, possibly has a confusing effect for struggling writers because we ask them to write stories and then ask them to turn their stories into something else. I want to explore that possibility by discussing a sample of student writing produced in response to the simply worded task, "Tell us something that happened to you," by a 10th-grade student I'll call Shawna:

> One night me and my two friends went to the store than we walked up to the store it was about 9:30. When we got to the pool we stay awhile then we went inside the fence. Then I pushed this boy in the water. then he started chasing me trying to throw me in the water. I started screaming, but he didn't throw me in the water. Then I started walking around the pool then I seen one of my friends flo so I pushed her in the water then her and this boy throw me in then he threw flo in she came in right behind me were soak and wet but we still kept going in the water. Then every one started to leave then I got throw back in the water everytime that I would get out somebody would throw me back in the water. So finally I got out so flo wanted to walk with me home then we went walking down the street soak and wet. We went right back to the pool got wet again and then we left. As soon as we got to Eastwood school it started to rain we were glad because we couldn't go home wet. Our sneakers were soak and wet.

Shawna's teacher responded to this piece by asking for more information. He pointed out, for example, that in the first sentence we can't tell which night, which friends, or which store the writer was referring to. By asking that the story be revised in the direction of fully explicit, context-independent prose, he responded to Shawna's story in the same manner in which he would respond to student writing in general. Such a response assumes that narrative writing, at least for school-sponsored purposes, should be as explicit as most other examples of academic writing, and it probably also assumes that revising stories for explicit meaning contributes to the achievement of what Gee (1990) and Farr (1993) call "essayist literacy." Stories, in other words, are really essays. The call for increased explicitness in Shawna's case, however, didn't work. She reluctantly revised her opening, then put the story away in her folder. By attempting to revise for explicit meaning, she lost interest in her story.

I'll take a closer look at Shawna's story in a moment, but first I want to point out that narrating is a default strategy we practice in spoken language long before we take up literacy, and this gives it a special status among our three default strategies. Copying and visualizing are basic ways of thinking and knowing, but they are not as likely as narrating to be influenced by experience within specific cultures because copying during writing processes frequently borrows from published materials and visualizing is mostly free of linguistic variation because it deals with imagery. Not only is narrating a way of thinking and knowing and therefore as "universal" as copying and visualizing, but it is also a way of speaking and therefore relatively more subject to cultural and social variation than copying and visualizing. In other words, some stories can be expanded and elaborated and others should be left in their original form, however abbreviated that may seem. The difference is determined by writers' goals for the stories they produce.

The appropriate response to Shawna's story is to ask her what she wants to accomplish. Patterns of language use such as oral storytelling are not only the bases of default writing strategies but also signs of group membership, indicators of degrees of familiarity and belonging, signs of status and power within and across cultural groups. Language has symbolic value beyond representing thought and word; it also tells who we are and what relation of power or solidarity is at work in a given communication situation (Labov, 1975). To borrow an economic metaphor from Bourdieu (1980), language patterns have cultural capital because they are symbolic of knowledge and status. The conventional patterns of language communities carry culturally significant attributes such as prestige and authority, and like all language conventions, "nonstandard" ones create a consensus within a community as to the significance of the social world. Language symbolizes power and status, and it does so in a manner that is deeply ingrained in cultural values. Conventional patterns in language may be arbitrary in abstract theory, but in the real world, they are culturally determined and serve as one of the major ways discourse communities symbolize power relations and legitimate status.

Given the fact of culturally influenced language systems and her teacher's request for revision in the direction of increased explicitness, the choices for Shawna appear to be three: to revise her story according to the expectations of the dominant language system represented by her teacher's advice; to preserve her story in its original, culturally influenced form; or to put it away. Shawna made the third choice. My point in sharing her decision is probably obvious: These three choices represent a dilemma not only for Shawna but for writing teachers as well. We need to teach struggling writers that communicative meaning matters more than conventional expression, and we need to build on their own default strategies, including culturally influenced linguistic forms such as personal narrative. But we also need to teach struggling writers that controlling conventional patterns of written language is important in a society that makes language standards one of the most significant trappings of social power and prestige.

My position in this dilemma, as I stated in Chapter 1, is that we should have it *both* ways. It is important to realize that genuine balance is needed in the teaching of writing. If we require Shawna to tell us a personal narrative and then tell her that it must be transformed into explicit, essayist writing, we are, in effect, telling her that her story is inadequate. This may amount to another "can't" for students' default writing strategies: "can't tell stories adequately" joins "can't copy" and "can't draw" as sensibilities struggling writers develop out of writing in school. On the other hand, if we don't tell Shawna about the problems in her writing, we are limiting her access to conventional written expression. By neglecting written standards and conventions too much, we may inadvertently reserve the primary benefits of literacy instruction for writers who are already familiar with literate language conventions. How do we strike a balance between teaching writing as communication and teaching it as convention?

In Chapter 5 I used a quote from Ochs (1979) to suggest that language strategies develop more by entailment than by replacement. Later developing language strategies are likely to build on and contain earlier ones, such as when Bereiter and Scardamalia (1987) describe their knowledge-transforming model of writing processes used by expert writers as containing the knowledge-telling model characteristic of novice writers. We noticed that this view of language development as proceeding by entailment rather than replacement offers a key principle for a pedagogy that seeks to connect old and new language strategies, or in the case of narrating, to connect the discourses of home and school: *language strategies are not replaced as development proceeds.* We certainly add to our linguistic resources as we go through life, but this does not mean we give up existing strategies as we acquire or learn new ones. Rather, we retain communicative strategies and go back to them when contexts and other conditions so require or when it suits our communicative purposes to do so. The important implication here is that teachers don't have to discourage the use of "old" strategies or "old" information to make room for new ones. The ongoing, agonized debates over issues such as grammar and usage, dialect variation, and ebonics could be a lot less politically and emotionally charged if we paused long enough to realize that we don't have to ask people to give up current language strategies and beliefs when we ask them to acquire new ones.

Ball (1992, 1994) describes one way of combining old and new strategies in her distinction between additive and subtractive models of language learning. Her research shows that the expository writing of adolescents is influenced by cultural preference, but perhaps her most significant contribution is her argument that teachers can view such culturally based preferences as either an obstacle to or as a resource in literacy learning. Viewing them as an obstacle is part of the subtractive model of language learning which argues that we must teach academic English at the expense of culturally or ethnically influenced language patterns. Ball points out that one reason many African American students decide to resist the use of academic discourse patterns may be their schools' tendency toward a subtractive model of language learning. She argues for an additive model of language learning, one that encourages teachers to develop language skills by adding to the linguistic the practices, text patterns, and communicative strategies students bring to the classroom. The list of culturally influenced writing strategies she found in her study include many that reflect possible workings of narrating:

1. Establishing a link or sense of rapport with the audience through the use of inclusive lexical terms like "we're"
2. Taking on a quality of performance in the style and delivery of the text
3. Using orally based organization patterns like narrative interspersion and circumlocution
4. Using interactive dialogue with the audience with phrases like "you know what I mean, man"
5. Linking topics through the use of personal anecdotes (Ball, 1994, p. 14)

We can further clarify the distinction between additive and subtractive models of language learning by returning to Shawna's response to the task, "Tell us something that happened to you":

One night me and my two friends went to the store than	1
we walked up to the store it was about 9:30. When	2
we got to the pool we stay awhile then we went inside	3
the fence. Then I pushed this boy in the water. then	4
he started chasing me trying to throw me in the water.	5
I started screaming, but he didn't throw me in the water.	6
Then I started walking around the pool then I seen one of	7
my friends flo so I pushed her in the water then her and	8
this boy throw me in then he threw flo in she came in right	9
behind me were soak and wet but we still kept going in the	10
water. Then every one started to leave then I got throw	11

back in the water everytime that I would get out somebody 12
would throw me back in the water. So finally I got out 13
so flo wanted to walk with me home then we went 14
walking down the street soak and wet. We went right back 15
to the pool got wet again and then we left. As soon as we 16
got to Eastwood school it started to rain we were glad 17
because we couldn't go home wet. Our sneakers were 18
soak and wet. 19

Shawna's story seems to be filled with problems stemming from an overreliance on the influence of spoken language, problems such as inexplicit meaning, vague pronoun references and sound-based syntax, and misspellings. In accordance with process teaching, Shawna's teacher postponed attention to spelling and mechanics and conferred with the writer about the need to make the content of the writing more explicit. As I said earlier, the teacher pointed out that the first sentence does not identify which night, which friends, or which store, a writing-conference move that seems justified because these words refer to people and to a time and place outside of the story itself. The words "night," "friends," and "store" are abbreviations for potentially fuller meanings. In the same vein, we don't know whether the character named *flo* (lines 9 and 14) is one of the original friends referred to in the opening sentence. Similarly, the phrase "this boy" (lines 4 and 9) points away from the text, and it is not possible to determine whether the same boy is meant in those two references or to which real person the phrase refers. The writing is context-dependent, and seemingly hopelessly so, because the writer appears reluctant or unable to provide access to the contexts of information necessary for the reader to fill out the story.

There is a long tradition, of course, of teachers telling writers to be specific, to identify characters, describe settings, and add details of events and sequence. In the case of nonnarrative writing, we tell writers to support generalizations with evidence, clarify main points with details, illustrate ideas with examples, and connect ideas with discernible patterns of logic. These traditional points of writing instruction certainly have merit, but this doesn't mean we need to bring them up every time we respond to student writing.

Take explicitness as an example. In secondary schools and

colleges, most writing assignments and test questions carry the expectation that students will respond in as much detail as possible, and because writing is often used as a means of examining students (Britton et al., 1975; Applebee, 1981), admonitions to be explicit seem to be always appropriate. Much theory and research, furthermore, support the focus on explicit content. Explicitness is recognized as a chief characteristic of written language (Vygotsky, 1934/1988, 1978), as a primary difference between spoken and written language (Collins, 1981; Collins & Williamson, 1981, 1984; Goody & Watt, 1972; Olson, 1977; Ong, 1979), and as a major component of writing development (Graves, 1975; Elsasser, & John-Steiner, 1977; Shaughnessy, 1977; Flower, 1979; Bereiter, 1980; Olson & Torrance, 1981; Bereiter & Scardamalia, 1982). The traditional call for revision in the direction of explicit content, however, could be inappropriate in the case of Shawna's personal narrative. Tannen (1985, 1986) suggests another reason why writing can resemble spoken language, and in Table 6.1 I describe her explanation by comparing it to the traditional one I just presented. The traditional approach is based on differences between talk and writing, and therefore I call it the "oral–literate hypothesis." The second is based on different degrees of interpersonal involvement in conversational styles, so I call it the "interpersonal involvement hypothesis."

TABLE 6.1. Comparison of Hypotheses on Speaking–Writing Relations

Oral–literate hypothesis	Interpersonal involvement hypothesis (Tannen)
Based on differences between talking and writing, especially differences between everyday conversation and formal expository prose.	Argues that spontaneous conversation and expository prose are by no means exclusive. Talk can be message-focused, as in a lecture, and writing can be relationship-focused, as in note passing in school.
Describes context dependence as a main feature of spoken dialogue and context independence as a main feature of written monologue.	Describes oral strategies as showing a relatively high focus on interpersonal involvement and literate strategies as showing a relatively low focus on interpersonal involvement resulting in more focus on the information conveyed.

The oral–literate hypothesis attributes the need for greater explicitness in writing to the fact that writing needs to be relatively autonomous and monological, owing to the absence of an interlocutor (as in Olson, 1977). Similarly, the interpersonal involvement hypothesis distinguishes between one-way and two-way communication which it sees as closely related to relative focus on information and involvement. The interpersonal involvement hypothesis, however, breaks with tradition in writing instruction because it suggests that teachers of writing should not assume that all writing that is "underdeveloped" (according to the oral–literate hypothesis) needs to be revised in the direction of greater explicitness because such writing might also be understood as serving an interpersonal involvement function, and in that case the writing deserves to remain relatively inexplicit. If Shawna is interested in writing down her story primarily to share the excitement, delight, and camaraderie evident in a minor series of events, the use of an interpersonal oral style is appropriate. Before recommending changes, in other words, it would be appropriate to ask Shawna to talk about her objectives for the piece and her perceived success with achieving them. Simply changing the story so that it begins more conventionally or academically—say, in accordance with a teacher's recommendation to say something like, "Last Tuesday night, Elaine, Flo, and I walked up to Smith's Variety Store at about 9:30 at night. On the way to the store we came to the pool and decided to stay a while"—might make it so formal and cumbersome as to detract from the writer's possible purpose, for example, of sharing her delight with her readers. It would also *subtract* Shawna's way of shaping her meaning and *replace* it with the teacher's way. And it would play a double trick on Shawna, first by asking her to relate an incident from personal experience, which she does by using the default form of narrating she knows best, and then by telling her that the story and its culturally inspired form are inadequate, which is what the teacher did by asking for more information without inquiring as to her purpose for the piece.

Re-presenting the original version of the story to show its resemblance to one presented in Gee (1990, pp. 119–120) suggests that form, not content, is Shawna's primary means for conveying her intended meaning in this piece (see Figure 6.5).

By thus following Gee's (1990) method of presenting the

	The cake story (Gee, 1990)	The pool story (Shawna)
Frame:		
Stanza 1		
1	Today	One night
2	it's Friday the 13th	me and my two friends went to the store
3	an' it's bad luck day	than we walked up to the store it was about 9:30
4	an' my grandmother's birthday is on bad luck day	when we got to the pool we stay awhile
Section 1:	**Making cakes**	**Going in the water**
Stanza 2		
5	an' my mother's bakin a cake	then we went inside the fence
6	an' I went up my grandmother's house while my mother's bakin' a cake	then I pushed this boy in the water
7	an' my mother was bakin' a cheese cake	then he started chasing me trying to throw me in the water
8	my grandmother was bakin a whipped cream cup cakes	I started screaming but he didn't throw me in the water
Stanza 3		
9	an' we bof went over my mother's house	then I started walking around the pool
10	an' then my grandmother had made a chocolate cake	then I seen one of my friends flo so I pushed her in the water
11	an then we went over my aunt's house	then her and this boy throw me in
12	an' she had made a cake	
Stanza 4		
13	an' everybody had made a cake for nana	then he threw Flo in she came in right behind me
14	so we came out with six cakes	were soak and wet but we still kept going in the water
Section 2:	**Grandmother eats cakes**	**Going home**
Stanza 5		
15	last night	then every one started to leave
16	my grandmother snuck out	then I got throw back in the water
17	an' she ate all the cake	everytime that I would get out somebody would throw me back in the water
18	an' we hadda make more	so finally I got out
Stanza 6		
19	an' we was sleepin'	so Flo wanted to walk with me home
20	an' she went in the room	then we went walking down the street soak and wet
21	an' gobbled em up	we went right back to the pool got wet again

(continued)

22	an' we had to bake a whole bunch more	and then we left
Stanza 7		
23	she said mmmm	as soon as we got to Eastwood school
24	she had all chocolate on her face, cream, strawberries	it started to rain
25	she said mmmm	we were glad because we couldn't go home wet
26	that was good	our sneakers were soak and wet

FIGURE 6.5. Comparison of the cake and pool stories.

story in a form that shows a frame, sections, and stanzas, we highlight the similarities between the cake and pool stories. Both stories were produced in school settings, but the cake story was spoken by a child in kindergarten on the West Coast, and the pool story was written by a student in 10th grade on the East Coast. These facts make it more than a little surprising that the only major difference between the two, other than subject matter, is that the cake story was 20 lines longer in its original version. That two stories produced a generation and a continent apart show such remarkable consistency of form suggests that the use of an interpersonal oral style in the pool story is not an accident or an error; rather, it probably derives from a reliance on a culturally regularized form which communicates strong delight through poetic repetition of events in a story. Its use by Shawna is not to be taken lightly and responded to automatically with advice for revision that *subtracts* from her attempt to express meaning in a form of her choice. From this perspective, it would be inappropriate to assume that Shawna has made a mistake by not translating from speech; instead, we should respect her achievement in capturing an oral style in writing and reserve for her the right to make any strategic decisions about the narrative form and content. We should ask her what she is trying to accomplish with the piece, and if she describes (in her own words of course) a goal of sharing a story by writing it down with an oral style, or a goal of conveying emotional or expressive meaning by sharing excitement, exaggeration, and repetition of ordinary events as if she were talking with a friend, we should help her do that instead of insisting on a conversion of the story to explicit, formal, essayist English. We can still work on some matters of standard written English, such as punctuation, capitalization, and spelling, but we can do this while we preserve the conversational format of the piece, if that is what the author is aiming for. This approach is completely consistent with the writing task ("Tell us something that happened to you") and has the advantage of using the additive approach to language learning because it respects the strategies Shawna is already using and because it adds considerations of mechanics and spelling to the writer's own sense of control over purpose and form.

In an article describing the evolution of collaborative strategy instruction with small groups of severely reading-delayed adolescents (ages 12–16), Anderson and Roit (1993) discuss the importance of respecting students' existing strategic knowledge:

> Approaches to strategy instruction have not been designed in ways that allow teachers to capitalize on adolescents' existing strategic competencies. Strategy instruction typically involves the passing on to students of one or more prescribed, experimenter-determined strategies, with little regard for whether learners have existing strategic knowledge. Adolescents, especially, cannot be viewed as strategic tabulae rasae. . . . (p. 126)

Even when narrative writing does function as a precursor to exposition, as in Jason's telling of his encounter with the Langston Hughes story in Chapter 2 and in my telling of my encounter with the Walter Loban book in Chapter 5, we should ask writers to clarify their purposes before advising them how to use writing in a narrative mode to serve an expository purpose. If a writer is using narrating to tell the story of a first encounter with difficult new ideas, as both Jason and I were doing, it is appropriate to look for ways to transform the narrative draft by revising it in the direction of exposition. It may also be appropriate to teach the writer how to use narrative writing, and perhaps other spoken-language-based forms of language such as everyday dialogue, in expository pieces. In the next chapter I present an example of a strategy for teaching a writer to make good use of an obvious strength with narrative writing by interspersing narration with exposition (much as I did in this book). In fact, using narrative forms within expository writing to clarify, illustrate, and exemplify one's meaning may be the most important "new" use of the narrative default strategy we can teach struggling writers. It is not the narrative form itself (which is a default strategy) that needs to be taught but, rather, the uses of narrative forms in creating, clarifying, and communicating meaning. This is where metacognitive control of writing processes is achieved.

Summary

In the case of narrating, the third of our three default strategies, cultural continuity between home and school is important because narration is often close to the oral language students use outside school. The more general point to be made in closing this chapter, however, is that in teaching "new" writing strategies, we should keep in mind the "old" strategies students bring to the classroom. The best way to do this is to keep in mind our overall purpose in strategy-based writing instruction, which is to help struggling writers to learn to manage their own writing. Strategic writing instruction teaches students to select from their own strategies and from new ones we suggest, always with an eye toward monitoring and managing their own writing. Default strategies are sometimes discouraged by teachers, as if copying is always cheating, drawing is always wasting time, telling the story of one's reading is always responding inadequately to it, and telling narratives of personal experience is something only beginning writers do. The ubiquity and usefulness of the three strategies, and the sheer power of borrowing and imagining and storytelling for sustaining creativity and expression and metacognitive control over writing, argue otherwise. Teaching new strategies by combining them with old ones is clearly sound advice, and it is consistent with what I said in Chapter 1 about the connection between classroom culture and identity and in Chapter 2 about achieving control over writing through declarative, procedural, and conditional knowledge. It is also consistent with helping writers to select goals and strategies that allow them to manage topics, genres, and levels of formality. Finally, it is consistent with the pedagogical stance in strategic writing instruction of co-constructing writing strategies with students and allowing a gradual transfer of responsibility for writing from teachers to students through personally and socially meaningful, goal-directed, strategic writing activities.

Chapter Seven

Adapting Strategic Writing Instruction to Particular Contexts

Whenever I talk with teachers about case studies from our research, they ask me how we know exactly which strategies to teach. In the case of Jason in Chapter 2, for example, I've been asked how we knew Jason would benefit from learning an organizing strategy consisting of drawing nested boxes for paragraphs and lines for topic sentences. My answer is that we didn't know that. *Jason taught us* about his ability to learn textual patterns by manipulating boxes and lines. What we did know, from studying his written products and observing his writing processes, was that Jason could use some help planning and organizing his writing. We tried a visual method of providing that help because our work with struggling writers had begun to suggest that visual means of representing text structures can be a useful alternative to the more commonly taught textual means, such as the standard textbook advice on paragraphs and topic sentences. The particular visual means of representing text structure, the boxes and lines, were co-constructed with Jason as we worked with him.

In our studies of struggling writers we have sufficient data to say that text-based writing instruction generally does not seem to help as much as instruction based in one or more of the three default strategies: copying, visualizing, and narrating. The logic for why that is the case seems fairly straightforward: Struggling writers may use various forms of these default strategies when faced with difficult writing tasks precisely because text-based rules and guidelines haven't worked for them. Text-based advice may not be remembered easily enough, or understood sufficiently or flexibly enough, to be immediately useful at points of need during their writing processes. Verbal explanations of a process tend to make much more sense *after* we have achieved some degree of expertise with performing the process; that, after all, is where all the standard textbook advice comes from.

I want to quickly add, however, that I am not recommending that we jump directly from our case studies to teaching all struggling writers to draw nested boxes for paragraphs and lines for topic sentences. I advocate instead, as I hope is abundantly clear by now, a much more collaborative process, a sociocognitive framework in which students and teachers build writing strategies together by co-constructing them as teachers work with individuals, groups, or whole classes. Copying, visualizing, and narrating are good places to begin looking for strategies to build on because students may already be using them as defaults to grapple with difficulties in writing. From there, the work of creating and implementing writing strategies happens at the intersection of instruction and learning. That's where co-construction takes place.

Strategic writing instruction is a creative business. Strategies are invented and adapted, and thus constructed, as teachers and writers work together. The instructional process initially should have a double focus: Teachers pay attention to both the difficulties struggling writers are experiencing during their writing processes and the expressive and communicative goals latent in their efforts. This double focus on difficulties and goals is what allows teachers to identify strategies struggling writers are using and to suggest new strategies for them to try. This is what permits us to combine "new" strategies with "old" ones, as I discussed in Chapter 6. In this chapter I present several examples of teachers adapting strategies to particular contexts, but first I want to make it clear that my intention is not to prescribe certain writing strategies to treat certain writing struggles. Rather, I hope the examples I selected will be read as a range of possibilities for co-constructing and customizing strategies with individual students, small groups, and whole classes.

Sometimes in the strategies literature and in content-area textbooks selected strategies are recommended in a seemingly prescriptive way. We are left thinking, for example, that any student who has problems of a certain kind will benefit from certain strategies, as if we need only discover some deep-structural one-to-one correspondence between struggles and strategies to make strategy instruction effective. Problems with reading comprehension? Teach a reading comprehension strategy such as SQ3R (for *Survey* the material to ask *Questions* based on subheadings, then *Read* to answer the questions, *Recite* the answers, and *Review* the answers). The trouble is, there is no magic in SQ3R. Students have to learn what it is and when and how to use it (declarative, procedural, and conditional knowledge) in connection with establishing and achieving goals, such as studying to prepare for a social studies test, and they have to practice the strategy repeatedly to learn to use it to monitor their reading (Caverly & Orlando, 1991). All of which is to say that students have to construct the strategy for themselves. The best we can do is to assist them in the construction process, by suggesting a strategy, modeling its use, and assisting with acquisition and learning and repeated practice.

If there is any "magic" involved in strategies-based writing instruction, it resides in the co-construction of strategies entailed in the four-step instructional process:

1. Identifying a strategy worth teaching.
2. Introducing the strategy by modeling it.
3. Helping students to try the strategy out with workshop-style teacher guidance.
4. Helping students work toward independent mastery of the strategy through repeated practice and reinforcement.

Without these four steps, a strategy is only an activity, something to be engaged in temporarily by students when the teacher requires it. For a strategy to function as a genuine metacognitive control over literacy processes the strategy must be constructed over time with diminishing amounts of teacher assistance and increasing amounts of student self-control. The strategy must also be retained so that it is accessible when students pause to consider their difficulties and what to do about them, as in Brandon's list of writing strategies in Chapter 4. This means that writing strategies must be understood and constructed by students in their own terms.

Making the Most of Modeling

Laurie L. Damba tried strategic writing instruction in a ninth-grade self-contained special education classroom where she teaches all four major academic subjects: global studies, general math, applied biology, and English. Her work with Samantha, a 15-year-old student classified as learning disabled, illustrates how Laurie adapted the approach. Samantha's area of greatest need, like most of Laurie's students, is in the area of written language. She has poor receptive and expressive vocabulary skills, and reading and text comprehension are extremely difficult for her. One of her test modifications is for all graded work to be read out loud to her. She has difficulty managing her time and often refuses to start homework in class, saying that she will do it at home, which she never does.

Laurie teaches writing by presenting writing assignments to her whole class and then by working with individual writers in a workshop environment. As she talks with individuals and reads their first responses to each task, Laurie concentrates on identifying the difficulties they are having. In doing this work she noticed that her students tend to become more open about discussing their writing problems as time goes on, and she attributes this to the privacy of her conferences with them, which she figures cuts down on the stigma and embarrassment involved in discussing writing difficulties. For each piece with each writer, Laurie focuses on one major difficulty and introduces a strategy to aid in overcoming the difficulty.

In the example I'm focusing on, Laurie and Samantha worked through the strategy together, with Laurie first modeling its use and Samantha following her model. After using the strategy, Laurie and Samantha always discussed how effective it was and why. They then planned how to use the strategy in subsequent assignments. Laurie was after conditional knowledge and metacognitive control of writing strategies in these discussions:

"I wanted each student to have more then one way to use a particular strategy and also more than one way to address a particular problem. Providing this allowed for greater student choice in deciding which form of which strategy to use when problems arose."[1]

Laurie began her diagnosis of her students' writing difficulties by asking them to list all the characteristics of a good essay they could think of. Their responses indicated a strong concern for problems with writing mechanics, especially spelling, capital letters, periods, essay length, and handwriting. These were the items her students worried about while writing, and Laurie knew she had to work on them, but she also noticed that few of her students suggested characteristics that had anything to do with planning, content, or structure. Laurie decided to work with her writers first in the general area of thinking processes writers use before, during, and after writing, and while doing that she discovered that for Samantha, and for many other students, the copying strategy helps with both thinking and mechanics.

Laurie began her work on writing strategies with a task she called "A Person I Admire": She asked her students to write to tell the class why they admire a person of their choice. She shared a model of an essay she wrote about her mother's admirable qualities. She gave each student a copy of the essay and reenacted the writing of it for them, modeling her thinking about purpose, audience, content, and structure while they took any notes they wanted. She then asked them each to choose three people they might write about, and she discussed with individual students how to select one or two to actually write about by thinking of admirable qualities and listing them as a prewriting exercise.

Samantha chose to write about her grandmother. Her pre-

[1]This quotation and other details of this example are from a case study of Laurie's classroom, which she wrote as part of our research on strategic writing instruction.

writing list shows a knowledge-telling or stream-of-consciousness quality, as in this excerpt:

```
    My grandparent have alot of money
They are really nice
They treat people with respect
They laugh alot
My grandma pretty
I get my look and hair color from her
My grandma is fun and talented is a good cook
She's in to craft and stuff like that
My grandpa into sports like football
```

Laurie asked Samantha to think about those things that made her grandparents good people: "What makes you look up to them? When other people meet them, what about them is likable?" With this guidance Samantha edited her prewriting, not by adding ideas but by deleting some which she decided were not appropriate for the task. Samantha then wrote about her grandmother. Laurie told her students to refer for help to her model essay, and she noticed that in its overall structure and in some details in the opening and closing paragraphs Samantha's draft was similar to the model. This modeling is apparent if we juxtapose the two pieces, as in Table 7.1.

In working on this draft, Laurie first conferred with Samantha to encourage her to say more, which led to modest additions to Samantha's third and fourth paragraphs in the second draft of the piece. Laurie next decided that Samantha was using two default strategies. Samantha used a narrative form to frame her essay by beginning both her introduction and conclusion with narrative statements: "I am wrighting about my grandma," to signal the beginning of the piece, and "I wrote about my Grandma," to signal the end. Laurie thought about building on Samantha's comfort with narration by asking for an example or two in story form, similar to what she did in her own piece (e.g., "When my mother and father got divorced about five years ago, my mother had to work to support herself"). Laurie also took Samantha's apparent dependence on the model essay as a positive sign, an indication that a copying strategy would be a good way for Samantha to learn more about editing her essay for improvements in sentences and wording. This is what Laurie

TABLE 7.1. Juxtaposition of Teacher Model and Student Essay

Laurie's model	Samantha's essay
There are many people in my life who have admirable qualities, but if I were to choose the one I admire most, it would have to be my mother. She has overcome many obstacles in the past few years and has never given up. She is brave, honest and extremely giving. I can only hope to be as wonderful and accomplished as my mother is when I am her age.	I am wrighting about my grandma. She has alot of good quality. She have over come things in the last cuple of years. I hope to be like her. She is nice, respectful, laughful and talented.
When my mother and father got divorced about five years ago, my mother had to work to support herself. She had been a full time mother and had not worked since she was 16 years old. She first got her GED and then started college. It was difficult for her to support herself while in college, but she never stopped plugging along. She was very brave to do the things that she had never done at her age. She never gave up or stopped believing in herself.	My grandma is nice and reaspectful. I think that because, she is nice to other people. She is really reaspectful because she Respect what people say and do even if its a little wrong.
The honesty that my mother displays is one of her best qualities. You never have to wonder if she is happy, proud or upset because she will be open and honest about her feelings. It's nice to know that I don't have to guess at how she is feeling or what she is thinking. Also, she is very honest at her job. My mother believes that they pay her to do her job so she always gives her best. Many times others will only do as much as is expected; however, my mom puts in more than enough to get the job done and get it done right. She is a strong believer that honesty is the best policy.	My grandma is laughful. She laughs at everything. She funny and she also makes people laugh. She loves making little kids laugh.
When I think of my mother, the first thing that comes to mind is all that she has done for me. She will always give before taking anything for herself. When I had my first apartment, my mom used to buy me food and give me things that I needed all of the time. She is also very giving of herself and her time. When I am sick, she would drive 1000 miles if she had to, to bring me some soup or to take care of me. She is always there to listen to me when I need to talk. My mother would give me anything that she thought I needed without a single thought. I find this a very admirable quality.	My grandma is talented. She loves cooking. She also loves crafes and other thing. She loves everything. She loves playing with people hairs.
My mother is like a solid rock in my life, and I know that many others feel the same way about her. Her admirable qualities are shared with everyone. All of these qualities add up to a make her a wonderful person and an excellent mother. I am lucky to have had her love and influence all of my life. I am proud to call her my mom!	I wrote about my Grandma. She has a lot of qualities in life. Shes good at everything almost. Some day I hope to be like her.

decided to work on. It was a judgment call; Laurie simply went with her sense that Samantha would benefit more from an editing strategy than from a content-generating strategy at this point. Remember, as I stated in Chapter 6, that writers' problems and challenges are of three general, overlapping types: generating content, structuring texts, and using conventions of the written language system. Part of the teacher's work is to decide which problems to work on with writers and to resist following rigid guidelines to do so (e.g., first work on content and save editing for later). The trouble with such guidelines is that later never comes for many struggling writers. A flexible approach will lead to greater success. Laurie "read" her work with Samantha appropriately; she tried a content-generating tactic when she encouraged Samantha to say more, and when that led only to modest gains, Laurie switched to editing rather than push harder for more content.

To show Samantha what her own essay would sound and look like without any structural or mechanical errors, Laurie rewrote Samantha's essay while talking with her about the content. Laurie then had Samantha copy this revision over in her own handwriting. Here's the result:

> I am writing this essay about my grandma. She has many great qualities that I admire. My grandma has overcome many obstacles in her life over the past couple of years. Someday, when I am older, I hope to be just like her. A few of the admirable qualities my grandma has is that she is nice to everyone, she is respectful of others, she has a great sense of humor and loves to laugh, and finally, she is talented in many ways.
>
> My grandma is both nice and reaspectful to others. The reason I think this is because I always see her treating other people well. She is also respectful because when others are talking, she will respect what they say, even if she does not agree with their ideas or thoughts.
>
> My grandmother has a great sense of humor and is always laughing. She will laugh at just about anything. She especially enjoys little children and making them laugh.

> Another quality that my grandma has is that she is talented in more than one way. Everyone enjoys my grandmother's cooking. Working on crafts is another talent that my grandmother has. She is good at and loves to do so many things. She even loves to play with people's hair.
>
> I admire my grandma for the many qualities that she has. Not only is she a pleasant person to be around, but she is good at almost everything. Many people enjoy my grandmother's company and benefit from her many talents. Someday in the future, I hope to be just like my grandma.

Laurie and Samantha next talked about the differences between Samantha's second draft and the latest revision. Samantha seemed to understand most of the changes Laurie had made, especially the verb tense changes, and she said that she wanted to model more of her sentences after Laurie's in future assignments. Laurie believes this modeling amounts to a way of combining learning by acquisition with learning by deliberate imitation. She claims that the modeling definitely led to improvements in Laura's sentences and lexical choices, and this seems like an accurate assessment if you compare "My grandma is laughful. She laughs at everything" in the initial draft to "My grandmother has a great sense of humor and is always laughing" in the final draft. Almost certainly this outcome would have been much more difficult to accomplish through textbook or workbook lessons on building more complex and mature sentences and vocabulary.

How do we know modeling in this case was not just a mindless act of imitation? Later in the year Laurie gave her students a persuasive task like the one they will have to complete on a statewide writing exam at the end of the year. This was the task:

"The situation: The principal of your school has asked you to suggest one way school life could be improved. She is interested in making some improvements in the school and would like to get some input from the students before deciding what those improvements should be. Keep in mind that the purpose of your composition is to persuade the principal to accept your suggestion.

"Your task: Write a composition of about 200 words persuading the principal to accept your one suggestion. Give at least two reasons why you believe this suggestion will improve school life. Explain each reason."

Laurie claims that Samantha's first draft written in response to this task showed the effects of learning to write fuller sentences and to choose words that carry clear meanings. Her sentences were substantial in the persuasive piece, and none of her words were made up (like "laughful" in the grandmother essay) or vague (like "other thing" and "everything" in the grandmother essay). Laurie adds that Samantha also continued to use the copying strategy, but this time she borrowed ideas and words from the assignment page rather than from a teacher-supplied model. Laurie sees this as a positive development because when Samantha takes her examination, she will have the task in front of her but will not have a model from which to copy content and structure. Samantha's learning to transfer her copying strategy to a new source is an example of a writer co-constructing a strategy by applying it in a novel and flexible way, just as Laurie had hoped. It is also a sign of progress toward success with the end-of-the-year exam. Laurie adds further that the evidence suggests we don't have to worry about Samantha's becoming too dependent on copying. This assignment was the first time since the grandmother essay that Samantha wrote an entire piece without having a model to copy from right in front of her, and still the essay is well structured across paragraphs and its sentences are well formed. Ironically, copying apparently helped Samantha outgrow the need to copy.

Samantha's draft of the persuasive piece was not without problems, however, and this led Laurie to look for a new strategy to share with her. Laurie noticed that Samantha's draft gave two reasons and explained them, as the assignment requested, but also repeated part of the explanation from the first reason in the second:

> I have many resones why I think this school needs to change. The one I choose is about

having more passing time it could improve our
school. I would like to suggest two resons why
i think that longer passing time would improve
our school.
    I think that we should have longer passing
time So we are not talking in our classes. When
we talk in our classes we interup the teacher.
We also get detension for being inconsidert to
other people.
    My other reson that I think we should have
more passing time is so that we are not late
to our classes. When we are late we get in
troble. Also if the time was longer we could
talk then. Then we wouldent have to go into our
classes and talk cause we would of talk in the
time we had for passing.
    The reson I choose that we should have more
passing time is so we're not late. And I think
that would improve our school. And so were not
interupting the teacher by talking.

In her explanation of her second reason, Samantha uses
information from the first; she mixes being late with being able to
talk. Laurie talked with her about this, and together they came up
with a "paragraph clubs" visual organizer to help Samantha look
globally at her writing. "Paragraph clubs" became a way for Samantha to look at how her ideas go together and to think of new ideas
which may join each "club." Figure 7.1 shows an example.

Using the paragraph clubs strategy, Laurie and Samantha
talked about how each supporting statement goes with a topic
sentence. By moving sentences from the second club to the first,
Samantha realized that she needed more information. Laurie
reports that Samantha "suddenly discovered that, amidst the
ideas on the organizer, there were the makings of two different
topic sentences to support her suggestion of more passing time.
These two topic sentences, [Samantha] said, would be easier to
explain and would make her paper more clear and persuasive."
This is an excellent example of co-construction at work. A
student writer, in this case a special education student with
serious writing difficulties, is taking over the construction of a
strategy to guide her writing process. Laurie and Samantha
quickly designed a second paragraph clubs organizer, as in
Figure 7.2.

Topic sentence: I think we should have longer passing time so we are not talking in our classes.

—interrupt teacher
—get detention
—talk in halls, not in classes

Additional ideas
—students usually on time and deserve more passing
 time

Topic sentence: I think we should have longer passing time so we are not late to our classes.

—get in trouble
—longer time wouldn't be late

Additional ideas
—need more time to go to the bathroom and to locker
 to get books together

FIGURE 7.1. The "paragraph clubs" organizer.

Samantha then wrote her final draft in accordance with the global planning she accomplished through the paragraph clubs strategy. Here is Laurie's evaluation of this draft:

> "Samantha's final draft of this piece shows some real strengths. Her paragraphs are cohesive. The introduction is appropriate and the conclusion, although brief, gets the point across and contains all the essential components. The length of the essay is just over the required 200 words. We also continue to see the increased sentence length and complexity. It appears as if the Paragraph Clubs organizer has helped Samantha to not only keep her paragraphs on topic, but to generate content as well."

Laurie adds that Samantha and her other students indicated their satisfaction with strategy co-construction and use. They are pleased with their progress and their confidence about writing has gone up. Laurie also believes that the focused one-on-one conferences which result in strategic control over written lan-

Topic sentence: I think we should have more passing
time because students deserve it.

> —show responsibility
> —respect teachers
> —go to class on time
> *spend lots more in class and deserve more time
> in halls to talk

Topic sentence: I think we should have more passing
time because it would cut down on misbehavior.

> —would give students longer time so they are not
> late. Kids get detention when they are late. They
> might get mad and refuse to go.
> —longer passing time would make kids happier
> because they would have more time to talk. When
> they come class they would do their work.

FIGURE 7.2. Revised "paragraph clubs" organizer.

guage allow her students to see that she cares about their
progress, and this in turn has positive effects on their behavior
and motivation.

Strategies for Writing Mechanics

Paul G. Lasch tried strategic writing instruction with students in
his 10th-grade English classes. Stephen, one of the students, has
marked difficulties with the mechanics of writing. His handwriting is nearly illegible, and it is especially difficult to distinguish
his lower- and upper-case letters. When Paul asked Stephen what
he thought his most serious difficulties with writing were,
Stephen identified spelling, paragraphing, and knowing when to
use periods and commas: "I don't know where to put them. I
just guess."[2]

The result of guessing where to put punctuation marks is
apparent in this two-paragraph excerpt from one of Stephen's

---

[2]This quotation and other details of this example are from a case study of Paul's
classroom which he wrote as part of our research on strategic writing instruction.

papers, an essay on playing chess written in response to an assignment to write to share with classmates a description of a process he was good at:

> The left flank moves in, The right front
> retreats, The center comes in, closing the trap.
> is this a battle plan? Right. but the name of
> this war is chess, SOUND interesting?
> Chess is a game of stratigy, planing, and
> inteligance. if you are a beginner to the game
> basic moves must first be learned, Let's start
> with pawns, Pawns are relatively simple movers:
> they only, go straight ahead and attack diago-
> nally, and if you want to get fancy about it,
> pawns can also attack to the side, this is known
> as impassing and can only be done once, like
> being able to go two spaces from their starting
> square.

Contrary to one of the basic tenets of process instruction, our belief is that work on writing mechanics should not always be put off until the end of the writing process. Paul and Stephen were both aware that mechanics were a particularly difficult challenge for Stephen, and they both knew that until Stephen improved his mechanics, his writing would be viewed as deficient because readers would have a hard time focusing on his meaning. Accordingly, Paul worked with Stephen on writing mechanics, and he started that work with punctuation, because it is Stephen's most obvious weakness. In response to this assignment, Paul worked with Stephen by having him copy a corrected version of the essay. The same two paragraphs in the corrected version looked like this:

> The left flank moves in. The right front
> retreats. The center comes in closing the trap.
> Is this a battle plan? Right, but the name of
> this war is "chess." Sound interesting?
> Chess is a game of strategy, planning, and
> intelligence. If you are a beginner to the game
> basic moves must first be learned. Let's start
> with pawns. Pawns are relatively simple movers:
> they only go straight ahead and attack diago-
> nally. If you want to get fancy about it, pawns
> can also attack to the side. This is known as

"impassing" and can only be done once, like being able to go two spaces from their starting square.

Paul gave Stephen the corrected version of his chess essay and asked him to copy it carefully and exactly. Paul's intention was to see what Stephen could pick up by imitation and acquisition by copying a version of his own writing with punctuation and spelling corrected. Paul thought Stephen understood how to copy the corrected draft, but the next day Stephen did not have the copied version with him. He hadn't done the work, he said, because he could see no differences between the corrected draft and his own original. Paul placed the two versions side by side and pointed out that where one had a comma, the other had a period. Stephen replied, "Oh, that doesn't matter. The ideas are what are important."

As they talked, Paul realized that Stephen did not see a difference in the two versions because the ideas were the same. Punctuation really was a matter of guessing for him. Paul explained to Stephen that punctuation is a set of arbitrary rules everyone is expected to follow in work and at school, and that these rules were created to make it easier for people to understand each other. Like it or not, we have to try to follow fixed conventions in formal writing. A breakthrough came when they talked about the reading Stephen was doing outside class. Stephen mentioned that the sentence structure he does know about he learned from reading and copying his favorite books. He would read a Stephen King story, for example, and try to write one just like it.[3] Paul pointed out that the copying strategy was the same in this exercise as in his work with Stephen King, and Stephen agreed to give it a try.

Stephen's copied draft showed that even when he copied Paul's corrected version, commas and periods were still a problem. In the first paragraph he left out the period after the introductory

---

[3]Interestingly, Stephen King reports using the same strategy: "The earliest writing I can remember doing was when I was stuck in bed with the flu and stared copying Tom Swift books into a tablet, changing the stories as I went along. Once you get a taste of that kind of power, you're lost forever" (Wells, 1989).

phrase, "Right but the name of the game is 'chess.' " Similarly, in the second paragraph he used a comma where the corrected draft used a period: "Lets start with pawns, pawns are relatively simple movers." Still, the copying strategy fixed many of Stephen's punctuation errors. As a bonus, his spelling errors were also repaired with this strategy. The real success, however, with using the copying strategy to call Stephen's attention to writing mechanics showed up during the next assignment, a task requiring the writing of a formal business letter to apply for a job.

For this second task, students had to research a career in the career center and then write a formal business letter to apply for a job in their chosen fields. Because they were planning for careers they would likely be applying for in the future, they were to imagine they already had the necessary credentials, and they could make up the experience they had in their letters. In class Paul reviewed the business letter format and discussed a beginning, middle, and end planning strategy for the parts of the letter of application: "Mention the job you are interested in, outline the qualifications and experience you have that make you right for that job, ask for an interview." They decided that this planning strategy could be easily broken up into three paragraphs in a letter of no longer than one page. Paul modeled the planning and organization by showing them his own letter of application he had sent to get his teaching job. This is the body of the first draft of Stephen's letter:

> Ever since I first discovered, and put together the skeleton of a miniature horse, I have wanted to learn about the past. Because of my excellent abilitys in palentalogy at harvard university I wish to pursue a career in archeology.
>
> I have a master's degree from cornell college. I traveled to utah to see the remains of Deinonychus, commonly known as the utah raptor. I am well trained for field resurch because of my traveling to Russia to study the newly-discovered spearpoints which date back 400,000 years.
>
> Due to my new book, relating to the evolutional theory of dinosaurs into birds, I have recived many invitations to atend meetings and debates involving the subject of evolution.

> Now that you have read my application,
> contact me and perhaps we can set a date for
> an interview. I will be available during the
> week of monday, augest 25th. Also included is
> the number that I can be reached at. my yearly
> wages is $22,000.

One of the first things Paul noticed in Stephen's letter of application was the sophistication of the information provided. Stephen included many details about paleontology and archaeology, showed a high degree of imagination, and showed he has plans for a future in the academic world. Paul was also happy to see that his problems with commas and periods had improved dramatically. The last sentence of the first paragraph—a complex sentence which, according to Paul, many of Stephen's classmates may have left as a sentence fragment without the independent clause after the dependent clause starting with "because"—was the only spot Paul had to tell him to add a comma. The copying strategy appears to have helped Stephen with periods and commas.

Stephen's draft still has problems with mechanics, especially capitalization and spelling. Paul and Stephen worked on spelling as a long-term project, using a personal spelling dictionary and the computer spell checker. Paul began working on capitalization in the letter of application by asking Stephen what words he thought should be capitalized. Stephen immediately knew that Harvard University and Cornell College should be capitalized. He was also sure that Monday, August, Utah, and Raptor should be capitalized. Apparently Stephen's difficulties with capitalization stem from monitoring other aspects of the writing process—perhaps punctuation in this case—and calling his attention to the need to work on capitalization and building his confidence in correcting his own errors in capitalization are all that's needed. Paul then asked Stephen which words he guessed he may have spelled wrong. Here again, Paul wanted to see how Stephen's self-monitoring skills were developing. Stephen guessed that "abilitys," "resurch," and "atend" were spelled wrong because "they didn't look right." Paul told him the correct spellings for those words, and he wrote them down in the essay and in his personal spelling dictionary. Paul pointed out that he spelled "college" as "collage" and that a spell checker would not catch that word because "collage" is a correctly spelled word.

Paul then decided that this was enough for Stephen to work on, and his next step was to type a final draft on a word processor. The following is the body of the final draft of Stephen's letter of application:

> Ever since I first discovered and put together the skeleton of a miniature horse, I have wanted to learn about the past. Because of my excellent abilitys in paleontology at Harvard University, I wish to pursue a career in archeology.
>
> I have a master's degree from Cornell College. I traveled to Utah to see the remains of Deinonychus, commonly known as the Utah Raptor. I am well trained for field research because of my traveling to Russia to study the newly-discovered spear points which date back 400,000 years. Due to my new book, relating to the theory of dinosaurs evolving into birds, I have received many invitations to attend meetings and debates involving the subject of evolution.
>
> Now that you have read my application, contact me and perhaps we can set a date for an interview. I will be available during the week of Monday, August 25th. Also included is the number that I can be reached at. My yearly wages are $22,000.

Paul concludes from his work with Stephen that Stephen is beginning to learn that mechanics are important and, furthermore, that writing mechanics are not that difficult to figure out. Stephen seems to be naturally able to mimic the reading that he does, so Paul believes that with some well-planned scaffolding between what Stephen does know and what he needs to learn, he will be able to improve quickly.

Paul remembers seeing Stephen's writing for the first time as a daunting experience because the presence of so many surface errors in the writing made it hard to decide where to begin. He chose to ask Stephen about his difficulties with writing: "Since it was Stephen I was trying to help, it was better to start with his concerns, not mine." Stephen was concerned that he did not know how or where to punctuate, and he expressed that concern as an admission that guessing is his main guideline. From there, Paul proceeded to break Stephen's problems down into smaller pieces, and he claims this made helping him much more manageable. They worked on commas and periods, capital letters, and spelling, in that order—spelling being the most enduring problem and thus the one to be worked on slowly over time. Paul concludes from using strategic writing instruction that struggling writers need to experience success. In his words: "Mechanical errors are good problems to work on because they are generally easy to correct. Easy, in that there is a strategy that can be learned and then applied to that one problem."

Strategies in the Writing Workshop

Angela Militello tried strategic writing instruction in an eighth-grade writing workshop. Angela addresses what she identified as skills her writers need to learn in minilessons, such as writing attention-getting introductions, well-formed paragraphs, and complete sentences (to eliminate run-ons and fragments). On a large chart in the front of her classroom Angela keeps an up-to-date list of the writing skills she and her students have worked on. She holds her students accountable for these items in all writing tasks. She has other requirements for all pieces, too: All formal pieces of writing (those taken beyond the first draft stage) must be word processed, all drafts must be turned in, revisions must be completed in a different color pen, and a checklist must be updated for each stage of the process of writing particular pieces. For each assignment, Angela also provides her students with a rubric she will use to grade their work.

Angela has found it easy to add writing strategies to her writing workshop because she thinks of strategies as the cognitive components of the skills she is teaching. She naturally observes her writers at work and talks with them about their writing, so finding opportunities to introduce writing strategies is not a problem. Angela believes strongly in helping her writers to take charge of diagnosing their own writing problems and devising strategies to overcome their weaknesses: "I didn't want to be a 'writing doctor' who was there to fix and bandage up their writing problems. Rather, I wanted us to be co-constructors of the writing strategies, working together to problem solve solutions to their writing weaknesses."[4]

Barry is an eighth-grader in one of Angela's classes who always takes a longer than average time to write. He procrastinates and has a hard time coming up with things to say, and he also has difficulty with what Angela calls "putting form and direction to his thoughts." She noticed this as they worked on their second writing task together. This assignment was a post-reading activity Angela devised for *The Diary of Anne Frank*. This is the writing task:

"In *The Diary of Anne Frank*, Anne states that 'In spite of everything, I still believe that people are really good at heart.' Despite Anne's conclusion, what is your view of humankind? Do you believe that people are mostly good or mostly evil beings? Respond to this question using examples from your personal life, from history, from recent events, or from literature. Express your thoughts in a well developed essay."

Barry's response to this task had a thesis statement, that people are mostly good, not evil, and one example. He lumped all of this into one paragraph, though, and couldn't come up with anything else to say. Angela suggested that he organize his ideas, and she suggested that he try a visual/spatial organizer using circles, as in Figure 7.3. This organizer is one Angela uses frequently as a global planning strategy to help students revise in the direction of fuller, more organized writing. Angela drew the visual organizer for Barry, and she explained that in the top circle he could write the main idea for his essay as a lead in his introductory paragraph (at this point he did not have an introduction) and that each separate circle represented a paragraph and supporting details (the "SD" circles in Figure 7.3). Angela

[4]This quotation and other details of this example are from a case study of Angela's classroom, which she wrote as part of our research on strategic writing instruction.

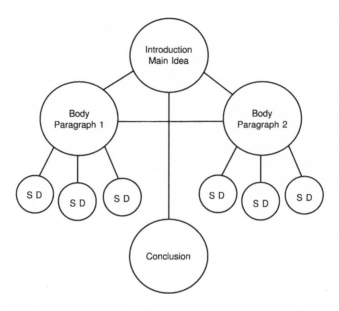

FIGURE 7.3. Visual organizer for global planning.

reports that the visual planning strategy helped Barry put structure and form to his thoughts and to express his ideas in an organized way.

On another piece Barry worked on, Angela again noticed that structure and direction were problems for him. When she asked him what the point or the goal of his piece was, he was puzzled and said that he didn't know. He also had difficulty deciding where to put paragraph divisions. She reminded him to use the circular visual organizer, and again Angela reports that it quickly helped him. What's more, it helped him in two ways which are reflected in his current writing: The visual organizer helps Barry have a point to his writing, for he knows that he must put the main idea of the piece in the top circle, and it imposes a structure on his writing, because Barry knows he must come up with an introduction, a conclusion, and body paragraphs with topic sentences and supporting details for each paragraph. Angela believes Barry's problem was that he couldn't "see," literally and figuratively, the point and direction of his writing. Before using the visual organizing strategy he would begin to write, without a point or direction in mind, not knowing where to form paragraphs. Angela concludes emphatically: "Now he knows how to do so!"

Strategies and Teacher–Writer Relations

In the case studies presented in this chapter, and dozens of others from our research, several patterns are noticeable. The first two are obvious: Teachers are learning to think strategically about the teaching of writing, and writers are learning to think strategically about their work. These patterns are what this book is about. In concluding this chapter, however, I want to point out that they are not all that matters.

Strategies-based teaching and learning do not happen in a vacuum. A third pattern in the case studies is seen in the extremely positive relations Laurie, Paul, and Angela established with their students. Earlier I said that any "magic" in strategic writing instruction is really the result of the workings of the four-step strategic teaching process—identifying a strategy, modeling it, assisting students in learning it, and providing repeated opportunities for practice with it. Adapting this approach to particular contexts humanizes it by emphasizing that caring teachers are what makes able students. Good teaching always has positive teacher–student work at its center. Writing strategies are simply a powerful way to focus that work on the improvement and self-regulation of writing abilities.

Perhaps Angela says it best. Her goal in her writing workshop classes is a traditional one for teachers who prefer a workshop format. She wants to put students in control of their own writing, but she has also discovered that developing strategies to help them allows them to feel in control of the process as much as possible. Angela wants writers to learn to assess their writing; to write rules, definitions, and writing tips in their own language; and to monitor themselves. She finds strategies and good working relations go together:

> "One of my personal strengths is that of being a good listener and a keen observer, and those attributes served me well. I found that the answers to the questions that my

writers posed were often found in the questions themselves if I were only listening carefully enough.

"I think that students know what their strengths and weaknesses are in writing; however, they don't always *know* that they know this! I wanted to give them the power of self regulation and self-assessment. I wanted them to think critically and problem solve about their own writing weaknesses, instead of me just handing them a quick fix to their writing problems. Thus, I wanted to impart to them *a new way of thinking about their writing* which they could take with them into other writing situations. I think that this is something that most struggling writers have never had before. Instead of always feeling baffled and overwhelmed by writing situations, I wanted them to assess their puzzlement and devise ways to overcome it."

Chapter Eight

Strategies, Identity, and Resistance

The studies, probes, and inquiries at the base of my thinking in this book used methods generally known as observational research. We observed what students do when they write and listened to what they told us about difficulties they were having while writing. We focused our observations especially on studying how teaching and learning work together to build an understanding of learning difficulties and strategies for overcoming them. Early on we decided *not* to separate teaching and learning, but instead to study how they combine together and work in tandem. We looked at how teachers and students negotiate understandings of texts and control of writing processes and how collaboration, especially in the form of co-construction of writing strategies, supports acquisition and learning. We paid particular attention to our emerging observation that certain key strategies, the ones I call "default strategies" throughout the book, show up repeatedly when writers are faced with challenging writing tasks. We recommended new strategies which were consistent with the default ones and with considerations of language and culture. Without exception, we found that students who cooperated with us in co-constructing new strategies took greater control of their writing processes, as indicated by improved quality in second and third drafts compared to first drafts and by sustainment of those differences over subsequent

tasks with diminishing amounts of assistance from us. Perhaps
the best evidence of the success of strategic writing instruction
was students' increased attention to planning before and during
writing, especially their use of plans based on the default
strategies. Planning before and during writing is a form of
control over writing processes; it tells us students are thinking
of writing as problem solving and using strategies to solve
problems. Planning is evidence of self-regulation; we are convinced that as students become more able to interrupt their
writing and tell themselves what to do to meet (or alter) their
plans for the piece, they are becoming more able to regulate
writing processes for themselves.

The disadvantage of observational research, of course, is
that there may have been differences in variables other than our
providing strategic writing instruction, such as differences in
writing abilities, in motivational levels of writers, or in the kind
and degree of instruction and collaboration provided by teachers. And those differences, rather than the co-constructed use
of writing strategies, could explain the differences we noticed in
quality across drafts and in the use of default strategies for
planning. Certainly this could be the case, and perhaps follow-up
studies using randomized "clinical intervention trials" would be
a good idea. To do this we would randomly assign writers to
receive strategy instruction or a control treatment and then wait
to see how many students in each group became better writers.
The strength of such clinical trials is that the only difference
between the groups would be strategic writing instruction, so it
would be less likely that anything else would explain any differences revealed by the research.

The trouble with clinical trials, however, would be exactly
that isolation of the experimental variable. We never theorized
or hypothesized that strategy instruction *by itself* would make a
difference, not before we started to study struggling writers at
work and certainly not after we decided to focus on the teaching–learning process as a single unit of analysis. In fact, our
major theoretical premise was exactly the opposite. We believed,
tentatively at first and then with increasing conviction as our
observations warranted, that strategic writing instruction im-
proves the writing abilities of struggling writers when used in
classrooms where students co-construct writing strategies with
teachers and peers and where such co-construction matches

strategies students bring to the classroom with the strategies they learn there. But we don't think writing strategies or strategy-based instruction made the difference. What mattered most, I am absolutely convinced, was a complex interaction among learning activities, classroom culture, and student identities. This is the same interaction that takes place at Special Olympic venues, boys' and girls' clubs, and other sites where adults and children work together to create an environment in which performance is enhanced by believing in self and others. Students who improved in our studies did so because they stopped standing outside the perimeter of the playing field and stopped participating in school only by running in place, all the while falling behind other, seemingly more "natural" learners. They started making progress as writers because their teachers took them into the circle of classroom discourse and worked with them to participate meaningfully while they learned to think of themselves as members of discursive partnerships and classroom discourse communities. Strategy instruction is good coaching; belief in self and others and membership on a team emerge along with writing development through an interaction between classroom culture and identity.

The basic principle in literacy learning appears to be quite simple: People become as literate as they need to be to participate meaningfully in the cultures in which they hold membership. That single principle combines the other two I identified in Chapter 2 as driving strategic learning:

1. The acquisition of increased ability can be assisted by the learning of strategies for managing performance.
2. Strategies for managing performance are best learned in social contexts which support both acquisition and learning.

Strategic writing instruction may have a fancy definition—a pedagogical stance focused on helping writers learn to identify and use strategies for writing through sociocognitive mediation of writing processes—but it really means combining social and cognitive aspects of writing, teaching, and learning. Control over writing strategies is a cognitive achievement, but it emerges most readily from co-construction of the strategies by students and teachers or peers, which means it is also a sociocognitive achievement. Thinking strategically about literacy becomes an emergent habit of mind when it is acquired and learned socially, in interaction with texts and other readers and writers.

Co-construction and collaboration are ways of helping students recognize the merits of strategic thinking and ways of helping them acquire and learn strategies that fit their own ways of thinking about the writing problem at hand; this in turn leads to a propensity for looking for new strategies and using them purposefully. I refer to this process as "thinking strategically about writing and writing difficulties" and "forming a strategic habit of mind" and as a foundation for a general problem-solving focus on literacy. This focus is extremely important because without it we would each have to carry around a huge quantity of individual strategies to deal with writing problems we encounter. Forming a strategic habit of mind lessens the burden by allowing us to look for or to construct strategies at the point of need, to invent strategies "on the fly" as we encounter new writing problems. Expertise with literacy, to the extent that it involves strategic thinking, is quite similar to other problem-solving behaviors. And becoming an expert with literacy, to the extent that communities impart expertise to and expect expertise from their members, is similar to gaining expertise with other problem-solving behaviors. Developing a strategic habit of mind is thus an integral part of individuals becoming as literate as they need to be to participate meaningfully in the communities in which they hold membership. Cognitive environments are sustained or modified as appropriate for full participation in cultural environments. Mind and culture, identity and community—these are the hallmarks of successful literacy learning.

Deciding What Strategies to Teach

Teachers, too, can benefit from "thinking strategically about writing and writing difficulties" and "forming a strategic habit of mind" as a foundation for a general problem-solving focus on literacy. There is no master list of literacy strategies, in spite of what textbook manufacturers want us to think when they present lists of strategies such as "using descriptive language" or "thinking critically" in their scope and sequence charts. Such lists encourage teachers to see strategies as fixed in form and finite in number and as neatly packaged in textbooks for delivery to students. I have argued in Chapters 4 and 6 against believing that we can "give" or "transmit" strategies to students.

In one of the best units I was ever involved with in strategies research (Blue & Collins, 1997), we had fifth-grade students rethink and rewrite sections of their social studies textbook in light of accounts of the same historical events by Native American and African American authors. We prepared a flexible template to guide their planning and writing, as in Figure 8.1.

I was unable to be at the school on the day the teachers used the template, and when I returned they reported to me that the "worksheet" I gave them "hadn't worked." Some students complained about not needing the template to write their essays, others tried to squeeze their thoughts directly into the paragraph-shaped boxes, and a few copied the topic sentences, including the [Say more] prompts and the direction to "Complete your essays according to your plan in the first paragraph." Clearly, students were not using the template to write strategically, nor were teachers using it to teach strategically. Of course, the fault was mine. I hadn't prepared the teachers for using the template as a means of helping students who need assistance in transforming class discussion into a coherent written argument. A device intended to assist strategic planning thus became nothing more than a piece of paper to write on or to complain about. I had not helped the teachers to think strategically about the task of assisting students in writing their social studies papers. We talked about writing strategies but apparently not enough about forming a strategic habit of mind. The teachers thought the strategy was equivalent to the template. Forming a strategic habit of mind has more to do with what teachers and students *do* with a template than with the template itself.

Forming a strategic habit of mind lessens the burden for teachers just as it does for students. It allows us to look for or to construct strategies at the point of need, to invent strategies as we observe student writing problems. I have seen teachers use strategic writing instruction in many ways, such as having students use various colors of highlighters to learn how to rearrange ideas in letters to Romeo or Juliet,[1] having students rearrange blocks in comic strips and then ideas in persuasive essays to learn

---

[1]Thanks to English teacher Meg Callahan.

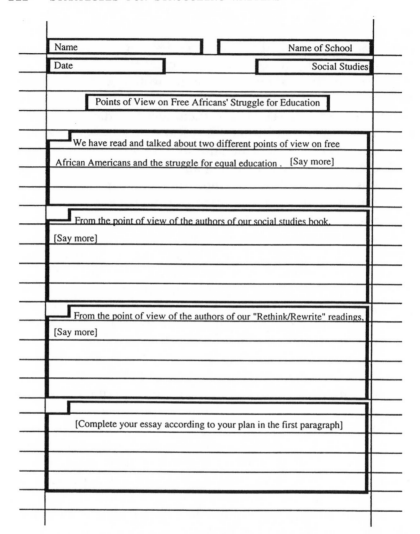

FIGURE 8.1. Planning and writing template.

about establishing patterns of logic in writing,[2] and having students work with partners to evaluate sample student essays for strong and weak uses of supporting details in preparation for revising their own essays.[3] Each of these projects and dozens of others used the four-step process we identified for strategic

[2] Thanks to English teacher Beth Welkly.

[3] Thanks to English teacher Moira Molloy.

writing instruction: identifying a strategy worth teaching, introducing the strategy by modeling it, helping students to try the strategy out with workshop-style teacher guidance, and then helping students work toward independent mastery of the strategy through repeated practice and reinforcement. Each also combined familiar and new strategies, visual and text-based strategies, and modeling with independent performance. Presenting these characteristics of good strategy instruction has been my main objective. Identifying strategies—beyond those that I've used to illustrate my main points—I leave to my readers.

Identifying strategies worth teaching is 10% personal and 90% observational. A personal strategy that works for me, for example, is to say "two *m*'s, dammit" each time I have trouble remembering that *recommend* has one *c* and two *m*'s. Of course, we should pay attention to our own writing strategies, including such personal ones, but the real focus of our attention should be on our students, their struggles with reading and writing, their cognitively and culturally inspired strategies, and their membership status in the classroom community.

Membership and Resistance in Classroom Communities

I referred several times to the interaction between what goes on in classrooms and the social formation of student identity, and now that I am near the end of this book I want to take a close look at that interaction. I will do so with a twist, however. Instead of just looking at a successful instance of identity formation, I want to present an unsuccessful one. In my discussion of culturally inspired strategies in Chapter 6, and in my saxophone lessons in Chapter 2, I noted a close relationship between the struggle to learn and resistance to learning. This relationship and the role of the teacher in fostering it are what I want to examine here. My point is that struggle feeds on isolation, on separation from positive and meaningful relations with others, such as the teacher–student relations we saw in Chapter 7. The final principle I want to discuss is this: No amount of strategic writing instruction will help if students are not full participants in classroom communities.

Steele (1992) presents a more general, more eloquent version of the same argument:

But if wise schooling is so obtainable, why is racial vulnerability the rule, not the exception, in American schooling?

One factor is the basic assimilationist offer that schools make to blacks: You can be valued and rewarded in school (and society), the schools say to these students, but you must first master the culture and ways of the American mainstream, and since that mainstream (as it is represented) is essentially white, this means you must give up many particulars of being black—styles of speech and appearance, value priorities, preferences—at least in mainstream settings. This is asking a lot. But it has been the "color-blind" offer to every immigrant and minority group in our nation's history, the core of the melting pot ideal, and so I think it strikes most of us as fair. Yet non-immigrant minorities like blacks and Native Americans have always been here, and thus are entitled, more than new immigrants, to participate in the defining images of the society projected in school. More important, their exclusion from these images denies their contributive history and presence in society. Thus, whereas immigrants can tilt toward assimilation in pursuit of the opportunities for which they came, American blacks may find it harder to assimilate. For them, the offer of acceptance in return for assimilation carries a primal insult: it asks them to join in something that has made them invisible. (p. 77)

The resistance to giving up one set of cultural patterns for another, which Steele describes, shows up repeatedly in studies of discourse patterns in schools, such as Michaels and Cook-Gumperz's (1979) study of sharing time narratives in a first-grade classroom, and in studies of the intersection of home and school cultures, such as Heath's (1983) study of three rural southern neighborhoods. These studies generally characterize the intersection of home and school cultures in terms of a continuum ranging from continuity to discontinuity (Emihovich, 1994), with the continuity end of the continuum being more characteristic of the experience of children from mainstream middle-class backgrounds and the discontinuity end more characteristic of the experience of children from nonmainstream backgrounds.

Bloome (1991), for example, points out that a dominant discourse pattern in schools—typically "I–R–E sequences" because teachers *I*nitiate discussion, students *R*espond, and teachers *E*valuate the response—serves many important functions, including providing feedback to students and identifying the setting as "doing school." However, he adds that research has shown that the asking of known information questions, like those in I–R–E sequences, is not compatible with the ways children use language in some cultures (e.g., Boggs, 1972; Dumont, 1972; Heath, 1982; Phillips, 1972; Smith, 1987). Bloome (1991) also points out that differences in how language is used at home and in school can confuse and distance minority children by structuring participation in events differently at school from the way it is structured in analogous events at home (e.g., Phillips, 1972; Shultz, Florio, & Erickson, 1982). Erickson (1987) goes even further by claiming that evidence from detailed studies of classroom discourse shows that lower-achieving students can at times actively resist learning language patterns and other behaviors they perceive to be typical of "doing school." Erickson (1984) defines *resistance* in terms of defiant classroom behavior on the part of students who are having difficulty with school tasks. In this view, a student's resistance is a way of countering or deflecting the possibility of being perceived as a person of less worth than others by not cooperating with requests to perform tasks that are difficult or otherwise likely to lead to judgments of weakness or failure. Resisting is better than attempting and failing because defiance provides a more acceptable self-image than does failed or inadequate performance, as defined by the school. Perhaps Greg's "Why do I have to do this writing?" question in Chapter 1 had some of this resistant quality; by choosing to stop writing, he may have been denying the school's control over his writing performance. Erickson (1984) adds that student resistance is self-defeating because it is likely to invite even harsher judgments by teachers and other school authorities.

In several studies I examined teacher–student discourse surrounding resistant student behavior (Collins, 1994a, 1994b, 1995b, 1995c), and I concluded that student resistance is a kind of cultural conflict co-constructed by teachers and students. In one of the studies (1994a), for example, an African American student repeatedly made apparently playful remarks during the course of a small-group literacy discussion; the teacher chose to ignore the remarks and to "isolate" the student from the discussion, the student became louder, the teacher became angry, and so on, until play turned into confrontation. Analysis of the discourse showed that the teacher asked known-answer questions within I-R-E sequences and that the resistant student substituted playful remarks for the inferences the teacher was attempting to elicit. Early in the discussion, the teacher exchanged playful banter with another one of the students in the small group and the resistant student joined in, perhaps thus setting the stage for one type of linguistic behavior—the skilled verbal challenge known as signifying (Smitherman, 1977; Lee, 1993, 1995)—to appear in the midst of another—a small-group literacy discussion. The two cultural forms bumped against each other, the teacher assumed the student should give up his discourse strategy, the student didn't do that, and conversation turned into conflict.

The concept of student resistance to learning is an important one in the education of students who struggle, and I will come back to it in a moment when I discuss classroom discourse and the social formation of student identities. First I want to point out that the process approach to writing instruction has not escaped the criticism that some school uses of language might confuse, distance, and call out resistance on the part of nonmainstream students. Kutz and Roskelly (1991), for example, claim that process approaches work best when learners come to school already in possession of the discourse strategies and styles of language used in mainstream literate discourse. They claim that the "process approach often fails to take into account learners whose discourse strategies and expectations may diverge from those of the mainstream" (p. 184). Gee (1990) similarly claims that the focus on voice and meaning, rather than on forms, typical of process and whole-language approaches can privilege students who already know the rules and forms for academic writing, especially if grading is based on how well writing matches traditional expectations.

African American scholars are among the most active critics of process approaches to writing instruction. Delpit (1986, 1988, 1995), for example, argues that many teachers of black children have their roots in other communities and therefore underestimate the fluent and creative aspects of the home language of many black children at the same time they underestimate the value of direct teaching of language skills and forms that are essential to exercising economic and cultural power. Siddle-Walker (1992) reviews the history of process teaching in composition studies and concludes that process approaches are oppositional to the cultural norms of teaching valued by some African American students, especially their valuing of teachers who are directive and "in charge" of their classes (see also Collins & Tamarkin, 1982; Comer, 1988). After Erickson (1984, 1987) and Foster (1987), Siddle-Walker (1992) sees possible sources of student resistance to instruction in teachers' patterns of questioning and suggesting rather than directly instructing. Siddle-Walker (1992) recommends that process teaching not be abandoned but, rather, that it be strengthened by including more attention to what she calls affective considerations, such as the preference in some cultural norms for teaching styles other than the nondirective, facilitative stance characteristic of process approaches. She also recommends including more specific suggestions for intervening in writing processes.

The Co-Construction of Resistance

An article entitled "Teacher Puts Boy Behind Partition" in the April 15, 1995, *San Francisco Chronicle* described a mother's shock at discovering that her second-grade son's school desk was "cordoned off on three sides by a 5-foot-high wooden partition" (Fimrite, 1995, p. A1). The mother accused her son's teacher of treating him "like a monkey in a cage." School officials described the partitions as part of a study carrel, and they said that the boy had "exhibited disruptive behavior numerous times in the past, forcing the teacher to separate him from his classmates several times this school year."

The physical isolation of students perceived as troublemakers is a common practice in classrooms, so common in fact that being sent to the principal or to the corner is the stuff of educational anecdote, lore, and legend. It happens in the comics to Dennis and Calvin and even to baby Marvin. Perhaps because we are so accustomed to the idea of isolating certain students in classrooms, being sent to the corner, to a "quiet chair" or a "time-out seat," is perceived in everyday perceptions of schooling more from the point of view of the school officials than that of the mother in the news report just mentioned. Isolation from the classroom community is generally perceived as temporary and positive, and the necessity of separating a young person is even seen as romantically reflective of a strong, individualistic, go-against-the-grain, all-American personality, a true "Dennis the Menace." The point I want to make here, however, is that isolation in classroom communities can also be seen as negative. Classroom discourse has participation structures some of which can be interpreted as the verbal equivalents of being sent to the corner, and when these structures operate repeatedly enough, educational authority and resistance become locked in ongoing opposition. The discursive details of classroom life are what constitute authority, resistance, and failure, which means that resistance is socially constructed in much the same manner as literacy is. The difference between success and failure in the literacy lesson I discuss next is mostly a matter of being included or excluded from the classroom discourse circle. The mother in the news article has a right to be concerned; her son's disruptiveness and isolation are forming a social identity that the second-grader may carry right through his remaining years of school.

For 6 years I was part of a school–university partnership designed to enhance the literacy learning of students in an urban middle school. The school serves an African American neighborhood and has approximately 600 students across two levels: an early-childhood center, grades pre-Kindergarten through 2; and an academy, grades 3 through 8. Through my involvement in this project, I developed a deep interest in classroom communities and in the ways in which classroom communities influence student success and failure.

In the main thrust of this research, I analyzed discourse in small-group reading and writing discussions to probe into the possibility that resistance and failure are co-constructed by teachers and students engaged in face-to-face interaction in classrooms. My study of educational resistance focused on playful scenes during small-group discussions involving middle-school students and their teachers. I took my data from observations, audiotapes, and transcripts of teacher-led small-group literacy discussions. In the brief excerpt presented here to illustrate the co-construction of resistance a teacher leads a discussion of part of *The Acorn People* (Jones, 1976), a nonfiction book about the capabilities of disabled children. Resistance takes two principal forms in the small-group literacy lesson. It shows up in brief comments when a resistant participant plays a different role from the one assigned by the classroom discourse structure, and it shows up in extended silences on the part of a resistant student and challenges to his resistance on the part of other members of the group, including the teacher. In both of these manifestations, resistance is initiated and sustained through interactive language processes. It is here that resistance is co-constructed within classroom discourse.

Each of the classrooms in the larger study had at least one "time-out chair" or "quiet seat." This is a student desk which has been removed from close proximity to other student desks and placed in a corner of the room or near the teacher's desk. Students are sent to the time-out chair or to the corner when their behavior, in the teacher's judgment, is sufficiently in violation of classroom rules to merit separation from the group. The time-out chair thus is a place to isolate single students from the classroom discourse community.

The small-group discussions that are the focus of my study frequently have events that are the dialogical equivalent of being sent to the time-out chair. Students displaying resistant behavior are often met with responses from the teacher or other students that contribute to and amplify their resistance. As the resistance grows, the resistant student becomes further removed from the business of the small-group discussion. Thus, a playful, mildly resistant comment can snowball into an incident that results in the resistant student being separated or isolated from the discourse. In this manner, a momentary display of resistance can become a lasting isolation from the group discussion. At the beginning of the following excerpt from the sixth-grade literacy lesson, for example, a student I'll call Mark has taken himself out of the discussion by lapsing into daydreaming.

In this excerpt Mark is caught "sleeping" by his peers, who briefly make him the object of their derision. I use italics to highlight the resistant portions of this segment from the small-group discussion because the segment shows what are really two separate but overlapping conversations: one the "official" or "business-like" group discussion and the other a side conversation commenting on the silent student's resistance to the official lesson. By highlighting the resistant portions of the excerpt, we notice how the silence of the resistant student is enforced and extended by the group:

(a) Teacher: OK, let me read it again.

(b) Tashay: [To Mark] Mark, why you ain't sayin' nuttin'?

(c) Darelle: [To Mark] Why are you tryin' to sleep?

(d) Tashay: I know. (Laugh)

(e) Teacher: –Mark, let's see if Mark can figure it out.

(f) Mark: –[To Tashay and Darelle] Quit buggin' me.

(g) Tashay: I know. Yeah.

(h) Teacher: Shh.

(i) Mark: [To Tashay and Darelle] Let's see you bug me . . .

(j) Darelle, Tashay, James: (Laugh)

(k) Teacher: —"He called down to us."

(l) Tashay: –(Laugh)

(m) James: –Oh god. (Laugh)

(n) Teacher: Martin called down to us, "Hey you guys it's easy." Martin was sitting down facing downhill. By moving his legs under him.

(o) Darelle: In a squat position.

(p) Teacher: In a squat position, pushing back, he edged up the hill in this sitting posture.

(q) Darelle: He probably had a, uh . . .

(r) James: Maybe he was handicapped.

(s) Teacher: Wait, shh.

(t) Darelle: He was probably using his legs and his hands.

(u) Teacher: OK, wait, let's see what Mark says.

(v) Mark: Maybe he, *(inaudible)*, and has his hand on the mountain, and pushed up.

(w) Teacher: He pushed himself up. How did he do that?

(x) Darelle: Good job, Marky.

This lesson is an exercise in making inferences based on information obtained from reading. In an I–R–E sequence just before the start of this segment of the transcript, the teacher asked how Martin, one of the handicapped characters in the story, managed to move up the mountain, and first Tashay and then James responded incorrectly. The teacher begins to repeat the reading that contains the information necessary for inferring the correct answer when Tashay asks, "*Mark, why you ain't sayin' nuttin'?*" Mark has been quiet for a little more than 2 minutes. Notice that there is a double layer of resistance here; Mark may be passively resisting the lesson by tuning it out and letting his boredom show, and Tashay may be actively resisting it by postponing the teacher's rereading of the passage while she playfully picks on Mark for his resistance. Darelle quickly joins the play with, "*Why are you tryin' to sleep?*" and Tashay agrees that they have, indeed, caught Mark sleeping: "*I know*" *(Laugh)*. Notice that the teacher picks up on the effort to make Mark feel uncomfortable for being caught daydreaming: "*Mark, let's see if Mark can figure it out.*" Quite without meaning to, I think, the teacher joins in the attempt to deride Mark by trying to restore the business function and wholeness of the group through a strategy of targeting the next I–R–E sequence directly at Mark. Perhaps intending to help Mark, Darelle and James try to provide the inference the teacher wants in (r) and (t), but the teacher silences them in (s) and (u). The question is intended for Mark alone, and answering it correctly is the price he must pay for readmission to the discourse circle. Mark makes an attempt to answer it, and the teacher repeats Mark's answer and asks for more information in (w): "He pushed himself up. How did he do that?" Here the repetition of Mark's words by the teacher suggests that the teacher is about to let Mark back into the discussion. Before Mark can answer, however, Darelle in (x) switches the discourse back to resistance and exclusionary derision with a sarcastic, *Good job, Marky*. Tashay answers the teacher's question, the lesson goes on, and Mark continues to be left out. About 4 more minutes go by before Mark speaks again, and when he does, his answer to one of the teacher's questions goes unheeded.

In the space of this segment, Mark stepped out, or "slept out," of the discourse circle and tried to get back in, but he found his way blocked, playfully at first by his friends, then powerfully by the teacher, and finally and most definitely by a resistant insider who chides Mark for unsuccessfully giving in to the teacher to gain readmission. Clearly in this example Mark's resistance is co-constructed by his peers and the teacher. In fact, it is the teacher who turns the resistance into a test of Mark's ability not only to make inferences but to make them quickly. By insuring that Mark fails the test, a fellow student helps the teacher turn resistance into gatekeeping (as in Gilmore, 1985).

Resistant behaviors are interwoven with other elements of classroom discourse, and membership in the community of discourse changes from moment to moment, at times in a manner quite independent of the official business of the discourse. The full exclusion of a resistant student, however, is only accomplished through cooperation between a resistant student and his or her teacher. In the excerpt, each of the students other than Mark resists and gets away with it; each one steps outside the circle of discourse with only one foot, and each knows when to step back in. Resistance in this view has a history; it begins with playfulness and boredom and only later turns into anger and frustration and the apparent formation of identity as a resistant student, all of which may be happening to Mark when he fails to gain readmission.

Perhaps most important, this classroom scene illustrates the way resistance is socially constructed by discourse in classroom communities. Resistant students are not resistant all by themselves. Resistance is constituted through discourse, and peers and teachers collaborate in its construction. Resistance can begin as play, or in Mark's case as daydreaming, but it is sustained in the same manner that positive educational outcomes, such as strategic literacy, are sustained. This is what makes my discussion of educational resistance relevant to this closing chapter. Struggling writers, owing to their struggles with literacy or other aspects of their schooling, may be inclined toward boredom or disruption. To my way of thinking, however, relegating them to the time-out chair or its discursive equivalent is inappropriate. Of course, there are degrees of misbehavior in classrooms, and teachers have to deal with disruptions for what they are. I am not arguing against classroom discipline. My point is simply that school success and failure are constituted through face-to-face language interaction. Just as Freedman (1987) bases her monograph on the theory that "the achievement of cognitive gain depends on the substance of social interactions" (p. 8), I am basing this book, finally, on the same notion but extending it to include both classroom success and failure, both cognitive gain and continuing struggle. Strategic literacy is a function of classroom discourse. It can flourish or disappear based on the quality of talk and membership in classroom communities.

Shifting the Paradigm

Sometimes I think we are so busy looking for major, sweeping changes in schools that we forget that what really matters most is the quality of interaction between teachers and kids. I suppose educational change can take place in two ways, in bits and pieces or by paradigm shift, but I believe that bits and pieces is the way it usually happens, as in the positive relations in strategic writing examples discussed in the last chapter.

Teachers, students, and classrooms change one step at a time. Paradigm shifts are preferred by educational reformers and researchers who expect one specific change, such as the current call for national standards, to enhance performance levels throughout schools. Sometimes teachers expect such changes too, as in whole language where the expectation was that literacy could be acquired as readily as speaking by everyone. Or in process writing, where the expectation was that students would develop naturally as writers if we just stopped worrying about skills. Such is not the case, we learned again. No single innovation or instructional approach matters more than teachers and students working together in collaborative, constructive communities of meaning makers. Why do we continue to place our faith in sweeping educational changes instead of in the ongoing hard work of teachers in classrooms? I'm not sure how to answer that question precisely, but I suspect the answer has something to do with "shifting the paradigm," as in the example I presented in Chapter 1 (Zemelman & Daniels, 1988) by citing a table to "identify the key points of contrast between the old and new paradigms" (p. 340), that is, between traditional teaching and process-based instruction.

In the late 1960's or early 1970's, Russell Baker wrote a column in which he examined the frequent news reports that claimed that the United States had finally turned the corner in Vietnam. Baker explained that a federal agency, the Office of Optimistic Prognosis (OOP), had built a huge corner in Washington and shipped it to Saigon where it was erected in a large room inside the American embassy. OOP claimed that people like to turn corners because the concept suggests change and progress. So, at times when nothing seemed to be changing or progressing in Vietnam, OOP would cable instructions to turn the corner, and officials rotated it on the set of cheap swivel casters on which it was mounted. News agencies could then write about how we were turning the corner in Vietnam.

Something comparable might be recommended for literacy education. We seem to have a similar need for change and progress and for reporting change and progress to various constituencies. Only instead of a turning corner mounted on wheels, we could build a huge paradigm and suspend it by a cable from the ceiling at the headquarters of the National Assessment of Educational Progress. Then, when events warrant, such as when another literacy crisis strikes, we could give the paradigm a push and write about how we're shifting the paradigm in the teaching of literacy. Or, in a less directive mode, we could walk beneath the swinging paradigm and write about how we're undergoing a paradigm shift in the teaching of reading and writing.

Educational research is obsessed with making progress. It seems that every innovation must signal a clean break with tradition, and every change in instructional practice must be thought of as reflecting or contributing to a paradigm shift. In research on literacy teaching we are in such a rush to embrace new approaches that we are forever turning our backs on what teachers are already doing and what we can learn from them. No wonder the shifting paradigm resembles a swinging pendulum. And no wonder a balance provides a more strategic image to guide our efforts.

References

Anderson, J. R. (1985). *Cognitive psychology and its implications* (2nd ed.). New York: Freeman.

Anderson, V., & Roit, M. (1993). Planning and implementing collaborative strategy instruction with delayed readers in grades 6–10. *Elementary School Journal, 94*(2), 121–137.

Applebee, A. N. (1981). *Writing in the secondary school: English and the content areas.* Urbana, IL: National Council of Teachers of English.

Applebee, A. N. (1984). *Contexts for learning to write: Studies of secondary school instruction.* Norwood, NJ: Ablex.

Atwell, N. (1987). *In the middle: Writing, reading and learning with adolescents.* Upper Montclair, NJ: Boynton/Cook.

Bakhtin, M. M. (1981). *The dialogic imagination: Four essays by M. M. Bakhtin* (M. Holquist, Ed.; C. Emerson & M. Holquist, Trans.). Austin: University of Texas Press. (Original work published 1975)

Ball, A. F. (1992). Cultural preference and the expository writing of African-American adolescents. *Written Communication, 9*(4), 501–532.

Ball, A. F. (1994, April). *Text design patterns in the writing of culturally and linguistically diverse students: The case of the African-American writer.* Paper presented at the meeting of the American Educational Research Association, New Orleans.

Bereiter, C. (1980). Development in writing. In L. W. Gregg & E. R. Steinberg (Eds.), *Cognitive processes in writing* (pp. 73–93). Hillsdale, NJ: Erlbaum.

Bereiter, C., & Scardamalia, M. (1982). From conversation to composition: The role of instruction in a developmental process. In R.

Glaser (Ed.), *Advances in instructional psychology* (Vol. 2, pp. 1–64). Hillsdale, NJ: Erlbaum.

Bereiter, C., & Scardamalia, M. (1987). *The psychology of written composition*. Hillsdale, NJ: Erlbaum.

Bernstein, B. (1975). *Class, codes and control* (Vol. 1). London: Routledge & Kegan Paul.

Bloome, D. (1991). Anthropology and research on teaching the English language arts. In J. Flood, J. Jensen, D. Lapp, & J. R. Squire (Eds.), *Handbook of research on teaching the English language arts* (pp. 46–56). New York: Macmillan.

Blue, E., & Collins, J. L. (1997, March 25). *Constructing critical learning processes in an urban school/university partnership.* Paper presented at the annual meeting of the American Educational Research Association, Chicago.

Boggs, S. T. (1972). The meaning of questions and narratives to Hawaiian children. In C. Cazden, V. John, & D. Hymes (Eds.), *Functions of language in the classroom* (pp. 299–330). New York: Teachers College Press.

Bourdieu, P. (1980). *The logic of practice.* Stanford, CA: Stanford University Press.

Braddock, R., Lloyd-Jones, R., & Schoer, L. (1963). *Research in written composition.* Urbana, IL: National Council of Teachers of English.

Britton, J., Burgess, T., Martin, N., McLeod, A., & Rosen, H. (1975). *The development of writing abilities (11–18).* London: Macmillan.

Bronowski, J. (1990). The reach of imagination. In F. Delaney (Ed.), *The folio anthology of essays* (pp. 202–209). London: The Folio Society.

Brown, A. L. (1980). Metacognitive development and reading. In R. J. Spiro, B. C. Bruce, & W. F. Brewer (Eds.), *Theoretical issues in reading comprehension* (pp. 458–482). Hillsdale, NJ: Erlbaum.

Brown, A. L. (1987). Metacognition, executive control, self-regulation, and other more mysterious mechanisms. In F. Weinert & R. Kluwe (Eds.), *Metacognition, motivation and understanding* (pp. 65–116). Hillsdale, NJ: Erlbaum.

Brown, R., Pressley, M., Van Meter, P., & Schuder, T. (1996). A quasi-experimental validation of transactional straegies instruction with low-achieving second-grade readers. *Journal of Educational Psychology, 88*(1), 18–37.

Bruner, J. (1983). *Child's talk: Learning to use language.* London: Oxford University Press.

Bruner, J. (1986). *Actual minds, possible worlds.* Cambridge, MA: Harvard University Press.

Calkins, L. M. (1994). *The art of teaching writing* (2nd ed.). Portsmouth, NH: Heinemann.

Caverly, D. C., & Orlando, V. P. (1991). Textbook study strategies. In R. F. Flippo & D. C. Caverly (Eds.), *Teaching reading and study strategies at the college level.* Newark, DE: International Reading Association.

Cazden, C. (1988). *Classroom discourse: The language of teaching and learning.* Portsmouth, NH: Heinemann.

Cole, M. (1985). The zone of proximal development: Where culture and cognition create each other. In J. V. Wertsch (Ed.), *Culture, communication and cognition: Vygotskyian perspectives* (pp. 146–161). New York: Cambridge University Press.

Collins, J. L. (1981). Speaking, writing, and teaching for meaning. In B. M. Kroll & R. J. Vann (Eds.), *Exploring speaking-writing relationships: Connections and contrasts* (pp. 198–214). Urbana, IL: National Council of Teachers of English.

Collins, J. L. (1984). The development of writing abilities during the school years. In A. D. Pellegrini & T. D. Yawkey (Eds.), *The development of oral and written language in social contexts* (pp. 201–212). Norwood, NJ: Ablex.

Collins, J. L. (1989). Computerized text analysis and the teaching of writing. In G. E. Hawisher & C. L. Selfe (Eds.), *Critical perspectives on computers and composition instruction* (pp. 30–43). New York: Teachers College Press.

Collins, J. L. (1991). Introduction. In J. L. Collins (Ed.), *Vital signs 2: Teaching and learning language collaboratively* (pp. v–viii). Portsmouth, NH: Heinemann-Boynton/Cook.

Collins, J. L. (1993). The development of writing abilities during the school years. In L. M. Cleary & M. D. Linn (Eds.), *Linguistics for teachers* (pp. 356–367). New York: McGraw-Hill.

Collins, J. L. (1994a, April 4). *Dialogue and resistance in small-group reading–writing instruction.* Paper presented at the annual meeting of the American Educational Research Association, New Orleans.

Collins, J. L. (1994b, November 18). *Overcoming the process–privilege connection: Strategy-based writing instruction.* Paper presented at the annual meeting of the National Council of Teachers of English, Orlando.

Collins, J. L. (1995a). Basic writing and the process paradigm. *Journal of Basic Writing, 14*(2), 3–17.

Collins, J. L. (1995b, April 22). *Discourse and resistance in two sixth-grade classrooms.* Paper presented at the annual meeting of the American Educational Research Association, San Francisco.

Collins, J. L. (1995c, March 12). *Resisting dominant notions of resistance.* Paper presented at the Sixteenth Annual Ethnography in Education Research Forum, Philadelphia.

Collins, J. L., & Godinho, G. V. (1996). Help for struggling writers: Strategic instruction and social identity formation in high school. *Learning Disabilities Research and Practice, 11,* 177–182.

Collins, J. L., & Miller, B. E. (1986). Presentational symbolism and the production of text." *Written Communication, 3*(1), 91–104.

Collins, J. L., & Williamson, M. M. (1981). Spoken language and semanatic abbreviation in writing. *Research in the Teaching of English, 15,* 23–35.

Collins, J. L., & Williamson, M. M. (1984). Assigned rhetorical context and semantic abbreviation in writing. In R. Beach & L. Bridwell (Eds.), *New directions in composition research* (pp. 285–296). New York: Guilford Press.

Collins, K. M., & Collins, J. L. (1996). Strategic instruction for struggling writers. *English Journal, 85,* 54–61.

Collins, M., & Tamarkin, C. (1982). *Marva Collins' way.* Los Angeles: Tarcher.

Comer, J. P. (1988). *Maggie's American dream.* New York: New American Library.

Cook-Gumperz, J. (1993). Dilemmas of identity: Oral and written literacies in the making of a basic writing student. *Anthropology and Education Quarterly, 24,* 336–356.

David, D. L. (1992). The literary experience: Reader-response theory in the community college classroom. In J. L. Collins (Ed.), *Vital signs 3: Restructuring the English classroom* (pp. 122–127). Portsmouth, NH: Heinemann-Boynton/Cook.

Delpit, L. D. (1986). Skills and other dilemmas of a progressive black educator. *Harvard Educational Review, 56,* 379–385.

Delpit, L. D. (1988). The silenced dialogue: Power and pedagogy in educating other people's children. *Harvard Educational Review, 58,* 280–298.

Delpit, L. D. (1995). *Other people's children.* New York: New Press.

Didion, J. (1984). Why I write. In E. G. Freedman (Ed.), *Joan Didion: Essays and conversations.* Princeton, NJ: Ontario Review Press.

Dillard, A. (1974). *Pilgrim at Tinker Creek.* New York: Harper & Row.

DiPardo, A. (1990). Narrative knowers, expository knowledge. *Written Communication, 7,* 59–95.

Dixon, J. (1967). *Growth through English.* London: Oxford University Press.

Dromey, R. G. (1982). *How to solve it by computer.* Englewood Cliffs, NJ: Prentice Hall.

Dumont, Jr., R. V. (1972). Learning English and how to be silent: Studies in Sioux and Cherokee classrooms. In C. Cazden, V. John, & D. Hymes (Eds.), *Functions of language in the classroom* (pp. 344–369). New York: Teachers College Press.

Dunn, P. A. (1995). *Learning re-abled: The learning disabilities controversy and composition studies.* Portsmouth, NH: Heinemann-Boynton Cook.

Dyson, A. H. (1983). The role of oral language in early writing processes. *Research in the teaching of English, 17,* 1–30.

Eisner, E. (1993). The education of vision. *Teaching Thinking and Problem Solving, 15,* 1–6.

Elbow, P. (1973). *Writing without teachers.* New York: Oxford University Press.

Elsasser, N., & John-Steiner, V. P. (1977). An interactionist approach to advancing literacy. *Harvard Educational Review, 47,* 355–369.

Emig, J. (1971). *The composing processes of twelfth graders.* Urbana, IL: National Council of Teachers of English.

Emihovich, C. (1994). Cultural continuities and discontinuities in education. In T. Husén & T. N. Postlethwaite (Eds.), *International encyclopedia of education* (2nd ed., Vol. 3, pp. 1227–1233). Oxford, England: Pergamon Press.

Englert, C. S. (1992). Writing instruction from a sociocultural perspective: The holistic, dialogic, and social enterprise of writing. *Journal of Learning Disabilities, 25*(3), 153–172.

Englert, C. S. (1995). Teaching written language skills. In P. Cigilka & W. Berdine (Eds.), *Effective instruction for students with learning difficulties* (pp. 304–343). Boston: Allyn & Bacon.

Englert, C. S., & Mariage, T. V. (1990). Send for the POSSE: Structuring the comprehension dialogue. *Academic Therapy, 25,* 473–487.

Englert, C. S., & Mariage, T. V. (1991). Shared understandings: Structuring the writing experience through dialogue. *Journal of Learning Disabilities, 24,* 330–342.

Englert, C. S., & Mariage, T. V. (1996). A sociocultural perspective: Teaching ways-of-thinking and ways-of-talking in a literacy community. *Learning Disabilities Research and Practice, 11,* 157–167.

Englert, C. S., Raphael, T. E., & Anderson, L. M. (1992). Socially mediated instruction: Improving students' knowledge and talk about writing. *Elementary School Journal, 92*(4), 412–449.

Erickson, F. (1984). School literacy, reasoning, and civility: An anthropologist's perspective. *Review of Educational Research, 54*(4), 525–546.

Erickson, F. (1987). Transformation and school success: The politics and culture of educational achievement. *Anthropology and Education Quarterly, 18*(4), 335–356.

Farr, M. (1993). Essayist literacy and other verbal performances. *Written Communication, 10,* 4–38.

Farrell, T. J. (1977). Literacy, the basics, and all that jazz. *College English, 38,* 443–459.

Fimrite, P. (1995, April 15). Teacher puts boy behind partition. *San Francisco Chronicle,* p. 41.

Finn, J. D., & Achilles, C. M. (1990). Answers and questions about class size: A statewide experiment. *American Educational Research Journal, 27,* 557–577.

Finn, J. D., & Voelkl, K. E. (1994). Class size: An overview of research. In T. Husén & T. N. Postlethwaite (Eds.), *The international encyclopedia of education* (2nd ed.; Vol. 2, pp. 770–775). Oxford, England: Pergamon Press.

Flower, L. (1979). Writer-based prose: A cognitive basis for problems in writing. *College English, 41,* 19–37.

Flower, L. (1985). *Problem-solving strategies for writing* (2nd ed.). New York: Harcourt Brace Jovanovich.

Flower, L. (1994). *The construction of negotiated meaning: A social cognitive theory of writing.* Carbondale, IL: Southern Illinois University Press.

Flower, L. S., & Hayes, J. R. (1977). Problem-solving strategies and the writing process. *College English, 39,* 449–461.

Foster, M. (1987). *"It's cookin' now": An ethnographic study of the teaching style of a Black teacher in an urban community college.* Unpublished doctoral dissertation, Harvard University.

Freedman, S. W. (1987). *Response to student writing.* Urbana, IL: National Council of Teachers of English.

Gardner, H. (1983). *Frames of mind: The theory of multiple intelligences.* New York: Basic Books.

Gee, J. P. (1990). *Social linguistics and literacies: Ideology in discourses.* London: Falmer.

Gee, J. P. (1993). What is literacy? In L. M. Cleary & M. D. Linn (Eds.), *Linguistics for teachers* (pp. 257–265). New York: McGraw-Hill.

Gilmore, P. (1985). "Gimme room": School resistance, attitude, and access to literacy. *Journal of Education, 167*(1), 111–128.

Goody, J., & Watt, I. (1972). The consequences of literacy. In P. Giglioli (Ed.), *Language and social context.* New York: Penguin.

Grandin, T. (1995). *Thinking in pictures.* New York: Doubleday.

Graves, D. (1975). An examination of the writing processes of seven year old children. *Research in the Teaching of English, 9,* 227–241.

Graves, D. H. (1983). *Writing: Teachers and children at work.* Portsmouth, NH: Heinemann.

Greenough, C. N., & Hersey, F. W. C. (1923). *English composition.* New York: Macmillan.

Harris, K. R., & Graham, S. (1992). *Helping young writers master the craft: Strategy instruction and self-regulation in the writing process.* Cambridge, MA: Brookline Books.

Harris, K. R., & Graham, S. (1996). *Making the writing process work: Strategies for composition and self-regulation.* Cambridge, MA: Brookline Books.

Hawkins, P. R. (1977). *Social class, the nominal group and verbal strategies.* London: Routledge & Kegan Paul.

Hayes, J. R., & Flower, L. S. (1980). The dynamics of composing: Making plans and juggling constraints. In L. W. Gregg & E. R. Steinberg (Eds.), *Cognitive processes in writing* (pp. 31–50). Hillsdale, NJ: Erlbaum.

Heath, S. (1982). Questioning at home and at school: A comparative study. In G. Spindler (Ed.), *Doing the ethnography of schooling: Educational ethnography in action* (pp. 102–131). New York: Holt, Rinehart & Winston.

Heath, S. B. (1983). *Ways with words: Language, life, and work in communities and classrooms.* New York: Cambridge University Press.

Hendrix, R. (1981). The status and politics of writing instruction. In M. F. Whiteman (Ed.), *Writing: The nature, development, and teaching of written communication* (Vol. 1, pp. 53–70). Hillsdale, NJ: Erlbaum.

Hillocks, G. (1986). *Research on written composition: New directions for teaching.* Urbana, IL: ERIC Clearinghouse on Reading and Communication Skills and National Conference on Research in English.

Hogan, K., & Pressley, M. (Eds.). (1997). *Scaffolding student learning: Instructional approaches and issues.* Cambridge, MA: Brookline Books.

Hughes, L. (1994). Thank you, ma'am. In *Prentice Hall literature, second course* (pp. 179–182). Englewood Cliffs, NJ: Prentice Hall.

Hunt, K. W. (1965). *Grammatical structures written at three grade levels* (Research Report No. 3). Urbana, IL: National Council of Teachers of English.

Jones, R. (1976). *The acorn people.* New York: Bantam.

Kantor, M. (1993). A man who had no eyes. In *Elements of literature, second course* (pp. 149–151). Orlando, FL: Holt, Rinehart & Winston.

Kimmel, K. L. (1996). *Silenced voices, signed visions: A phenomenological study of the role of literacy in the lives of five deaf individuals.* Unpublished doctoral dissertation, State University of New York at Buffalo.

Kirby, D., & Liner, T. with Vinz, R. (1988). *Inside out: Developmental strategies for teaching writing.* Portsmouth, NH: Heinemann-Boynton/Cook.

Koontz, D. (1984). *Darkfall.* New York: Berkley Books

Krashen, S. (1982). *Principles and practice in second language acquisition.* Hayward, CA: Alemany Press.

Kroll, B. M. (1980). Developmental perspectives and the teaching of composition. *College English, 41,* 741–752.

Kutz, E., & Roskelly, H. (1991). *An unquiet pedagogy: Transforming practice in the English classroom.* Portsmouth, NH: Heinemann-Boynton/Cook.

Labov, W. (1975). *The study of nonstandard English.* Urbana, IL: National Council of Teachers of English.

Lee, C. D. (1993). *Signifying as a scaffold for literary interpretation: The pedagogical implications of an African American discourse genre.* Urbana, IL: National Council of Teachers of English.

Lee, C. D. (1995). A culturally based cognitive apprenticeship: Teaching African American high school students skills in literary interpretation. *Reading Research Quarterly, 30*(4), 608–630.

Livingston, J. (1996). *Effects of metacognitive instruction on strategy use of college students.* Unpublished paper, State University of New York at Buffalo.

Loban, W. (1976). *Language development: Kindergarten through grade twelve* (Research Report No. 18). Urbana, IL: National Council of Teachers of English.

Michaels, S., & Cook-Gumperz, J. (1979). *A study of sharing time with first grade students: Discourse narratives in the classroom.* Proceedings of the 5th Annual Meeting of the Berkeley Linguistics Society, Berkeley, CA.

Moshman, D. (1982). Exogenous, endogenous and dialectical construcivisim. *Developmental Review, 2,* 371–384.

Noden, H. R., & Vacca, R. T. (1994). *Whole language in middle and secondary classrooms.* New York: HarperCollins College.

Ochs, E. (1979). Planned and unplanned discourse. In T. Givon (Ed.), *Syntax and semantics: Vol. 12. Discourse and syntax* (pp. 51–80). New York: Academic Press.

O'Donnell, R. C., Griffin, W. J., & Norris, R. C. (1967). *Syntax of kindergarten and elementary school children: A transformational analysis* (Research Report No. 8). Urbana, IL: National Council of Teachers of English.

Ohlhausen, M. M., & Roller, C. M. (1988). The operation of text structure and content schemata in isolation and in interaction. *Reading Research Quarterly, 23,* 70–88.

Olson, D. R. (1977). From utterance to text: The bias of language in speech and writing. *Harvard Educational Review, 47,* 257–281.

Olson, D. R., & Torrance, N. (1981). Learning to meet the requirements of written text: Language development in the school years. In C. H. Frederiksen & J. F. Dominic (Eds.), *Writing: The nature, development, and teaching of written communication* (Vol. 2, pp. 235–255). Hillsdale, NJ: Erlbaum.

Ong, W. J. (1979). Literacy and orality in our times. In *Profession 79.* New York: Modern Language Association.

O'Rourke, P. J. (1996, November). Dr. Hunter S. Thompson. *Rolling Stone*, pp. 64–75.

Palincsar, A. S., & Brown, A. L. (1984). Reciprocal teaching of comprehension-fostering and monitoring activities. *Cognition and Instruction, 1,* 117–75.

Paris, S. G., Lipson, M. Y., & Wixson, K. K. (1983). Becoming a strategic reader. *Contemporary Educational Psychology, 8,* 293–316.

Phillips, S. U. (1972). Participant structures and communicative competence: Warm Springs children in community and classroom. In C. Cazden, V. John, & D. Hymes (Eds.), *Functions of language in the classroom* (pp. 370–394). New York: Teachers College Press.

Pressley, M. (1996). *Getting beyond whole language: Elementary reading instruction that makes sense in light of recent psychological research.* Paper presented at the meeting of the American Psychological Association, Toronto.

Pressley, M., Borkowski, J. G., & O'Sullivan, J. (1985). Children's metamemory and the teaching of memory strategies. In D. L. Forrest-Pressley, G. E. MacKinnon, & T. G. Waller (Eds.), *Metacognition, cognition and human performance: Vol 1. Theoretical perspectives* (pp. 111–153). Orlando, FL: Academic Press.

Pressley, M., Harris, K. R., & Marks, M. (1992). But good strategy instructors are constructivists! *Educational Psychology Review, 4*(1), 3–31.

Pressley, M., Rankin, J., & Yokoi, L. (1996). A survey of instructional practices of primary teachers nominated as effective in promoting literacy. *The Elementary School Journal, 96*(4), 363–384.

Resnick, L. B. (1989). Introduction. In L. B. Resnick (Ed.), *Knowing, learning and instruction: Essays in honor of Robert Glaser* (pp. 1–24). Hillsdale, NJ: Erlbaum.

Roller, C. M. (1996) *Variability, not disability: Struggling readers in a workshop classroom.* Newark, DE: International Reading Association.

Romano, T. (1987). *Clearing the way: Working with teenage writers.* Portsmouth, NH: Heinemann.

Rose, M. (1984). *Writer's block: The cognitive dimension.* Carbondale, IL: Southern Illinois University Press.

Scardamalia, M., & Bereiter, C. (1986). Research in written composition. In M. C. Wittrock (Ed.), *Handbook of research on teaching* (3rd ed., pp. 778–803). New York: Macmillan.

Schuder, T. (1993). The genesis of transactional strategies instruction in a reading program for at-risk students. *Elementary School Journal, 94*(2), 183–200.

Searle, J. (1984). *Mind, brains and science.* Cambridge, MA: Harvard University Press.

Shaughnessy, M. P. (1976). Basic writing. In G. Tate (Ed.), *Teaching composition: Ten bibliographical essays* (pp. 137–167). Fort Worth, TX: Texas Christian University Press.

Shaughnessy, M. P. (1977). *Errors and expectations.* New York: Oxford University Press.

Shultz, J., Florio, S., & Erickson, F. (1982). Where's the floor? Aspects of the cultural organization of social relationships in communication at home and in school. In P. Gilmore & A. Glatthorn (Eds.), *Children in and out of school* (pp. 88–123). Washington, DC: Center for Applied Linguistics.

Shuy, R. W. (1981). Toward a developmental theory of writing. In C. H. Fredericksen & J. F. Dominic, (Eds.), *Writing: The nature, development, and teaching of written communication* (Vol. 2, pp. 119–132). Hillsdale, NJ: Erlbaum.

Siddle, E. (1988). *The effect of intervention strategies on the revisions ninth graders make in a narrative essay.* Unpublished doctoral dissertation, Harvard University.

Siddle-Walker, E. V. (1992). Falling asleep and failure among African-American students: Rethinking assumptions about process teaching. *Theory into Practice, 31*(4), 321–327.

Smith, D. (1987). Reading and writing in the real world: Explorations into the culture of literacy. In R. Parker & F. Davis (Eds.), *Developing literacy: Young children's use of language* (pp. 173–189). Newark, DE: International Reading Association.

Smith, V. (1994). Finding the path with the help of a friend. *Voices from the Middle, 1*(2), 11–18.

Smith, W. L., & NCTE Task Force on Class Size and Workload in Secondary English Instruction. (1986). *Class size and English in the secondary school.* Urbana, IL: ERIC and the National Council of Teachers of English.

Smitherman, G. (1977). *Talkin and testifyin: The language of black America.* Boston: Houghton Mifflin.

Steele, C. M. (1992, April). Race and the schooling of black Americans. *The Atlantic Monthly,* pp. 68–78.

Strickland, K. (1995). *Literacy not labels: Celebrating students' strengths through whole language.* Portsmouth, NH: Heinemann-Boynton/Cook.

Tannen, D. (1985). Relative focus on involvement in oral and written discourse. In D. R. Olson, N. Torrance, & A. Hildyard, (Eds.), *Literacy, language, and learning: The nature and consequences of reading and writing.* Cambridge, MA: Cambridge University Press.

Tannen, D. (1986). *That's not what I meant! How conversational style makes or breaks your relations with others.* New York: William Morrow.

Trudeau, G. B. (1996, May 19). Doonesbury flashback. *Buffalo News,* §2, p. 1.

van Dijk, T. A., & Kintsch, W. (1983). *Strategies of discourse comprehension.* New York: Academic Press.

Vygotsky, L. S. (1978). *Mind in society: The development of higher psychological processes* (M. Cole, V. John-Steiner, & E. Souberman, Eds.). Cambridge, MA: Harvard University Press.

Vygotsky, L. S. (1986). *Thought and language* (A. Kozulin, Ed. and Trans.). Cambridge, MA: MIT Press. (Original work published 1934)

Warriner, J. E. (1986). *English grammar and composition: Complete course* (Liberty ed.). New York: Harcourt Brace Jovanovich.

Weinstein, C. E., & Mayer, R. E. (1986). The teaching of learning strategies. In M. C. Wittrock (Ed.), *Handbook of research on teaching* (3rd ed., pp. 315–327). New York: Macmillan.

Wells, R. W. (1989). Interview with Stephen King. In T. Underwood & C. Miller (Eds.), *Feast of fear: Conversations with Stephen King.* New York: Warner Books.

Wilhelm, J. D. (1995). Reading *is* seeing: Using visual response to improve the literary reading of reluctant readers. *Journal of Reading Behavior, 27,* 467–503.

Willoughby, T., & Wood, E. (1995). Mnemonic strategies. In E. Wood, V. E. Woloshyn, & T. Willoughby (Eds.), *Cognitive strategy instruction for middle and high schools* (pp. 5–17). Cambridge, MA: Brookline Books.

Yolen, J. (1991). The route to story. *The New Advocate, 4*(3), 143–149.

Zemelman, S., & Daniels, H. (1988). *A community of writers: Teaching writing in the junior and senior high school.* Portsmouth, NH: Heinemann.

Author Index

Subject Index